Directory of _____
CLASSIC SPORTS-
RACING CARS

Directory of
CLASSIC SPORTS-RACING CARS

Mike Lawrence

Aston Publications

Sole distributors for the USA
Motorbooks International
Publishers & Wholesalers Inc.

Published in 1987 by Aston Publications
Limited,
Bourne End House, Harvest Hill,
Bourne End, Bucks., SL8 5JJ

ISBN 0 946627 21 5

Designed by Chris Hand

Photoset and printed in England by
Redwood Burn Limited,
Trowbridge, Wiltshire

Sole distributors to the
U.K. book trade,
Springfield Books Ltd,
Norman Road, Denby Dale,
Huddersfield, West
Yorkshire, HD8 8TH

Sole distributors for the USA,
Motorbooks International,
Osceola, Wisconsin 54020,
United States

Giannino Marzotto, seen here at Brescia, won the 1953 Mille Miglia with this Tipo 340MM Ferrari. (Publifoto)

Contents

Introduction	9	Kieft	117
A.C. Ace	11	Lagonda	120
Alfa Romeo Disco		Lancia	123
Volante	14	Lister	128
Allard	19	Lola Mk I	135
Aston Martin	23	Lotus	137
Borgward	36	Maserati	145
Bristol 450	40	Mercedes-Benz	159
Connaught	44	Nardi	166
Cooper	48	Nash-Healey	168
Cunningham	53	OSCA	171
D.B.	58	Pegaso	176
E.M.W.	65	Porsche	179
Elva	68	Salmson	190
Ferrari	71	Scarab	192
Frazer Nash	89	Skoda	195
Gilby	92	Stanguellini	198
Gordini	94	Talbot	200
H.W.M.	99	Tojeiro	204
Jaguar	104		

In formation through the Esses early in the 1954 Le Mans race go the complete team of Tipo 375 Plus Ferraris driven by Rosier/Manzon, Maglioli/Paolo Marzotto and Gonzalez/Trintignant.

Introduction

The cars included in this book are mainly those which took part in the first World Sports Car Championship, 1953–61, though some earlier models are also included. The Le Mans victory of Mercedes-Benz in 1952, for example, is hardly less meritorious because it didn't count towards a championship.

The year 1961 brings us more or less to the end of the front-engined era, a time when special builders, working by instinct, could still build successful cars. The likes of Lister, D.B., Allard, Tojeiro, Stanguellini, and Cooper were all special builders, but as the Fifties came to an end, their days were numbered as a more scientific approach to racing became the rule rather than the exception.

The cars of this period have a special attraction for several reasons. One is that they are *understandable*. Most of us can readily appreciate the principles on which they are built. There are no exotic materials, there is no electronic wizardry, there are no hidden secrets. Very few of us can fully understand all the parts on many modern production cars, features such as computer diagnosis, ABS, and engine management systems are the preserve of a few specialists, but there are no mysteries in a Lister-Jaguar.

Then again, the art of aerodynamics as applied to cars was still in its infancy, so the stylist had more of a free hand. This resulted in a much wider range of expression than one sees in the equivalent category, Group C, today. There is some justification in the gripe that nowadays all the cars look the same, for when one tries to solve a problem purely scientifically the number of solutions is limited and, besides, the regulations defining a category are now so tight that a designer has less room for expression.

Finally, the cars of the period were not only expected to often race on public roads but the regulations called for them to be 'street legal' and to provide for the carriage of a nominal amount of luggage. A Jaguar D-type might be a sports-racer, but it was one which could be, and frequently was, driven on the road. John Bolster wrote a memorable series of road, not track, tests for *Autosport* of cars which at weekends were battling for racing honours. A Lotus Eleven or a Ferrari Testa Rossa was *approachable* in a way which a Porsche 962 or a Jaguar XJ-8R is not.

Makers of the period divide into two types, the constructors who created the entire car, and the special builders who used proprietary components. In France special builders turned to Panhard and Renault units with the result that, at Le

9

Mans, the 750 cc class and the Index of Performance became largely a battle between French special builders. In Italy, Fiat components tended to form the basis of cars, which again led to an emphasis on the smaller capacity classes. In Britain there was a much wider choice of proprietary engines and when one emerged which was powerful, reliable and available, there tended to grow up around it a class of racing.

There was an intrinsic difference between British and European special builders. Racing in Britain was on ex-airfield circuits, which by their nature were open, flat, and smooth. In Europe cars often competed on public roads and had to be constructed to withstand indifferent surfaces, cobblestones, manhole covers and such.

The continental special builder therefore had to make his cars rugged enough to last the distance and tended to find his advantage in engine power. The British special builder, while obviously seeking any edge he might find in power, put a greater emphasis on chassis development.

The airfield circuit, however, was destined to be the precursor of most future tracks since, following major accidents at Le Mans in 1955 and in the 1957 Mille Miglia, pure road racing rapidly began to go into decline and there was an emphasis on purpose-built circuits which naturally had the best possible surfaces.

Grand constructor or special builder, the makers of the period built a wider variety of cars than we've become used to in sports car racing and with their greatly differing approaches to the problem created one of the richest periods in postwar motor racing.

A.C. Ace

By the early 1950s, the long-established firm of A.C. Cars was in decline. Apart from a reasonably successful line in invalid cars, its range consisted of the Petite, a three-wheeler with a 300 cc Villiers engine, and a terribly old fashioned 2-litre sports saloon (and convertible) with non-independent suspension which sold in small numbers while the postwar sellers' market remained. Although A.C. was known as a motor manufacturer, it was kept going by general engineering contracts.

A.C. Cars employed a Polish engineer named Zdzislaw Marczewski, who designed an astonishing number of engines which never saw the light of day. Apart from the fact that they were all horizontally-opposed units, they ran the whole gamut of variations. There were twins, fours and sixes, some air-cooled and some water-cooled, some with push rods and some with overhead camshafts. Some were built and some run in cars but none saw production.

It is hard to see why this work continued in such profusion, for A.C. had neither the plant nor the capacity to produce the engines, or the cars which might use them in numbers to be economically viable. It is equally hard to detect a coherent policy running through A.C.'s postwar work so far as cars are concerned. For all its research, A.C. had a thin range and the company looked in poor shape when chance revived its fortunes and it went into production of what had been little more than a club racing special.

Meanwhile in Cambridge John Tojeiro made simple ladder-frame chassis with transverse leaf spring suspension, front and rear, for which customers specified their own engine and body. These chassis were mainly bought by club racers, who created a minor reputation for Tojeiro. Perhaps a dozen had been made when, in late 1952, a London car dealer called Cliff Davis bought one.

Davis was loaned Sid Greene's Bristol FNS engine and had Gray and Rich build a copy of the Ferrari 166 Barchetta body. The result was a practical, pretty, sports car (LOY 500) which won an enormous number of races in Britain in 1953 and 1954. In passing, Davis was portrayed in the film *Dance With A Stranger* and LOY 500 featured in the racing sequences.

One of Tojeiro's customers, Vin Davison, ordered a similar car, but had a 2½-litre Lea-Francis engine installed. Davison was a friend of the Hurlock family, owners of A.C., and he introduced them to Tojeiro and allowed Cliff Davis to demonstrate his car to Marczewski and Derek Hurlock along the Kingston bypass, the 'test track' for a number of British constructors of the day. It impressed them so much that it was decided to put the car into production. It was a machine which they could easily make without investment in further plant or machinery and, thanks to LOY 500, it started with a fine reputation and a successful competition record.

At the same time Davis was also keen to produce the car, but Tojeiro, who admits to being commercially naïve at the time, accepted a deal from A.C. He would loan the firm Davison's car, which was then re-engined with A.C.'s own 6-cylinder 1,991 cc engine, and also make a show chassis. These were to be paid for at the going rate and, in addition, he would receive a royalty of £5 for each car built by A.C., up to a limit of 100 vehicles. In view of the success of the car, 'commercially naïve' was an understatement.

The car was displayed at the 1953 Earls Court Motor Show, where it received a favourable reception (to put it mildly), but by the time it went into production the following year it had been productionized and extensively restyled by A.C.'s

Don Levy's appropriately registered Ace-Bristol leads an Elva Mk II during practice for a race at Mallory Park in 1957. (T.C. March)

Alan Turner. Turner lightened and balanced the lines so though they were recognizably descended from the Barchetta the car had a distinct presence of its own. Its wheelbase and overall length increased by two inches in each case and weight increased from 10½ cwt (LOY 500) to nearly 16 cwt (production Aces). Wire wheels replaced the original alloys which Tojeiro bought from fellow special builder Jack Turner.

Before the Motor Show, A.C. was, with Ford, the only company in Britain selling a car with non-independent front suspension. With the Ace it leapfrogged its rivals and became the first British company to sell a sports car with all-independent suspension.

Under the curvaceous bonnet was A.C.'s venerable s.o.h.c. aluminium engine, designed by A.C.'s founder, John Weller, in 1919, which gave 90 bhp at 4,500 rpm and this was mated to a 4-speed Moss gearbox. Few engines have enjoyed so long a production run, but it restricted the car for competition use though making it a reasonably rapid road car. In 1956, the Ace was offered with Bristol's 1,971 cc engine as an alternative and most buyers took the option, though it was not until 1960 that the last A.C.-engined car was made, a production run of a staggering 41 years. It is thought that 228 A.C.-engined Aces were made. From 1955 a coupé version, the Aceca, was offered, but this was perceived as a tourer and few were raced.

Even in standard trim, a 125 bhp Ace-Bristol (a 105 bhp version was also avail-

Designed by John Tojeiro and styled by Cavendish Morton, this special A.C. was driven by Peter Bolton and Dickie Stoop to eighth place at Le Mans in 1958 but it had no apparent advantage over the standard Ace. (Geoffrey Goddard)

able) had a top speed of a shade under 120 mph, but others, notably Ken Rudd, an A.C. agent, fitted more powerful versions and these cars achieved much success in British and American club racing. In 1957 Rudd, partnered by Peter Bolton, competed at Le Mans and in the 2-litre class finished second to a Ferrari. This was more or less a standard car except that the nose section had been smoothly drawn round a smaller grille.

Encouraged by this unexpected turn of events, A.C. commissioned Tojeiro to build a special car for the 1958 Le Mans race. It was in the manner of the space-frame competition cars he was currently building, with coil spring and unequal wishbone front suspension and a de Dion axle at the rear. It was styled by Cavendish Morton, an architect, artist, and motor racing enthusiast, who had become involved with Tojeiro. 'Cavvy' would paint a picture of how he saw a finished car and this would then be turned over to the chosen body builder as the 'blueprint'.

Morton's paintings resulted in a stream of very pretty Tojeiros and the special A.C. was no exception. Although it was commissioned at short notice and Tojeiro himself was never happy with the rear suspension, it was good enough to finish second in the 2-litre class (to the Behra/Herrmann 1.6 Porsche RSK) and finish eighth overall, in the hands of Dickie Stoop and Peter Bolton. A production Ace of Swiss privateers Patthey and Berger finished next up in ninth place so, as it turned out, there was no need for the special car and, indeed, it detracted from a fine performance by a customer.

Perhaps this influenced A.C.'s thinking, for the Tojeiro car was entered by the works in only one other event, the 1958 Tourist Trophy at Goodwood. Driven by Mike Anthony and Ted Whiteaway, it suffered from a succession of cooling problems, and though it finished, it was down in 19th place having covered only 105 laps to the winning Aston Martin's 148 laps.

No further work was done on the A.C. 'Toj' which was sold on, survives, and is still to be seen occasionally in British Historic racing. Production A.C. Aces became popular, and very successful, in SCCA racing, winning their class championship five successive times between 1957 and 1961. In the Sebring 12 Hours race, Aces won the 2-litre GT class in 1958 and in 1959 scored a 1-2-3 in class.

A private A.C. Ace, driven by Whiteaway and Jack Turner, ran at Le Mans in 1959, and though this was a low-budget, strictly amateur, effort, they brought it home a splendid seventh overall and first in the 2-litre class. It was a tribute to the durability of its Bristol engine, for it achieved its splendid result by being one of only 13 finishers.

In 1959 the Moss gearbox was replaced by a new unit using Triumph internals in an A.C. casing, which gave a much lighter gear change. Two years later, Bristol ceased production of its own engine (466 Ace-Bristols were made) and the car underwent another motor transplant, this time receiving a tuned 6-cylinder 2.6-litre Ford unit, courtesy of the Zephyr saloon. At the same time, front disc brakes were specified for the first time. Though the engine could be very highly tuned, and the car retained its timeless looks, there were few takers for it cost more than a Jaguar E-type and the larger engine took it out of the 2-litre Production Sports Car class making it much less attractive for racing. Only 36 Ford-engined cars were made.

A.C.'s many ambitious projects remained only projects, and sales were declining when Carroll Shelby approached the firm with a scheme to ship chassis/body units to the States, where they would receive American Ford V-8 engines. So was born the Shelby Cobra. . . .

Alfa Romeo Disco Volante

It is difficult today to see Alfa Romeo as it was in the immediate postwar era for, by attempting to become a volume producer, the company became a shadow of what it once was. The Alfa Romeo which marketed the ghastly Arna (a Datsun Cherry with an Alfasud engine) is not the same Alfa Romeo of the early Fifties. Then the very name was redolent with excitement. It stood for the essence of the Italian car: style, tradition, wonderful engineering, sheer motoring pleasure. A visit to the firm's museum in Milan is an unforgettable experience for any lover of motor cars.

When Ferrari was still an interesting newcomer making its way, Alfa Romeo set the standard it had to match. It was as though a single company combined the values we now associate with Ferrari, Porsche and the McLaren F1 team.

The war left the factory virtually demolished, but even as Alfa Romeo struggled to recover, it kept alive its long and distinguished tradition of motor sport. As early as 1946 it had a racing department which built a competition version of the production 6-cylinder 2500 Freccia d'Oro (Golden Arrow). Considerably lighter than the standard car, and with 145 bhp, it was run by the works and a few private customers with some success and its tally included two third places in the Mille Miglia (1948 and 1949) and second in the 1949 Targa Florio.

Alfa Romeo dominated Formula One racing with its Alfettas in the immediate postwar period (with the exception of 1949 when it withdrew for a season following the deaths of its two best drivers, Achille Varzi and Jean-Pierre Wimille) and Farina and Fangio won the first two World Championships with them. In 1950 Alfettas won all six races and followed that by winning the first races of 1951 but then, ominously, Ferrari won the remaining three. At the end of that year Alfa retired from F1, aware that the 1½-litre straight-eight supercharged Tipo 159 had reached the end of its development and could offer no answer to the 4½-litre normally aspirated Ferraris.

Alfa Romeo's racing department was not, however, wound up and was busy at work on a new sports car. This had a multi-tubular chassis, and suspension was broadly similar to the production 1900 with coil springs and double wishbones

The Alfa Romeo C-52 Disco Volante in its original form. The shape worked well in a wind tunnel but under-car airflow caused destabilising lift.

Juan-Manuel Fangio drove this 3.6-litre Colli-bodied Alfa Romeo coupé into second place in the 1953 Mille Miglia despite a broken track rod. It was one of the great Argentinian's greatest drives. (Publifoto)

at the front and a de Dion rear end located by radius arms, a Watts linkage and coil springs.

When the car was shown in late 1952 it caused a stir because of the startling shape of its Touring-built body. Officially designated C-52, it was immediately dubbed Disco Volante (flying saucer – there was a UFO craze at the time) and has been known as such ever since. The greatest car company in Italy appeared to have taken a giant step forward. If what looks right is right, then Alfa Romeo was heading in an exciting new direction.

Italy had never been at the forefront of aerodynamics applied to motor cars, but Alfa Romeo had carefully wind tunnel-tested the shape and fitted a convex undertray intended to reduce undercar drag and turbulence. The result was low drag, but an unfortunate tendency to lift the rear wheels as huge amounts of air were efficiently channelled under the car.

Alfa Romeo built five C-52s, three with 1,997 cc d.o.h.c. 4-cylinder engines which produced 158 bhp, while the other two had 6-cylinder d.o.h.c. 3-litre units. Each had a 4-speed gearbox mounted at the rear in conjunction with the final drive, but by the time the cars appeared in competition an extra ratio had been added. Since the whole vehicle weighed just 1,600 lb it had a very favourable power/weight ratio and, on paper, looked promising, but the aerodynamics were wrong.

It is generally believed that none of the first five cars, the genuine Disco Volante, was raced, but we understand from a source within Alfa Romeo that the cars did appear in a couple of minor events in Italy, but beyond that our informant was vague. Certainly the cars did not appear in the sort of high-level competition for which they were designed.

They were tested and found wanting, but the lessons learned were applied to a

The Alfo Romeo coupé of Kling/Riess at Le Mans in 1953. It was running third after eight hours when it retired with clutch trouble. (LAT)

This 3-litre Disco Volante Spyder was driven by Fangio to victory in the 1953 Supercortemaggiore Grand Prix, the type's only win when run by the works.

second generation built to the same theme. Two C-52s are retained by Alfa Romeo's own museum, one is in the Schlumpf collection, a fourth in the Biscaretti Museum in Turin while the fifth, a 3-litre car, was dismantled.

The style and nickname of the original car so caught the imagination that its derivative, the 6C 3000 CM, was always known as the Disco Volante even though none of those which actually raced looked remotely like the original. In fact the only Disco Volante-shaped car which raced regularly was a Cooper-based special built for an English privateer, John Risely-Prichard, which had a 1½-litre Connaught engine.

Eight cars, mainly fitted with 3½-litre engines, were made for the 1953 season and these had several different types of body during their careers. There was a coupé version of the original shape, a much more conventional coupé built by Colli and at least one open 2 seater, only the front end of which bore any relationship to the first body.

Four Colli coupés were entered for the 1953 Mille Miglia. Freddy Zehender's 2-litre car retired early in the race, but Consalvo Sanesi led nearly all the way to Pescara, when he had to retire with transmission troubles. Karl Kling, on loan from Mercedes-Benz, took over the lead and was still in front by Rome, but then had to retire with a cracked transmission housing.

Juan-Manuel Fangio, still recovering from his 1952 Monza crash, then led but quickly had a track rod break, which meant only one of his front wheels was steering. Instead of giving up he drove one of the greatest races of his career to finish second to Giannino Marzotto's 4.1-litre Ferrari.

Three cars started Le Mans, but the Fangio/Marimon car lasted only two hours when a burned-out piston eliminated it from sixth place. After eight hours, though, Kling/Riess lay third and Sanesi/Carini fourth, but both retired after ten hours with transmission troubles.

A single car, for Fangio and Sanesi, appeared in the Spa 24 Hours race and Fangio had it in third place after two hours, but when Sanesi took over he spun in the wet and retired. During private practice for the first Nürburgring 1,000 Km race, Kling had the steering break and crashed and the factory withdrew its cars.

Three cars were entered for the non-Championship Supercortemaggiore race, but only one, with an open body, appeared. With it, Fangio won against strong Lancia works opposition. It was the last time that the factory entered the cars.

One Colli coupé was later sold to Swedish Alfa Romeo dealer Jo Bonnier, who fitted it with an open Zagato body. With it, Bonnier ran in the 1955 Swedish GP but retired when eighth with brake trouble. A second International sports car race, also at Karlskoga the following weekend, saw him third, still with brake trouble. In the final race of the short series Bonnier gave the car its first win. Bonnier raced the car extensively in 1956 (Ken Wharton drove it a couple of times in England), but without success and sold it at the end of the year.

Several of the cars were dismantled, one was 'sold' to President Peron of Argentina (he never paid for it) and is now in America, as is the Bonnier car. Another, frequently re-bodied during its life, is also in America, while the Alfa Romeo museum houses the Supercortemaggiore-winning car.

By all accounts the Alfas were a delight to drive and would have repaid further development.

Ironically, although the special competition models were short-lived and unsuccessful, modified versions of Alfa Romeo's production saloons, and some with custom bodies, were very successful in both saloon car racing and the Turismo classes in events such as the Mille Miglia and the Carrera Panamericana. On the back of these successes, it was clear that a market existed for a production Alfa Romeo competition car for privateers.

It was with this in mind that the 1900 Sportiva was conceived as a development of the 3000 CM programme. The Sportiva was more compact than the 3000 CM, but followed similar principles with a multi-tubular frame, 1900 front suspension, a de Dion rear axle located by an A-frame and Panhard rod, and a 4-cylinder engine giving 138 bhp.

Bertone provided stylish bodies in open and coupé form which were then handed over to the racing department for aerodynamic testing using tufts of material and a slow-motion camera. As a result, the style was rationalized.

The car's competition history was a single hill-climb in 1955, where it finished second to a Mercedes-Benz 300SL. Spyder and coupé models were displayed at the 1956 Turin Show and the works prepared to produce at least 100 Sportiva spyders. Then Alfa Romeo's management cancelled the project.

The company was expanding in a new direction as a volume manufacturer of cars with above-average quality and specification and it built a further prototype based on Giulietta components and was thinking of building racing cars which reflected the future of its production range rather than the established past.

This was the 1½-litre Tipo 750 Competizione, a joint project with Carl Abarth, who designed the chassis frame, and Baono, which supplied the bodywork. The heavily modified Giulietta engine gave 145 bhp (close to the 100 bhp/litre which was the engine tuner's lodestone). This car might have been the racer for which Alfa Romeo was searching. Although heavier and, to the eye, less aerodynamic than the opposition in what was a popular and keenly contested International class, it had a distinct power advantage and its lovely lines were the sort to capture the imagination.

Unfortunately, the pressure on the company to build production cars saw this promising project first squeezed, then abandoned after two prototypes were built and neither driven in competition.

It was to be a long time before Alfa Romeo again entered serious racing, but its great tradition was kept alive in races and rallies with its production cars, some of which had limited production special bodies created by the best of Italian stylists. In the early Seventies it tried further expansion with the Alfa-Sud, but was neither big enough, or small enough, to ride the late Seventies recession, hence the Arna, an act of sheer desperation.

For some time Alfa Romeo was in a precarious position, kept going by government subsidies, and it lost its traditional values of innovation and quality. With the company's future now assured as part of the Fiat empire it has a chance of once more rediscovering its great tradition and sadly dented reputation which, postwar, was never better expressed than in its prototypes of the Fifties.

Allard

Sydney Allard was a no-nonsense Londoner with a passion for cars and racing. While learning his trade as a garage apprentice, he owned a couple of three-wheeled Morgans which he was soon entering in trials and sprints and was just 19, in 1929, when he won his first race at Brooklands. When he had served his time his father bought him a garage business which happened to be called 'Adlard's', a coincidence which was occasionally to cause confusion.

By the Thirties, American cars had developed into a distinct breed which found little acceptance in Europe. Allard, however, was an admirer of the Americans' ability to mass-produce large, cheap, torquey engines and rugged chassis and he bought a succession for use in trials. It was not long before standard cars did not meet his ambitions and in 1935 he built his first Allard Special.

This was based on the Ford Model 48, but the chassis was shortened and narrowed, the live front axle split, the engine moved back in the frame, and the rear of the body came from a Bugatti; Sydney had no time for 'purism'. The car was an immediate success in competition and Allard soon had people wanting replicas. By the time the war broke out, Allard was a small-scale constructor and a leading figure in British motor sport with a reputation for fearlessness behind the wheel. Friends of Sydney's are on record as believing he would not make old bones.

During the war Adlard's landed a contract for the maintenance of military vehicles, and prospered, and when peace returned the company had large premises and the opportunity to buy a great number of Ford spare parts at a ridiculous price. In 1946 Sydney registered the Allard Motor Co Ltd and was in a position to supply cars almost immediately.

Since new cars of any description were rarer than hens' teeth, Allard could sell everything he made and he began with a 2-seater sports model, the K1. It followed the general principles of his pre-war special with a box-section chassis, swing-axle front suspension with a tranverse leaf spring, a solid rear axle on semi-elliptical springs, and a V-8 engine, in this case Ford's 3,662 cc side-valve 'Pilot' unit. Later some K1s used 3.9-litre Mercury engines. An aggressively styled aluminium body completed the package.

Almost immediately a long-wheelbase 4-seater version, the Allard L, was offered. Both cars reflected their maker; they were big, powerful and rather basic. As a driver Sydney was forceful and somewhat lacking in finesse and much the same can be said about his cars.

The following year the range was further expanded to include the Mercury-engined J1, basically a shorter, slimmer and lighter K1, for competition use. These were initially successful in trials and sprints, which were then both important mainstays of the sport in Britain, and some of the 12 made were exported to the States. Production reached 176 cars that year, leaping to 432 in 1948, by

19

which time there was yet another variation on the basic theme, the M, a more refined 4-seater drop-head coupé.

Production never again equalled the high point of 1948, as customers had a much wider choice of car and tended to opt for more modern designs. Still production remained at a respectable level (5–7 cars a week) for the next three years, when it began to decline sharply.

For 1947 Allard built a single-seater hill-climb car around an Austrian Steyr 3.6-litre air-cooled V-8 engine. It had a mixed first season, but was well sorted the following year, by which time it had a de Dion rear end. Allard was one of the fastest men on the hills in 1948 and was almost unbeatable in 1949 after he had developed the engine with new cylinder barrels and JAP heads.

Meanwhile work was in hand on a new Allard base design with a modified chassis, retaining established dimensions and weight distribution, but with coil spring front suspension and Ford transverse leaf rear springing. In 1949 a 4-seater sports saloon, the Allard P, was marketed and it was with such a car that in 1952 Sydney became the only driver/constructor to win the Monte Carlo Rally. Also in 1949 came the J2, successor to the J1, but using the new short-wheelbase chassis and a de Dion back axle to cope with all the power the cars were putting down on the road.

Various engines were fitted to the 90 J2s made. The standard unit was a 4,375 cc sv Mercury V-8, but most J2s which went to the States were sold without engines and customers tended to fit either the 5.4-litre ohv Cadillac V-8 or the Mercury V-8 fitted with the ohv Ardun conversion developed by Arkus Duntov. A Halibrand quick-change final drive unit which gave a total of 38 different

In 1952 Allard tried again with the J2X with full-width bodywork but retired with brake problems. (Geoffrey Goddard)

ratios was an option and these, imported by Allard, were also sold to such as H.W.M. and Cooper

J2s were widely raced and were especially successful in America. In 1950 Allard partnered Tom Cole in the latter's J2-Cadillac at Le Mans. After 11 hours they lay second to Rosier's Talbot, but then lost first and second gears and had to motor around in top. Their determination was rewarded with third place, just 50 miles behind the winning Talbot. Later that year, a J2 won the Watkins Glen Grand Prix for sports cars.

In 1951 Allard entered the Tour of Sicily with a 4-litre Mercury-Ardun in his J2, but he retired with a holed piston. The Tour of Sicily was a tough race, almost

At Silverstone in May 1953 Sydney Allard struggles with the unwieldy J2R-Cadillac. Like all Allards, it handled no better than it looked. (T.C. March)

21

on a par with the more famous Targa Florio, and it was unusual to say the least for any British driver to enter, let alone one in a car of his own manufacture. The Mille Miglia likewise saw few British contestants, even in its later years, but Allard entered. For this he had a Cadillac engine in the car, but went over an embankment and down a considerable drop. The escapade did nothing for the car, but did not diminish the driver's enthusiasm.

Two J2s were entered at Le Mans, but there was to be no repeat of the previous year's success. One went off the road and ended in a sandbank while Allard and Cole again lost their bottom two gears and finally retired with a burned-out clutch. American manual gearboxes were not designed for heavy use and some manufacturers recommended that the bottom two gears were only to get the car moving, whereupon the driver stayed in third and relied on the torque of the engine.

Racing experience led to revisions of the car and at the end of 1951 came the J2X with Al-fin drum brakes and the engine fitted 7½ in. forward in a new tubular chassis which retained the 100 in. wheelbase and suspension layout of the earlier car. Handling was greatly improved, but since power outputs had been increasing rapidly, some improvement was necessary, for the J2 was fairly agricultural.

Again this car sold well in the States (83 were built between 1952 and 1954), but Allard's overall production was slipping, for the cars were crude and ungainly and had been overtaken by much more modern designs. A Ford Consul-engined tourer, the Palm Beach, was introduced in 1952 but was quickly superseded by such as the Triumph TR2, which was cheaper and much quicker.

From 337 cars sold in 1951, production dropped to 143 in 1952, despite the win in the Monte Carlo Rally, and having reached a mere 36 two years later, Allards were available only to order. Too late Allard revised his styling and offered Jaguar-engined cars, which at least came with the glamour of Le Mans successes. Unfortunately these cars were expensive and offered nothing which could not be bought cheaper elsewhere. A strange motor-cycle-engined three-wheeler, the 'Clipper', came in 1955, but there were few takers.

The trouble with Allards was that they were (rightly) perceived merely as ready-made specials. When the sellers' market began to disappear in 1952, the company had nothing on the stocks to compensate and, being a small outfit, its cars were naturally expensive and the marque lacked sufficient 'badge' to attract customers.

Allard's remaining International competition career is briefly told. Two J2Xs with full-width bodies were entered at Le Mans in 1952, one retiring with a leaking fuel tank, the other with no brakes. Cars with these bodies were sold as J2X 'Le Mans' models. In 1953 Sydney entered Le Mans with a further variation on the J2 theme, the J2R, this time with wishbone and torsion bar front suspension. Its Cadillac engine had 275 bhp on tap and Sydney led the field first time round, but was soon out with no brakes.

As production declined, Allard took to rallying Fords and marketing various conversion kits for them, including superchargers. In 1961 he made what was probably the first custom British dragster, and until his death in 1966, at the age of 56, channelled his competitive urge into what was for Britain a new sport. That Britain now has a healthy drag-racing scene is due to Allard and his admiration of the American way of making machines.

Aston Martin

To say that the fortunes of Aston Martin have been variable is to use English understatement and that is appropriate because AM is the most English of companies. In the James Bond films, the eponymous hero has used many cars, but the one that sticks in the mind is the Aston Martin DB5 he used in *Goldfinger*. It was the right car for the character. In Ian Fleming's books, Bond drove Bentleys, but when updating the details for a modern film, an Aston Martin was perfect.

The company has had its ups and downs, and many owners, but its most successful period was as part of the David Brown empire. Brown bought it in 1947 after seeing a small ad in the Personal Column of *The Times* which offered a sports car company for sale, a steal at £20,000.

David Brown had built up a thriving corporation which made tractors and gears, and other worthy, but unglamorous, examples of engineering. By contrast, Brown enjoyed the style and advantages which come with wealth and that included an element of risk. Despite having no competition driving experience, he once put himself forward to drive a works Aston Martin at Le Mans, but was dissuaded. When the V-12 Lagonda was first tested, Brown was behind the wheel.

Given the man and the history of the company he bought, it was natural that Aston Martin should continue its tradition of racing with a particular aim to win Le Mans, a resolve strengthened by Jaguar's success in the race.

In the pre-Brown era, Aston Martins had always been superbly constructed, if heavy, 1½-litre sports cars (with the exception of one 2-litre model) which were stylish, expensive, and reliable, and which were ideal for long-distance racing. Soon after buying Aston Martin, Brown also bought Lagonda, another company with a chequered corporate history, and a reputation for quality performance cars. Indeed Lagonda had won Le Mans in 1935.

With the acquisition of Lagonda came a 2.3-litre d.o.h.c. engine designed by W. O. Bentley. With Aston Martin came a prototype for a new 2-litre car, the 'Atom', designed by Charles Hill. A marriage between the two elements was in prospect, but not before works test driver, St John Horsfall, partnered by Leslie Johnson, took an 'Atom' to the 1948 Spa 24 Hours race and won outright. It was the first major victory for the marque. A Spa Replica was offered for sale together with the DB1, a coupé based on the 'Atom'.

For the 1949 Le Mans race a new model, the DB2, was prepared. It had styling by Aston Martin's own Frank Feeley and was based on the 'Atom' chassis, which was welded from square-section tubes. Front suspension was by coil springs and trailing arms while the live rear axle was located by coil springs, parallel trailing arms and a Panhard rod. Two of these cars had the 1,970 cc (82.55 × 92 mm) 95 bhp pushrod 'Atom' engine, while the third had the Lagonda LB6 unit, enlarged to 2,580 cc (78 × 90 mm), which gave 116 bhp.

The 2.6-litre car ran well, but retired after six laps with a faulty water pump. Pierre Maréchal in one of the 2-litre cars crashed and was killed (the only fatal accident the works team ever suffered), while the remaining car, driven by Arthur Jones and Nick Haines, had a troubled run but finally finished seventh. A privately entered DB1 finished 11th.

A return to Spa saw the 2.6-litre DB2 finish third overall (second in class) and one of the 2-litre cars finish fifth.

If it had not been a spectacular start, it had been instructive. Fitted with either

The first of the 2.6-litre DB2s, LMA/49/3, at Silverstone after its days as a works car were over. (Guy Griffiths)

George Abecassis and LML/50/9 on their way to 11th place in the 1951 British Empire Trophy on the Isle of Man. (Guy Griffiths)

World Motor Cycle Champion, Geoff Duke, had a brief car racing career with Aston Martin. Duke showed promise but never became happy on four wheels partly due to the fact that his reputation put a few noses out of joint. Here he drives DB3/1 in the Production Sports Car Race at Silverstone, May 1952, before its retirement with steering problems. (T.C. March)

engine, the DB2 was reliable and had excellent roadholding. It was clear, however, that the push-rod engine was not worth developing further and when the cars returned to Le Mans the following year, the 2.6-litre DB2 had become the backbone of Aston Martin's range.

Overseeing the team's return to France was John Wyer, a respected team manager who had agreed to go to Aston Martin for a year and remained for 13. By the time Wyer left to go to Ford, he had become one of the handful of managers in the history of the sport to achieve star status. The three team cars he now supervised were fitted with the optional 'Vantage' engine, which gave 125 bhp.

As production road cars they were driven to the circuit, and on the way Jack Fairman crashed his, so the prototype 2.6 DB2 was pressed into service, but it broke its crankshaft after eight laps. The other two ran like trains, George Abecassis and Lance Macklin brought one home fifth overall, shared the Index of Performance with a Monopole-Panhard and won the 3-litre class in the process. Reg Parnell, partnered by Charlie Brackenbury, a competent amateur, finished sixth, second in class and third in the Index.

Later in the year, in the Tourist Trophy run at Dundrod, Parnell and Abecassis finished fourth and fifth overall (it was a handicap race) and, with Lance Macklin in the third car, scored a 1-2-3 in class.

Aston Martin was on its way. Dr Robert Eberan von Eberhost, the former Auto Union designer, joined the company from E.R.A. and was given a brief to design a 'pukka' sports racing car, the DB3. Until that was ready the team built two lightweight DB2s which shed 450 lb and had 138 bhp engines thanks to Weber carburettors, the first time a British firm had used them. Joining the two lightweights was VMF 64, the Index-winning car of the previous year, which was also given the more powerful engine.

It was VMF 64 which took all the glory as Lance Macklin and Eric Thompson brought it home third overall, first in class and fourth in the Index. There was nothing wrong with the lightweights, which finished fifth and seventh and gave the team a 1-2-3 in class, but VMF 64 had by far the strongest driving team. Macklin was a brilliant talent who raced as part of a raffish life-style and who did not concentrate on building a career as a racer.

Two private cars finished 10th and 11th, so with five starters and five finishers, Aston Martin made a fine showing and, with the DB3 in the background, could look forward to 1951 with some confidence. Nobody at the time could know it, but it was to be many years before AM was to do as well again at Le Mans. It is, anyway, arguable that even the 1959 win at Le Mans equalled the team's achievement with a production sports saloon in 1950.

When the DB3 was first seen, in the summer of 1951, it bore the unmistakable signature of von Eberhorst. There was a ladder-frame chassis made of large-diameter tubes which cranked up at the rear to accommodate a de Dion rear axle suspended by trailing arms, tranverse torsion bars and a Panhard rod. Front suspension retained the trailing arms of the DB2, but these were sprung by transverse torsion bars.

Lance Macklin drove DB3/1 in the Tourist Trophy, but the engine ran its bearings. Abecassis' lightweight DB2 retired with clutch trouble and Brian Shawe-Taylor in the other lightweight could finish only seventh and give best in the 3-litre class to Bobby Baird's Ferrari. By the standards the team had come to expect, it was a poor showing, but it was also an omen for 1952.

Modifications to the rear suspension geometry had greatly improved the DB3's road-holding, but for the first race in the team's greatly expanded programme, the Mille Miglia, DB2s were used. The previous year Tommy Wisdom had been loaned VMF 64, which had become David Brown's personal transport, and he had brought it home 11th overall and first in the 3-litre GT class. VMF 64 was again entrusted to Wisdom, who brought it home 12th and repeated his class win (he also won a Coupe des Alpes with the car later in the year) and Parnell brought one of the lightweights home 13th and second in class.

The works raced the DB2s only once more that year, in the Prix de Berne. There World Champion motor-cyclist Geoff Duke drove brilliantly to finish fourth behind the Mercedes-Benz 300SLs and was offered an M-B contract on the strength of his drive. Reg Parnell brought the other car home fifth.

From then on, AM concentrated on the DB3. Its first showings were promising and the three team cars finished 2-3-4 to Moss's Jaguar C-type at Silverstone in May. Duke was given one to drive in the British Empire Trophy on the Isle of Man, a course he knew intimately. He recorded fastest lap but retired with a broken crankshaft.

For the Sports Car GP at Monaco, the team was back to full strength and this time the cars had 2,922 cc (83 × 90 mm) engines which gave 147 bhp. Bentley's original engine had been of 2.3 litres and the cylinders were closely grouped. To enlarge them, they had to be bored slightly offset to the crank and to compensate the small ends of the con rods were slightly offset. In the race, Parnell's engine threw a rod and he spun into the barriers at St Dévote on his own oil, as also did half of the field. Macklin's car lasted 73 laps before it threw a rod, and newcomer

Peter Collins was classified seventh – after a con-rod broke on lap 93 of 100.

It was back to the 2.6-litre-engine while the larger unit was modified (the solution was to offset the big ends), but the team's next race, Le Mans, was a disaster. Parnell and Thompson had a very pretty coupé DB3, intended to reduce drag, and this went well – for ten laps. An extra high back axle ratio had been specified and it seems that the batch was faulty. One car retired with a broken water pump (31 laps), though the Macklin/Collins car held third after 20 hours, when it, too, went out with a broken transmission.

In the only other important race the team entered in 1952, the Goodwood Nine Hours, one car went out after catching fire during a fuel stop and one retired with clutch trouble, but Peter Collins and Pat Griffith took the third to an encouraging win, though there was no serious foreign opposition.

It was clear that the DB3 was not the winner the team had hoped it would be, mainly because it was too big and, at 2,010 lb, too heavy. AM anyway began every race with a power disadvantage because the LB6 engine could not be extended beyond 3 litres. Willie Watson, a senior design engineer at Aston Martin and a man whose experience went back to the 'WO' Bentleys, proposed and drew a more compact chassis which followed the broad outlines of the DB3, though a central slide replaced the Panhard rod in locating the de Dion tube.

Along with shedding 160 lb, the 2,922 cc engine had been developed to give a reliable 160 bhp, and the stylish new body presented less frontal area. Together with improvements in these three vital areas went better handling. Watson's DB3S was a huge all-round improvement on its predecessor, but its aerodynamics still lagged behind the science as applied in Germany and France.

The new car was not to appear until Le Mans and in the meantime the team drew on the pool of five DB3s. Two went to Sebring in March 1953 and should have won, but Duke crashed the leading car he was sharing with Collins, while Parnell, driving with Abecassis, made an uncharacteristic mistake at the start when he stalled the engine on the line. Making up for lost time he had an off-track excursion in which he damaged a headlight. It was to prove critical and the car finished a close second to the winning Cunningham, though it has to be said there was not a great deal of opposition.

For the Mille Miglia three DB3s were entered, along with a lightweight DB2 for Tommy Wisdom which retired with a broken back axle. It was the DB3's last appearance for the works and, despite a broken Panhard rod and a broken throttle cable, which meant he had to drive on the ignition switch, Parnell brought his car home fifth. It equalled the highest placing ever achieved in this race by a British car.

Parnell's engine had been fitted with a new camshaft, which increased power to 182 bhp and all three DB3S cars entered for Le Mans had the modification. The race was to be the darkness before the dawn. All three retired, Parnell crashed one, another had a slipping clutch and the third dropped a valve. Thereafter the team won all five races it entered in 1953.

Parnell won the British Empire Trophy, a minor race at Charterhall, and headed a 1-2-3 at Silverstone. Partnered by Eric Thompson he led home Collins/Griffith for a 1-2 in the Goodwood Nine Hours, while the pairings finished in the reverse of that order in the Tourist Trophy at Dundrod. While these wins were a welcome fillip, it should be remembered they were against only National competition and the main opposition was the Jaguar C-type which, though excellent at Le Mans and Reims, was not a great competitor on either difficult circuits or in sprint races.

The promise of late 1953, and the performances *were* promising, was destined to be dashed the following year. Aston Martin's racing department was not a very big operation and its resources would have been stretched to adequately develop the DB3S, but a great deal of energy went into David Brown's 'Ferrari-beater', the Lagonda V-12.

In parallel with the Lagonda, work went into a supercharged version of the LB6 engine and the development of a coupé body to achieve lower drag at Le Mans. The normal winter breathing time which the small racing department relied on for development was cut into by the WSCC and the opening round was the Buenos Aires 1,000 Km on 24 January. In those days a race in Argentina meant a very long sea voyage.

The use of Av-gas in Buenos Aires allowed a higher compression ratio to be used (9.4:1 instead of the normal 8.5:1) and this allowed the engine to produce 194 bhp, but apart from that small improvement, an advantage shared by all the runners, the cars began 1954 in exactly the same specification as they ended 1953. Two of the three Astons retired, but Collins and Griffiths finished third, five laps behind the winning Ferrari, and two laps behind a 3-litre Ferrari. It looked a decent performance on the results sheet but in reality was not.

At Sebring, new automatic brake adjusters which had worked in Argentina gave problems. Two cars retired with brake trouble while the third broke a con-rod.

Both entries crashed in the Mille Miglia, but Le Mans was to be the real disaster area. The team had five entries and when one of the Lagondas was withdrawn, it entered a 1953 DB3S. Two of the other cars were coupés with new twin-plug heads which increased power to 225 bhp, but while the DB3 coupé had worked, the DB3S version did not. They had lower drag, sure, that much was proved in the wind tunnel, but as Alfa Romeo had discovered with the Disco Volante there is more to aerodynamics than low drag. The cars showed an alarming tendency to lift at speed and both were eliminated by crashes almost certainly caused by this. They were anyway no quicker than the previous year's open cars which had 43 bhp less. All this should have been discovered before the race, not during it.

Aided by excellent pit work, Peter Collins and Paul Frère (seen here) brought DB3S/6 home second overall and first in class at Le Mans in 1955. (T.C. March)

When the coupés were rebuilt, it was with open bodies, but three coupés were later sold as road cars. As a road car the coupé was sensational, but Aston Martin did not promote them, preferring to concentrate on its DB2/4 range.

The 240 bhp supercharged DB3S was the fastest of the quintet, but with a top speed of 150.2 mph it was a long way from being on the pace. After eight hours it began to blow a gasket, which should have been predictable, for the bridge between the tops of the engine bores was very narrow. The last-minute entry broke a stub axle.

During 1956 works Aston Martins featured re-styled bodywork in an attempt to improve their competitiveness. Peter Collins drove DB3S/9 at Rouen before retiring with run bearings. (LAT)

Stirling Moss was the greatest asset of the Aston Martin team. Here he is seen at the May Silverstone meeting in 1956 with DB3S/8. On this occasion he was beaten into second place in the Sports Car race by team-mate Roy Salvadori. (T.C. March)

The DBR1 Aston Martin seen on its debut in 2.5-litre form at Le Mans in 1956. (LAT)

A minor race at Silverstone which saw a DB3S 1-2-3 with a Lagonda fourth restored morale sufficiently for the team to run three cars in the Tourist Trophy. They should not have bothered, one crashed, one retired with a broken differential, and the third finished 13th.

Later that year the DB3S was offered for sale with a 'single-plug' engine which gave 180 bhp (later 210 bhp) and by 1957 21 had been sold, including the three coupés. Since the works team used a total of ten different cars, it brings total production to 31, most of which survive.

A great deal of work was clearly needed if Aston Martin was going to be at all competitive in 1955 and it was decided to miss the first two rounds of the WSCC, Buenos Aires and Sebring, so it was not until the Mille Miglia in May that a DB3S appeared again. It was a singleton entry, driven by Collins, and for the first time Aston Martin used disc brakes. Collins had a tyre blow out and, driving in a temper, later over-revved his engine.

At the International Trophy Meeting at Silverstone Parnell and Salvadori had new cars incorporating a lot of detail modifications, Girling disc brakes and ZF differentials. They came first and second, beating the works Jaguars, and on the same day Paul Frère won the Spa sports car race in one of the customer cars.

At Le Mans the cars were slow in a straight line compared with the best opposition. Still, with disc brakes and the car's superb handling, they stayed in contention and though only one of the three team cars finished, it was second not far behind the winning Jaguar.

At Aintree, in the British Grand Prix Meeting, a 1-2-3-4 ahead of Hawthorn's Jaguar confirmed that the new cars could be very good on the right circuit, but in 1955 the standard was set by Mercedes-Benz, and of the seven races M-B entered, the Astons met them in only four. There was the Mille Miglia, Le Mans (where Mercedes withdrew its cars after the horrendous crash), the Swedish GP (Salvadori finished a poor seventh) and the Tourist Trophy.

Three team cars entered the TT and two finished, in fourth, behind three Mercedes-Benz 300SLRs, and seventh. In the third, and last, Goodwood Nine Hours race, Dennis Poore and Peter Walker completed a hat-trick for the marque this time against a field which included three works 750 Monza Ferraris. One could point to several wins in 1955, but these were never against full International fields. At World Championship level the tally was a second, a fourth, and a seventh. The DB3S had also reached the end of its development and its successor was some way from being ready.

Going some way to balance the equation in 1956 was the driver line-up, which included Stirling Moss and Tony Brooks, arguably the finest sports car drivers the sport has known. In fact the team as a whole with Collins, Parnell, Salvadori, Carroll Shelby and Peter Walker was perhaps the strongest assembly of driver talent that any sports car manufacturer has been able to call on in any one season. In 1956 the drivers probably flattered the car for apart from the introduction of a smoother nose section with faired-in headlights, the DB3S made no advances.

Most of the races entered were comparatively minor ones, but even then Aston Martin had to be content with place finishes. Three of the five WSCC rounds, Buenos Aires, the Mille Miglia and the Swedish GP were missed (Le Mans was not included in the Championship that year). In the two rounds which Aston Martin did enter, Moss battled for the lead at Sebring, but the only team finisher was Salvadori/Shelby in fourth place. Collins/Brooks came fifth in the Nürburgring 1,000 Km but not on the same lap as the fourth placed 1,500 cc Porsche of von Trips/Magioli.

If Brooks and Collins (who won two Grands Prix for Ferrari that season) could not do better than that on a 'drivers' circuit' on which they both excelled, then Aston Martin was in deep trouble, although the next race, Le Mans, did flatter the team.

Following the previous year's Le Mans accident the organizers introduced safety regulations which allowed 'production' sports cars of unlimited capacity, but restricted 'prototypes' to 2½ litres and this led to the race being dropped from the WSCC. As a listed 'production' car the DB3S was eligible, as was the Jaguar D-type.

In the Championship or not, it was Le Mans the team wanted to win. Aston Martin nearly managed it, too, the Moss/Collins DB3S finishing only a lap behind the winning D-type. In the three-car team was an interesting prototype, the DBR1/250, and though it did not finish (it retired when it ran its rear axle bearings), and though most came away merely with the impression that it was the *noisiest* car in the race, it was the direct forebear of the car which was to win three years later.

The DBR1/250 ran with a new engine of 2,493 cc (83 × 76.8 mm), the smaller capacity from this natural 3-litre unit being achieved with a short-throw crankshaft. Even so, it gave a healthy 212 bhp when tuned to cope with fuel consumption regulations imposed for the 1956 race (the DB3S had 219 bhp for that year's race).

The new engine was designated 'RB6' and as before it was a d.o.h.c. straight-six with a two-plug 60-degree head. There were many detail differences such as an aluminium crankcase and different main bearings, and though initially it gave only slightly more power than the LB6, by 1959 it had 30 bhp more. The engine was helped by having a 5-speed gearbox for the first time, and this was mounted in unit with the final drive. It was ironical, in view of the fact that a significant part of the business of the David Brown group was gear making, that the transmission was never very good and though its drivers recall the car with affection they shudder when the gear change is mentioned.

Though the DB3S had initially been much lighter than the DB3, by 1956 it had put on 200 lb. By contrast, the DBR1's space-frame was 50 lb lighter than the old ladder-frame and the body was of magnesium alloy. At 1,760 lb, the whole was 301 lb lighter than the final version of the DB3S. Its designer, Ted Cutting, retained the old front suspension and while the rear suspension remained broadly the same, a Watts linkage replaced the sliding guide and the torsion bars ran longitudinally, not transversely.

In case the new car did not work, the works built up two more DB3S cars, bringing the 'works' total to ten, and one had double wishbone front suspension. All but one of the four 1956 team cars were sold.

Aston Martin faced 1957 with two distinct models of 3-litre cars, but had yet

At the International Trophy meeting at Silverstone in September 1957 Brooks (DBR1) leads Salvadori and Cunningham-Reid (DBR2s). (T.C. March)

another string to its bow, the DBR2. Although outwardly similar to the DBR1, under the skin was the Project 166 (Lagonda) semi-backbone space-frame and a 6-cylinder, 3.7-litre engine which was being developed for the DB4 road car. This was, unusually for Aston Martin, a 'square' (92×92 mm) unit with a single-plug 80-degree d.o.h.c. head and, depending on its state of tune which was varied from circuit to circuit, gave up to 287 bhp. Suspension was similar to the DBR1, but the 5-speed gearbox was in unit with the engine.

For a 'parts bin special' it was a very effective machine with a great deal of potential, but since WSCC regulations imposed a capacity limit of 3 litres from the end of 1957, its International racing career was brief. The two DBR2s made can be distinguished from the four DBR1s by the fact that the exhaust pipes emerge under the passenger door.

Aston Martin competed in only two of the seven WSCC rounds in 1957 and began the season with a couple of races in Britain. In both events the expensive thoroughbreds had to give best to Brian Lister's Jaguar-powered special driven by Archie Scott-Brown, though on both occasions the DBR1s were using 2.5-litre engines. Then Brooks and Salvadori went to Spa for a non-Championship sports car race and, with 3-litre engines in their DBR1s, came first and second.

As is so often the case in the history of the marque, it was an encouraging result, but it was not at the very top level. The crunch would come at the Nürburgring 1,000 Km on 25 May. There, Brooks, revelling in a real driver's circuit, took an early lead and pulled away a 39-second advantage by the time he handed over to Noel Cunningham-Reid, who was driving in his first major event.

Despite huge pressure, Cunningham-Reid had actually increased the lead by the time he handed back to Brooks for the final leg. Brooks, a supreme stylist, went on to win by over four minutes from two works Ferraris. It was Aston Martin's first WSCC victory, its first in a classic race outside of the British Isles,

Stirling Moss again, this time with the experimental DBR3 that he drove at Silverstone in May 1958. The engine seized and as it was developing far less power than anticipated, it was never raced again. (T.C. March)

*Stuart Lewis-Evans at the wheel of the DBR1 that he shared with Tony Brooks in the
1958 Nürburgring 1000 Km race. The blistered paintwork on the door was caused by an
engine blow-back resulting from too rich mixture.* (LAT)

and it was the first leg of what was to be a hat-trick.

Le Mans, the team's next race, was a different matter. All three cars, two
DBR1s and a DBR2, had gearbox troubles which caused the DBR2 to retire and
Brooks to crash when wrestling with the gear change. The third car retired with a
broken oil pipe. The failure of the team was hardly noticed at home with the triumph of Jaguar and Lotus to celebrate.

At Aintree, Salvadori's DBR1 was again beaten by Scott-Brown's Lister;
Brooks went to Spa for the second time that year and won the Belgian GP against
a good field; and at Silverstone in September, Salvadori finally defeated the
Lister, the only time that year when Scott-Brown was beaten fair and square.

It had been a good year, but the significant thing was that all three overseas victories had been by Tony Brooks, a driver of sublime talent and outstanding mechanical sympathy. There have been greater drivers but never a better one.

With a 3-litre limit in the WSCC, 1958 saw Aston Martin in good shape. Moss
had rejoined the strength and a new 95-degree cylinder head gave 255 bhp when
required. After giving the first round of the Championship, Buenos Aires, a miss,
two DBR1s ran first and second at Sebring until one retired with a broken chassis
frame and the other with gearbox problems.

As usual the team turned out for a number of British events with mixed fortunes and in one, at Silverstone, a car designated DBR3 was driven by Moss. This
had a short-stroke (92 × 75 mm) 3-litre engine derived from the DB4 unit. It
revved up to 7,000 rpm, 1,000 rpm more than the RB6 engine, and Aston Martin
was hoping for 300 bhp, the magic 100 bhp/litre. In the event, it gave no more
power than the RB6, dropped a valve in the race, and was never seen again.

A single car was entered in the Targa Florio for Moss and Brooks, but it retired
after five laps with (what else?) gearbox trouble, though Moss did set fastest lap.
At Spa Frère and Shelby brought their 3,910 cc (95 × 92 mm) DBR2s home
behind Masten Gregory's Lister. It was the last time the works ran a DBR2,
although later, in private hands, these appeared with engines up to 4.2 litres.

Back to the Nürburgring and Moss drove brilliantly to win the team's second
1,000 Km. He was partnered by Jack Brabham, who had virtually no practice
and drove only eight of the 44 laps. One car went out with gearbox failure on the
second lap and the other, driven by Brooks and a newcomer, Stuart Lewis-Evans,
lost time early on to extinguish a fire which dropped it to 14th, but Brooks was
about to take third in the final stages when he was forced off the road by a backmarker. Once again the DBR1 demonstrated it had all the ingredients of a potential champion.

Le Mans was a different story. Moss led the race for 30 laps when his engine threw a rod, Lewis-Evans crashed, and the third car went out with transmission troubles. Complete catastrophe, however, was averted by the Whitehead brothers, who drove their private ex-works DB3S into second, the same car which had finished second in 1955. For the third time in four years an Aston had finished runner-up, but always a victory eluded the cars.

Ferrari had clinched the World Championship at Le Mans, so did not enter the final round, the Tourist Trophy at Goodwood. With no real opposition, AM staged a reliability run and all three cars crossed the finishing line in echelon. Still the race, a four-hour affair, gave half points for the WSCC and the team thus tied with Porsche for second place.

Ten times Aston Martin had tried to win Le Mans and ten times it had failed. It was decided therefore that all the team's efforts would go into the one event and there would be no distractions. Work went into improving the transmission and the tail of the cars was raised to improve air flow, rather as Costin had modified the Lotus Elevens in 1957. Spats covered the rear wheels and the front wheels were partly enclosed too. The team was at last catching up on the sort of aero-dynamic tweaks the Germans had been using pre-war.

After pleas from the organizers, a single car was sent to Sebring, where it failed to finish. Then Moss persuaded the works to enter one car at the Nürburgring, and despite his partner, Jack Fairman, losing time by landing in a ditch, Moss drove brilliantly to secure a hat-trick of wins for AM and take the second leg of a personal hat-trick in the race.

Apart from these diversions everything was directed at Le Mans, where three cars were entered. Two had slightly detuned engines, giving 240 bhp, while the Moss/Fairman car, which was to act as the 'hare', had the maximum 255 bhp. Moss led the race at first, but shortly after Fairman took over, part of an air duct broke and found its way into the engine, which it wrecked.

Then the Ferrari of Oliver Gendebien and Phil Hill led, until it retired in the

Stirling Moss turned in one of the finest drives of his career in the 1959 Nürburgring 1000 Kms. Moss did most of the driving and, despite Jack Fairman putting the car into a ditch, completed a hat-trick for Aston Martin. (LAT)

20th hour with overheating problems which allowed the DBR1s of Salvadori/ Shelby and Frère/Trintignant to sweep home first and second overall and second and third in the Index of Performance.

At last the great goal had been achieved, and in doing so Aston Martin suddenly found it was, with Ferrari and Porsche, capable of winning the WSCC, for there was only one round and that was at Goodwood, a circuit which had been kinder than any other.

For the Tourist Trophy on-board pneumatic jacks were fitted to the three race cars, while the spare had a Maserati 5-speed gearbox. In the race Moss and Salvadori led the sister car of Shelby and Fairman until the second fuel stop on lap 94 of 224. The circuit's primitive refuelling system caused petrol to spill on the hot exhaust pipes and ignited the car. Though the fire was quickly extinguished, the leading car was out of the race.

Moss was then given the Shelby/Fairman car and he drove the remainder of the race single-handedly, putting in another virtuoso performance to win a lap ahead of the Porsche of Bonnier and von Trips. Moss is sometimes called the 'greatest driver who never won a World Championship' but in fact he won two, for Mercedes-Benz in 1955 and Aston Martin in 1959.

With Le Mans and the WSCC under its belt, Aston Martin then withdrew from sports car racing to pursue a fruitless F1 programme. In the early Sixties it ran some special coupés, the Projects 212, 214 and 215, in a handful of races. Handsome and very fast, it is hard to imagine why they were not put into at least limited production.

With the works retiring, the cars were sold on and all six (four DBR1s, and two DBR2s) are still in existence. In British sprint racing the cars were outclassed by the new rear-engined Climax-powered cars made by Cooper and Lotus, but in 1961 Clark and Salvadori finished third at Le Mans in a DBR1. The following year Salvadori and Tony Maggs were lying fourth in one after 17 hours, when a leaking petrol tank side-lined them and in 1962 McLaren and Maggs took fourth in the Nürburgring 1,000 Km.

Aston Martin's list of victories at the highest level was a short one and then mainly due to the genius of Moss and Brooks. The cars, however, were so attractive and well turned out that they caught the imagination. Further, unlike the majority of British sports-racing cars of the Fifties, they were thoroughbreds and the team drivers were frequently stars.

Borgward

Borgward was something of a curiosity among postwar volume car makers because it was owned and controlled by one man, Carl Borgward, an autocratic individual with a passion for building motor cars. His enthusiasm was a double-edged blade so far as his business was concerned. On the one hand he was obsessed with quality and his cars reflected this, on the other hand this obsession did not always translate into healthy balance sheets. The combine collapsed in 1961 due to poor management.

Just prior to World War II, Borgward acquired the Hansa, Lloyd and Goliath companies and, briefly, marketed a Hansa with a Borgward badge. In 1949 the

The Borgward Hansa coupé of Hartmann/Brudes at Le Mans in 1953. It retired and shortly afterwards was destroyed in an accident though one of the three Hansa coupés built remains in Sweden. (NMM)

first 'pukka' Borward appeared and created something of a sensation, being the first German saloon car to have a fully-enveloping body. In the market it occupied a place similar to Audi today.

Production of Borgwards was never high, the best year's production being 38,000 cars, a third of the group's total, but sales were rising consistently until the firm's collapse and tuned versions of the Isabella TS (introduced in 1954) were successful in saloon car racing both in Germany and Britain.

Given Carl Borgward's obsession with motor cars, it was more or less inevitable that his company would turn its hand to motor sport. While most British constructors were still making sports cars with cycle wings, the Germans understood the value of aerodynamics and, in 1950, a standard Hansa chassis fitted with a streamlined body had taken a clutch of International records at Monthléry which included 1,000 km at 107 mph, impressive for a car with a standard 66 bhp engine.

Encouraged, Borgward had Karl Brandt develop a 1,500 cc Rennsport using a modified 1,498 cc (72 × 92 mm) production engine. This had hemispherical combustion chambers, inclined valves operated by push-rods, and two downdraught Solex carburettors. By 1952 it developed 100 bhp at 5,500 rpm, a respectable figure for the day.

For the chassis, Brandt chose a conventional twin-tube layout with front suspension by coil springs and double wishbones and, at the rear, coil springs and swing axles located longitudinally by an A-bracket. To save weight, the frame was extensively drilled (there were, count 'em, 2,000 holes in the frame) so parts of it ended up looking like the protective shield over an external exhaust pipe.

The car was clothed in a slippery aluminium body which could be fitted with spats over the rear wheels, and metal discs over the headlights, for high-speed circuits.

Driving was entrusted to Hans Hugo Hartmann, who pre-war had been a cadet driver with Mercedes-Benz and had driven for the team in the 1939 Eifelrennen. Then, like so many others, he had seen the prospects of a fine career disappear with the onset of war. 1952 was a limited season but, during it, Hartmann won at the Grenzlandring (at an average speed of 121.54 mph) and Avus, and finished second to a 2-litre BMW-engined Veritas in the Eifelrennen. In the Carrera Panamericana he had the misfortune to be disqualified for finishing the final leg seven seconds over time. At the time he was running over two hours clear from the next man in class. The car was also used to take five Class F International records.

Borgward's little racing department was always under-resourced, but one must bear in mind that total production of Borgward in 1952 was only 7,000 cars. Still, the racing programme always seemed to lack any consistent policy. It would have been advantageous, for example, to have sold examples to privateers to increase representation on the grid and benefit from feed-back, but Borgward sold none of its Rennsports.

After a promising debutant year, cars appeared only spasmodically in 1953, but two finished second and third to Helm Glöcker's push-rod 1,500 cc proto-type Porsche 550 in the Eifelrennen and Bechem/Helfrich finished a fine third in the Nürburgring 1,000 Km (a WSCC round) behind a 4.5-litre Ferrari and an Ecurie Ecosse Jaguar C-type. In the Freiburg-Schauinsland hill-climb, Bechem finished second to Hans Herrmann's push-rod 1,500 cc Porsche 550. Since these Porsches had, at best, 98 bhp to the Borgward's 110 bhp, it would appear that the Borgward chassis was not quite in the same class.

That same year the company showed a special Hansa coupé, made with exten-sive use of light alloy and looking rather like a front-engined Porsche 356. A top speed of 144 mph was claimed, but even with Bosch-fuel injection its engine was giving only 110 bhp, so it was a claim which few took seriously. Along the Mul-sanne Straight at Le Mans the car was actually timed at 114 mph.

Three of these cars were entered for Le Mans, but one was written off shortly before the race, so then there were two. One, driven by Hartmann and Brudes, retired in the third hour having ran out of fuel, while the other, driven by French-men Poch et Mouche, was holding 18th place with thirty minutes to go when the overheating engine gave up the ghost.

Joachim Bonnier on his way to second overall (and tying with team-mate Hans Herrmann) in the 1958 Trento-Bondone hill climb. Borgward's 16-valve 1500cc fuel injected engine had enormous, but unfulfilled, potential. (Autosport)

A Borgward Rennsport *undergoing preparation.* (Autosport)

Shortly after the race one of the cars was destroyed in a crash in Germany, but the other, the Poch/Mouche car, later found a home in Sweden, was raced in national events, underwent a lot of rough treatment, but now is happily restored.

Borgward entered a few races in 1954, and the cars featured a new d.o.h.c. engine, based on a standard block, which had first been exhibited at the 1951 Frankfurt Show. Then it had been claimed to deliver 135 bhp, but in 1954 was producing 150 bhp (the magic 100 bhp per litre) at 7,200 rpm.

Despite a severely restricted season, Gunther Bechem won the Eifelrennen and the two cars of Bechem and Hammernick led all the Porsches in the Carrera Panamericana when crashes eliminated them. At the time he crashed, Bechem was lying third overall, behind the Ferraris of Phil Hill and Umberto Magioli, in the toughest race ever to have featured in the WSCC. Either Bechem was an extraordinary driver or the Borgward was an extraordinary car.

Borgward did not re-enter racing until 1957. Progress from prototype to fully developed racing engine had been slow, but when it came it proved worth the wait. Indeed the engine was so good that one is led to speculate how the history of the sport might have been had it been backed by proper resources and made more widely available. More than that, it was designed from the beginning to be simple to mass produce and, had it been productionized and fitted to road-going cars, Borgward could have had its own Lotus-Cortina years before Ford.

Details of the engine were released in 1956, by which time it had discarded standard components though retaining the overall layout. It was a four-in-line d.o.h.c. unit with four valves per cylinder, twin magnetoes, two plugs per cylinder and Bosch direct fuel injection. Commentators prophetically suggested it would make an ideal unit for the new F2 which was due to come into force the following year.

When the engine was finally ready to do serious battle, in 1957, it was decided to concentrate on the European Hill Climb Championship and Hans Herrmann took two second places, at Gaisburg and Monte Parnes, and two thirds, at Freiburg and Aôsta-Gran St Bernard, to finish third in the series behind Daetwyler (Maserati) and von Trips (Porsche).

The following year the upper limit for the Championship was raised to 2 litres so the two cars which were run, mainly for Jo Bonnier and Herrmann, started with a disadvantage. They still gave a good account of themselves and had a fierce season-long battle with the larger-engined Porsche RSK of 'Taffy' von Trips.

Driving brilliantly, Bonnier set a new outright record for the Freiburg climb with Herrmann third. Bonnier took second place to von Trips at Gaisburg (Herrmann third), Ollon-Villars and Trento-Bondone, where he tied with Herrmann. Herrmann came second at Monte Parnes with Cabianca, replacing Bonnier for the one event, third. Von Trips emerged Champion with the Borgwards of Bonnier and Herrmann second and third.

It was a good showing which suggested that the cars might have been competitive in 1,500 cc circuit racing. Indeed, at the 1958 German GP meeting, Borgwards finished second, fourth and sixth in a sports car race with Porsches filling the other places. Since Porsche was the cream of the category, Borgward's performance was impressive. It was reported in the press at the beginning of 1958 that Borgward had started work on its own F2 car, but like the promise of the sports-racing cars, this came to nothing.

It was a pity that the cars were not given more opportunities, more backing, and allowed to prove themselves in International racing. At the end of 1958 Borgward withdrew from competition but allowed its engines to be used by others and it was as a F2 unit that the worth of the RS engine became widely apparent.

In 1959, three Cooper F2 cars were fitted with Borgward engines, two for the British Racing Partnership for Ivor Bueb and Chris Bristow to drive, and one for Rob Walker, Stirling Moss's entrant. Moss won at Siracusa, Reims, Clermont-Ferrand and Rouen, four circuits of incredible diversity. Bristow took two wins in Britain and Bueb a second and a third.

So far as motor racing was concerned, it was the marque's swansong, though experiments with four-valve cylinder heads continued. Unfortunately, although its engineers had shown themselves capable of advanced design, the Borgward group was mismanaged and was already sliding into the crisis which ruined it in 1961. Carl Borgward, who was both creator and destroyer of the company which bore his name, died two years later.

Bristol 450

On the face of it, the story of the Bristol 450 is the most simple imaginable. Three cars were built using an engine based on a production unit. They were entered in just five races in three years, took three wins in the poorly supported 2-litre class and broke a few International class records. The story of the cars, however, is rather more complicated and interesting than the bare bones would suggest.

The Bristol Aeroplane Company made its decision to build cars while World War II was still in progress and as soon as peace returned it established a Car

Division. Broadly speaking, the new company was a partnership between Bristol and H. J. Aldington of A.F.N. Ltd, the pre-war B.M.W. importer and maker of Frazer Nash cars.

Aldington went to Munich with one of the teams which picked over German technology and carried off some as war reparations. From these forays came the elements which, in 1946, produced the first Bristol car, the 400 coupé with its chassis derived from the B.M.W. 326, its body from the B.M.W. 327/80, and its engine from the B.M.W. 328.

None of these elements were precise copies, though, for B.M.W.'s drawings first went through Bristol's drawing office, which, as one of the world's foremost aircraft manufacturers, was an outfit which knew a thing or two about engineering. We need not concern ourselves with Bristol road cars, or with the constitution of the company, except to say the cars were superbly constructed and the partnership with A.F.N. Ltd was short-lived. One reason for the split was that A.F.N. wanted 50 per cent more power than Bristol was prepared to provide. Pre-war, B.M.W. had been obtaining 140 bhp from competition versions of the 2-litre 328 engine, but for its road cars Bristol was content with little more than half of that.

When the partnership split up A.F.N. obtained an exclusive deal to use special Bristol FNS (Frazer Nash Special) engines in its cars. These had been developed by an ex-B.M.W. engineer, Fritz Fiedler, who was on A.F.N.'s staff, and they formed the basis for all Bristol competition units.

Both the Bristol and B.M.W. engines were straight-six 1971 cc (66 mm × 96 mm) units with hemispherical combustion chambers and inclined valves operated by a system of push-rods activated by a single camshaft located low in the cylinder block.

Before long, Bristol engines found their way into various sports and formula cars. As so often happened in the Fifties, when a powerful and reliable engine became available, there sprung up a class of racing around it. Quite apart from

The Bristol 450 of Tommy Wisdom and Jack Fairman leads the Talbot of Pierre Levegh and Charles Pozzi at Le Mans in 1953. During this, their debut race, all three Bristols retired but the company responded quickly and within three weeks the engine had reliability and the front end had been restyled. (Geoffrey Goddard)

the fact that the Bristol engine was eligible for Formula 2, firms such as Lister, Lotus, Cooper and Tojeiro used them in sports cars and, for a period, the 2-litre sports car class became one of the most competitive in British National racing.

One F2 car built using a Bristol unit was the G-Type E.R.A. Pre-war, E.R.A. had been successful in Voiturette racing, had then been bought by Leslie Johnson, a successful amateur racer, and operated as an engineering and consultancy company. Johnson wanted to restore E.R.A's former racing reputation and laid plans for an F1 car to be ready when the 2½-litre Formula began in 1954. While E.R.A. set to work on a 6-cylinder engine based on the Norton motor cycle unit, Johnson decided to make a start with an interim Bristol-engined F2 car.

This was designed by David Hodkin, who had assisted Robert Eberan von Eberhorst in the design of the Jowett-E.R.A. which became the Jowett Jupiter sports car. It is not surprising then that the G-type had a chassis frame bearing more than a passing similarity to the Jowett, with two large-diameter tubular main members, but there were some distinctive features. The frame was made from magnesium alloy and the de Dion rear axle, mounted on trailing links, could be adjusted to alter the car's handling. Front suspension was by coil springs and double wishbones, the rear (drum) brakes were mounted inboard, and the wheels were of cast alloy.

Hodkin designed a fairly wide car, so the driver could sit alongside, rather than on top of, the prop-shaft and though this kept the height down, it still resulted in a large, too large, frontal area. Despite the use of magnesium alloy, the car was overweight and even with Stirling Moss behind the wheel, its performances were feeble compared with Mike Hawthorn's Cooper-Bristol. It was not until years later it was learned that quite apart from Hawthorn's brilliance as a driver that his car had been assisted by the use of a nitro-methane-based fuel which gave him a considerable power advantage.

The E.R.A. project was brought to an end when Leslie Johnson suffered a heart attack and, on medical advice, sold up. Johnson's illness also brought to an end a racing career which had been unusually successful in events such as Le Mans and the Mille Miglia. E.R.A. was bought by Solex, the carburettor company, and still operates as an engineering company, and the G-type and its spares went to Bristol, which had decided it would like to run cars at Le Mans. For evaluation purposes, Bristol built a startling coupé body on the E.R.A. chassis and was sufficiently encouraged by the results to proceed with its own version.

The chassis followed the same lines as the E.R.A. but without the adjustable rear suspension, and the frame, though made from steel rather than magnesium, was actually lighter. While the E.R.A. had been too wide for a single-seater, the Bristol was a little too narrow for a sports-racer, so the driving position was fairly high. Still the end result was a car which was beautifully detailed, was one of the very first British competition cars to employ *serious* aerodynamics as opposed to 'streamlining' and was perfect for its task, which was to secure class wins at Le Mans and in the Reims 12 Hours races.

At Le Mans in 1953, the two cars entered were slow, due to being over-geared, and both retired in the race after crankshaft balance weights flew through the crankcase causing oil to ignite on the exhaust pipe. In one instance this caused the car to crash, injuring its driver, Tommy Wisdom.

It was a set-back, but just three weeks later not only were two cars ready for the Reims 12 Hours race, but they had undergone fairly extensive modifications to the front bodywork and the engine fault was cured. Thereafter no works Bristol ever suffered an engine failure.

The 2-litre class at Reims was not well supported, but one 450 outlasted the opposition to win it and finish a creditable fifth overall, while the other retired with clutch trouble.

Back at the factory, further bodywork modifications resulted in a superbly clean front end and a car was dispatched to Monthléry to successfully tackle some International class records.

Three cars were entered at Le Mans in 1954, these having the rear panel between the fins raised two inches and the engine power increased. Running to team orders, which meant that the drivers were restricted to a pace which was enough to see them secure a class win, the cars finished 1-2-3 in class and seventh, eighth and ninth overall. Shortly afterwards at Reims, they were beaten by a 2-litre Ferrari, but finished 2-3-4 in class and 10th, 11th and 12th overall.

It was Bristol's policy to employ competent club racers rather than professional drivers and the most successful of its drivers, a test pilot called Peter Wilson, had a racing career which in its entirety comprised less than ten races, all

The Bristol team before the start of the 1954 Le Mans race in which it scored a 1–2–3 in class. (The Bristol Aeroplane Co Ltd)

For 1955 the three team cars were converted into roadsters for another 1–2–3 in class at Le Mans. Here the class-winning car of Peter Wilson/Jim Mayers leads the Ferrari 121LM of Maglioli/Phil Hill. (Geoffrey Goddard)

of them at International level. One reason for this policy was that Bristol did not want to detract attention from its cars but, in any case, few professionals would sign for so restricted a season.

Another two-race programme was planned for 1955, and it was now part of a longer-term plan which included a F1 car. This time Bristol cut off the roofs to improve aerodynamics and eliminate some of the problems associated with closed cars such as misting, wiper failure and oil on the windscreen. It was another splendid demonstration run, the cars finishing seventh, eighth and ninth overall (one had been running as high as fifth but had been slowed on team orders) and again, there was a 1-2-3 in class, which was the object of the exercise.

1955 was the year of the terrible crash at Le Mans which saw the Reims race cancelled, so Le Mans was the 450's last appearance. Later in the year, the deaths of two of the team drivers, Mike Keen and Jim Mayers, in separate races, and neither in a Bristol car, helped to persuade Bristol to abandon racing altogether and so a future sports-racer was stillborn along with the proposed F1 car.

The two E.R.A. chassis Bristol had bought and two of the team cars were sawn up, for in those days obsolete racing cars had little value. Bristol did not need the money from a sale and, besides, did not want to place its reputation in other hands, which is what would have happened had the cars been sold. The cars anyway were designed solely for endurance racing on two smooth high-speed circuits and would probably have been embarrassed in sprints. The single survivor has recently been restored by the factory.

Connaught

Connaught Engineering was established on 1 January, 1949, primarily to provide machinery for a gentleman amateur driver, Kenneth McAlpine, and to sell replicas of his cars to like-minded drivers. The company was never registered as such but was McAlpine trading under the Connaught name.

'Connaught' derives phonetically from the 'Con' of Continental Cars, and 'aut' of 'automobile'. Continental Cars was a garage business set up by Rodney Clarke during World War II after he had been invalided out of the RAF. After the war he was joined by Mike Oliver, another ex-flier.

Both men were first-rate intuitive engineers and as well as trading in exotic cars, especially Bugattis, prepared racing cars for customers. A hoped-for Bugatti agency did not materialize after the war, indeed, new cars of any description were scarce on the home market, though rolling chassis were readily obtainable. To have something to sell, Clarke bought chassis from Lea-Francis and made minor modifications to them while Oliver extensively re-worked the engines. They were then fitted with simple, but hardly attractive, enveloping aluminium bodies. Two models were offered, the L1 and the more powerful L2.

No L1 was made, for customers preferred the performance of the L2, and these cars were quick for their day, thanks to Mike Oliver's painstaking work on their engines. McAlpine, who had been first impressed by the work the partners had done in preparing his Maserati 8CM, then by the Connaught L2 for which he was the first customer, set up Connaught Engineering and commissioned Clarke and Oliver to build him an F2 car.

This car, the Type A, appeared late in 1950 and in it McAlpine finished second to Stirling Moss's H.W.M. at Castle Combe in the only race he tackled with it that year. It was a promising debut for a car fitted with a modified alloy-block 1,750 cc Lea-Francis engine driven by an amateur.

Meanwhile the L2 performed quite well in British club events and one, using a 1,500 cc engine and a simple cycle-winged body, was very successful in the hands of Ken Downing. When Lea-Francis began employing ifs, Connaught had to follow suit and the cars using this chassis were designated 'L3'. Three examples of a stripped-down car, the L3/SR, were also made but achieved no great success. In all, 14 of these cars were made and all but one is accounted for.

After McAlpine's debut with the F2 car, the engine was enlarged to 2 litres, and during the next three years, a total of nine Type As were built. Though they scored no major International successes, they took numerous wins in lesser events in Britain and also picked up a few World Championship points. At a time when small constructors built by intuition, Connaught did things properly to sound engineering principles and employed up to eight men in its drawing office, a number which some F1 teams today would envy.

Clarke was a man of astonishing originality and, had Coventry Climax re-leased its V-8 Godiva engine, would have had a rear-engined monocoque F1 car ready for the 1954 season, eight years before Colin Chapman re-wrote design parameters with the Lotus 25. When it became clear that this engine was not going to be released on schedule, Clarke's advanced design was put on ice until a suitable power unit became available and the team proceeded with a front-engined stop-gap, the Type B.

Because of the length of time it took to develop and prepare, to Connaught's exacting standards, the dated Alta engines which were to power this car, the Type B did not begin its racing career until 1955. In the meantime, the company built up two AL/SR sports-racing cars using surplus long-wheelbase Type A components.

The Type A chassis was a simple ladder-frame built around two 3½-in. tubes, but like all Connaughts was carefully detailed, one of the cross-members doubling as an oil tank, for example. Suspension was by torsion bars all round, with double wishbones at the front and a de Dion tube located by single trailing arms and a transverse link at the rear.

As with the single-seater cars, the wheels were of cast magnesium and it says much about Connaught's approach to engineering that those still in Historic racing are still able to use their original wheels while other magnesium wheels of the period have generally had to be discarded.

Connaught's chief draughtsman, 'Johnny' Johnson, sketched out the aluminium body which he cribbed from magazine photographs of contemporary Italian sports racers.

Though the 1,500 cc engine was basically Lea-Francis, Oliver's modifications were so comprehensive that Connaught might justifiably claim them as its own. Almost all internal components were either specially made for Connaught or else machined in the team's workshops. Carburation was by four Amals mounted on ram pipes. The unit's alloy block was originally intended by Lea-Francis to form the basis for an engine for American midget racing, but the cylinder head was standard Lea-Francis cast iron with camshafts mounted high in the block operating the valves via short push-rods. As with the formula cars, transmission was via a rear-mounted 4-speed preselector gearbox designed by the Self Changing Gear Company to Wilson patents.

The first car went to John Coombs, but he found that the chassis, though sweet, was too heavy for British sprint events and by mid-1954 had transferred the engine to a Lotus Mk 8. The rest of the car was sold and fitted with a new Connaught engine. A second car appeared during 1954 and this was used by Kenneth McAlpine but without any notable success.

Although the chassis design was five years old when the first AL/SR appeared, Connaughts had a reputation second to none for their road-holding. They were often outclassed in British sprint races on the faster circuits, but they did take a number of wins and the probability is that they would have shown well in continental road races, for they were solidly built and powerful.

McAlpine's car was rebodied the following year with a startling but properly conceived aerodynamic shell resembling the original 'streamliner' body with which the F1 Type B Connaught first raced. At Le Mans the car was rapid, touching 135 mph down the Mulsanne Straight, 7 mph faster than the 1,500 cc Lotus-Climax Eleven was to achieve the following year. Though showing well in the early stages, it retired in the sixth hour with gearbox problems.

A couple of months later, during the Dundrod Tourist Trophy, it was driven
by a promising young driver, Bill Smith, who was involved in a multiple crash in
which he lost his life. The car was destroyed.

The first AL/SR, though, driven by Les Leston and Archie Scott-Brown, came
home sixth overall and first in the 1,500 cc class in the Goodwood Nine Hours
later that year. It was the only International success the model achieved, but that
was not the fault of the car, which was basically a very sound design. The trouble
was that it was a merely a stop-gap, built from available spares, to fill in the time
before Connaught had its F1 car ready. As such it had received limited attention
and an all-too-brief racing programme.

Later the survivor was rebodied with a proprietary Rochdale fibreglass body
and raced in British club events. Now owned by Gerry Walton, who drives it in
Historic races, it has an aluminium body closely resembling its original shell.

Connaught was always under-funded and was frequently threatened with clos-
ure, so few of Clarke's many brilliant ideas saw the light of day. Not only did he
conceive, and partly build, an F1 monocoque car years before anyone else, his
schemes included a mid-engined GT car – in 1950! His first Type B F1 car had a
fully-enveloping body of good aerodynamic characteristics which he developed
simultaneously to Mercedes-Benz, and among other developments which Connaught explored was an anti-lock braking system six years before one appeared
on any car.

Connaught looked doomed for the axe at the end of 1955 when Tony Brooks
drove a Type B to victory in the Syracuse GP trouncing a strong Maserati works
team. This decided McAlpine to keep the team going a little longer and in 1956
Type Bs put in some good performances including second in the International
Trophy at Silverstone (Archie Scott-Brown) and third and fifth in the Italian GP
(Ron Flockhart and Jack Fairman).

1957 began with Stuart Lewis-Evans winning a F1 race at Goodwood, largely
due to others' retirements, and finishing fourth in the Monaco GP, but despite
these successes, and strong showings in non-Championship F1 races, McAlpine
felt he could no longer support the team. He had retired from racing and no
longer had the same impetus to spend his income on other men's sport.

Connaught closed down and all its effects were auctioned. Clarke continued as a motor trader until his death in 1979. Oliver returned to flying, became a respected test pilot, and now lives in retirement in Devon.

Cooper

Charles Cooper, a former racing mechanic, had pre-war set up a small garage in Surbiton on the Kingston bypass. When World War II ended, some of the ideas which had been chewed over during six years without motor racing came to fruition and one was the introduction of a class for 500 cc racing cars intended for the impecunious special builder.

Together with his son John, Cooper was one of the first to build a car for the category. The Coopers took the front suspension of two scrap Fiat Topolinos, made a basic frame to hold the two ends apart, installed a JAP engine at the back and clothed it with a basic but attractive body.

A second car followed for Eric Brandon and he and John Cooper were soon among the silverware. The car itself was not outstandingly the best in the embryo class, Colin Strang's special built on a Topolino chassis was probably its equal, but the Coopers were able to put their car into production.

The problem facing any constructor at the time was the scarcity of materials, most of which were earmarked by the government for more serious purposes. The Coopers, however, were nothing if not resourceful. They bought up redundant Morrison air raid shelters (a sort of steel table under which it was possible to obtain protection from falling masonry) and the tops were converted into the castles on which the transverse leaf springs were located, while the legs were made into welding jigs.

Wheels were difficult to come by, so the Coopers cast their own from aluminium from a scrapyard filled with redundant military aircraft, and this also furnished the material for the cars' bodies. Brake drums were made by sawing up the wet liners of marine diesel engines, again obtained from a scrapyard. One of the Coopers' customers was in the steel business and was able to help in other ways.

The upshot was a batch of 12 cars which swamped the opposition, and this led in turn to another batch, and then another. The company was established and made over 400 such cars over the next ten years or so.

By 1949, the Coopers wanted to diversify and they constructed a front-engined, M.G.-powered sports car which was built on the same basic lines as the 500 cc cars. The success of the half-dozen or so built gave them sufficient confidence to build, in 1952, a Bristol-engined F2 car (T20) and despite their relative lack of power they were surprisingly successful, especially when driven by Mike Hawthorn, who finished fourth in that year's World Championship.

Some of these cars were eventually converted to sports cars, most of which have since been re-converted to F2 cars for reasons not unconnected to current market values. The outstanding Cooper-Bristol, no matter which way you view the cars, is the ex-Hawthorn car converted to sports form in 1952–3, with a body copied from a Ferrari 212, which Alan Brown owned until recently. Among his many successes with it, Brown won the 1954 British Empire Trophy and, the same year, the 2-litre race at the (sports car) Dutch GP meeting.

The 500 cc Formula Three cars continued to be the company's main line of business, but it did make half a dozen Bristol-engined (T22) sports cars, broadly based on the F2 design, and a similar number of Jaguar-engined cars, which departed from previous Cooper practice by having multi-tubular frames.

The first Cooper-Jaguar (T33) came about as a result of a commission from Peter Whitehead, a wealthy amateur who had started racing before the war. Since Whitehead was in the wool trade, he could fit in racing 'Down Under' with his business activities and was a regular visitor to the Antipodes usually with his privately owned Ferraris. Though not an 'ace', he drove occasionally in Grands Prix, was good enough to be a works driver for both Jaguar and Aston Martin and, in 1951, shared the winning Jaguar at Le Mans.

Whitehead's idea was to make better use of the Jaguar engine's power with a chassis which would be lighter and handle better than the C-type.

Peter Whitehead with the first Cooper-Jaguar, Silverstone, May 1954. Note the ducting for the low-mounted radiator. (The Motor)

Suspension on the new car followed traditional Cooper practice with transverse leaf springs and telescopic dampers but it had double wishbones front and rear. Disc brakes, then still something of a novelty, were fitted all round and the finished car had similar dimensions and weight to the Jaguar D-type, which was then nearing completion in Coventry, though, naturally, its components derived from the heavier (by 150 lb) C-type.

In one obvious way it was very different. John Cooper was another designer to have been influenced by Taruffi's twin-boom Tarf record car and though the Cooper-Jaguar was not outlandish in the same way as the Nardi and Pegaso interpretations of the theme, the driver sat very far to the right, outside the main chassis tubes, while the nominal passenger seat was equally far to the left. As with aerodynamics, weight distribution was still regarded as something of a black art.

In Whitehead's hands the car had a fairly lacklustre career, a win in the Wakefield Trophy in Ireland against thin opposition and an undistinguished third in the Oporto GP, two laps down from a pair of works Lancias, were the highlights of the year. Two other cars were sold to a couple of British club drivers who did not make names for either themselves or their cars.

A revised Mk II version (T38), with more conventional bodywork and a dry-sump engine, was made in 1955, but it stuck to the odd seating location of the first car. Undeterred by his experiences with the Mk I, Whitehead bought one and its highlight came when he ran it at Le Mans with his half-brother, Graham, who was also a more than averagely competent amateur racer. The car retired after three hours when lying 14th.

Peter returned to Oporto and motored steadily to finish fourth in a thin field, and in the equally low-key Lisbon GP the Cooper ran in third place before retiring with transmission trouble. It next appeared in the Tourist Trophy, but retired after 44 laps with a broken chassis.

Whitehead took it to New Zealand that winter and after he raced without particular distinction in the 'International' races, sold it to Stan Jones (father of Alan) who had better fortune in Australian national events. The car is still Down Under, one of the five survivors of the six made.

Tommy Sopwith bought a Mk II but raced it only occasionally before chang-

David Shale's ex-Sopwith Cooper-Jaguar Mk II leads an Austin-Healey in the 1957 British Empire Trophy at Oulton Park. (T.C. March)

The 1100cc Cooper-Climax 'bobtail' of Wadsworth/Brown which finished last at Le Mans in 1955 or, if you prefer, third in class. (T.C. March)

ing his racing policy, while a third went to Michael Head (father of Williams designer Patrick Head), who used it both as a tourer and for club racing, in which he enjoyed some success. Whitehead's first car appeared again in the 1957 Mille Miglia driven by Dick Steed and John Hall, but it did not last long.

It is difficult to assess the Cooper-Jaguar because the cars only ran as private entries and no top-line driver ever used one. It can hardly, though, be regarded as a success and the most probable reason is that John Cooper and his draughtsman, Owen Maddocks, were out of their depth. It was something Charles Cooper suspected all along, which is why he did not give the project his whole-hearted blessing.

The Coopers were not scientific designers such as Chapman or Broadley but were, rather, special builders who had a shrewd idea of what would work and who normally were able to work from feedback given them by good drivers. It is no coincidence that Cooper's greatest glory came when the team drivers were Jack Brabham and Bruce McLaren, both fine natural engineers, and the company's fortunes declined when first Brabham, then McLaren, went off to build their own cars.

If the Jaguar-powered car was a failure, Cooper's next sports car redressed the balance. The Coopers had been quick to see the potential of the Coventry Climax FWA engine which made its racing debut in 1954 and decided to build a Climax-powered sports car for 1955. The performance of the Costin-bodied Lotus MK8 had convinced them of the desirability of an aerodynamic shape and they had already produced a 500 cc record-breaking car fitted with a streamlined body

51

after the style of John Cobb's Napier-Railton Special.

John Cooper knew an aerodynamacist at Hawker Aircraft who took drawings of the record car in to his boss for comment. His boss suggested that the overall shape would be suitable for a racing car, while cutting off the tail behind the back wheels and making the rear panel slightly concave would give an aerodynamic advantage while making the car more practical. Having arrived at the shape, John Cooper and his draughtsman/designer, Owen Maddocks, produced a simple multiple-tube frame, with curved tubes, to go beneath it.

Because the 500 cc car was rear-engined, this sports car would be rear-engined. Because the driver of the record car sat in the middle, the sports car would have a central driving seat with a passenger seat, fit for an undernourished midget, to the driver's left. As with most previous Coopers, suspension was independent all round by transverse springs and lower wishbones, and the brake drums were cast into the magnesium alloy wheels. The gearbox, in unit with the final drive, had French E.R.S.A. gears in a Citroën casing.

It was a tiny car, with an overall length of 10 ft 10 in, a wheelbase of 7 ft 5 in, and a dry weight of just under 900 lb. When asked to explain the sawn-off tail, John Cooper described the theory and said he called it a 'Camm tail', for it had been done at the suggestion of Hawker's great designer, Sir Sydney Camm. By an extraordinary coincidence, it fitted the aerodynamic theories of the German scientist Dr Wunibald Kamm, so in print it has generally been called a 'Kamm tail', which is also correct. Its official designation was T39, but nobody ever referred to Coopers by their type numbers and it was always known as the 'Bob-tail'.

Initially works cars were made for Ivor Bueb and Jim Russell, both graduates from F3, and the first customer car went to Tommy Sopwith. Since the car cost just £1,350 other customers soon arrived at Surbiton.

It was impossible to know in 1955 that the 1,100 cc sports car class in Britain was witnessing a significant battle as the Cooper took on Chapman's Lotus Mk 9. On balance it was Cooper's year with a large number of wins and fine performances. Most of these were in club events, but they included class wins in the Goodwood Nine Hours (Ivor Bueb/Jim Russell), the International Trophy at Oulton Park (Russell) and the Tourist Trophy (Bueb/Mike McDowell), while privateers Wadsworth and Brown finished third in class at Le Mans.

A Bristol-powered version was entered as a F1 car for Jack Brabham in the British GP, where it was comprehensively outclassed, but it had a couple of decent runs in minor events later that year. A similar car was sold to Bob Chase, but his driver, Mike Keen, crashed it at Goodwood and died.

In 1956, an 1,100 cc Bobtail won its class at Sebring and another came eighth overall, and second in class, at Le Mans. Overall, the cars were no match for the new Lotus Eleven, for Cooper did not have the same aggressive works programme, but in private hands they managed a fair number of wins in British and American club racing.

That same year, however, when fitted with Coventry Climax's 'stop-gap' 1,460 cc s.o.h.c. FWB engine, and driven by top-class drivers, Bobtails were quite successful in second division sports car races. Roy Salvadori took two outright wins at the 1956 Easter Monday Goodwood International Meeting, a class win at the *Daily Express* International Trophy Meeting at Silverstone, and the City Cup in Oporto, Portugal. Salvadori came third in a race at the Nürburgring, Jack Brabham finished second in the Imola sports car Grand Prix, and Stirling Moss won the British Empire Trophy at Oulton Park.

Stirling Moss on his way to winning the 1956 British Empire Trophy in this Cooper fitted with an sohc 1460cc Coventry Climax FWB engine. (T.C. March)

By 1957 production of these cars had reduced to a trickle as customers turned to Lotus and Cooper turned to F2, its single-seater being a direct derivative of the Bobtail. That year Cooper cars opened a racing drivers' school and made some Bobtails with conventional seating and an open cockpit. Records do not exist to pinpoint precisely how many were made in all, but an educated guess would be between 40 and 50.

Though the Bobtail's successful period covered just two seasons, it was the direct forebear of the car with which Jack Brabham won the 1959 World Championship and led the rear-engine revolution in single-seater racing.

Cunningham

Despite many appearances to the contrary, motor racing can be one of the most romantic of sports and nowhere is this better illustrated than in the attempts of Briggs Cunningham to win Le Mans in the early Fifties. The fact that Cunningham was American was enough to attract interest at the time, for racing in the States had grown apart from Europe, but more than that the team's performance on and off the track won it many friends and admirers. Had Cunningham fulfilled his dream, it would have been a popular victory.

In the days when the entries for Le Mans reflected the race's original intention of proving road cars, there was frequent American participation. Indeed, in 1928 Chryslers finished second, third, and fourth behind the sole surviving Bentley, but as the nature of the competition changed, American interest waned and no Yankee cars appeared after 1935 until Cunningham arrived in 1950.

The cars he brought over raised a few eyebrows, for one was a virtually unmodified Cadillac Model 61 coupé, while the second car was another Model 61, this time in a higher state of tune and fitted with a startling streamlined body designed by Grumman Aircraft. The French nicknamed them 'La Petite Pitaud' (Little Elephant) and 'Le Monstre,' respectively, but monster or not, the streamliner was a serious attempt at aerodynamics.

The coupé (Sam and Miles Collier) finished 10th and 'Le Monstre' (Cunningham/Walters) 11th, after spending time in a sandbank, and the average speed of both cars was within 8 mph of the winning Talbot.

Encouraged, Cunningham returned home, rented a factory, and had Bill Frick and Phil Walters start work on a prototype sports car, the C-1. This led on to the more advanced C-2, which was offered for sale as a practical road car, with Cadillac or Chrysler V-8 engines, which could also be raced. They were large cars, rugged and well made and, given their bulk, gracefully styled.

Three of the four made were earmarked for the 1951 Le Mans race and were designated C2-Rs. They had 5.3-litre Chrysler engines which were tuned to give 270 bhp, though the inferior fuel supplied by the organizers knocked about 50 bhp off this figure. The team cars were barely finished in time for the race (their testing was little more than a run around the block), and they were heavy because of Cunningham's insistence that they be real sports cars, but they acquitted themselves well in a very wet race.

Two cars retired after crashing, but the third car (Walters/John Fitch) held second place to the Walker/Whitehead Jaguar after 13 hours. Unfortunately the official fuel which was of low quality, but heavily leaded to raise the octane rating, played havoc with the big Chrysler unit and eventually the car was forced to trickle round, overheating, with burned valves and with a con-rod about to go. Its eventual 18th place did not reflect its performance. After returning to the States, the three cars finished 1-2-4 at Elkart Lake.

The Cunningham Le Monstre (a re-bodied Cadillac) driven at Le Mans in 1951 by Briggs Cunningham and Phil Walters. (Geoffrey Goddard)

This Cunningham CR-4 was driven at Le Mans by Fitch/Rice in 1952 but retired with engine troubles. (Geoffrey Goddard)

The Cunningham CR-4K (K-Kamm) with which Moran/Benett finished tenth at Le Mans in 1953. (Geoffrey Goddard)

In order to qualify as a *bona fide* manufacturer, Cunningham created the C-3, a Vignale-bodied 2+2 road car, styled by Giovanni Michelotti. Its chassis was derived from the C-2, being a tubular frame with independent front suspension by coil springs and wishbones and a de Dion rear axle. It had a modified 5.3-litre Chrysler V-8 engine producing 210 bhp and most examples were fitted with the Chrysler Fluid-Torque semi-automatic transmission. Though the C-3 was handsome and very quick, its $9,000 (and rising) price tag restricted its sales and no more than 27 were sold.

Cunningham's road car was to establish the firm's credentials, but the main effort went into the racing side and the C-4R. Like the C-3 this was developed from the C-2, but was about 1,000 lb lighter and used a live rear end in place of the de Dion axle. Chrysler had begun to take an interest in the project and was helpful to the team which arrived at the 1952 Le Mans race with 300 bhp on tap.

For Le Mans 1954 Cunningham entered this modified Ferrari with water-cooled brakes. Driven by Walters/Fitch it retired early on with engine troubles perhaps caused by extra load on the engine to run the pumps for the braking system. (Geoffrey Goddard)

The team's entry consisted of two open cars and a coupé, the C-4RK, the 'K' standing for Dr Wunibald Kamm, the German aerodynamicist whose theories were put into practice with a sharply cut-off tail. In practice for the race, the new 5-speed transmissions proved unreliable, and were hastily replaced by 3-speed gearboxes. Then the brake drums cracked and, lacking replacements, had to be repaired with the team starting the event knowing that it had to go easy on them.

Lap one saw Phil Walters lead in the coupé, followed by Fitch in one of the roadsters, but the 3-speed transmission caused the engines to over-rev and both cars were out with valve trouble after eight hours. Briggs Cunningham himself, driving with Spear, ran steadily to finish fourth.

Returning home, the three cars were successful in SCCA races and took the first three places at Elkhart Lake. The following year, Fitch and Walters took a C-4R to victory in the Sebring 12 Hours race. Though there was only one other works team at Sebring, Aston Martin, which should have won had not its drivers thrown the cars at the scenery, the win augured well for Le Mans.

Four cars were entered for the 1953 French classic, the three C-4Rs and a new design, C-5R. This followed the practice of USAC roadsters in that it had a solid front axle, a sort of reverse de Dion. While it raised eyebrows at the time, being considered a retrograde step, it should be remembered that Ferrari has experimented quite recently with a similar set-up for F1. Cunningham himself believed it was the best chassis his team made, pointing out that the car ran 24 hours without changing a front tyre.

It was a quick car, too, clocking 154.8 mph on the Mulsanne Straight, which made it the fastest car in the race. 1953 was the year Cunningham came closest to victory, Walters and Fitch bringing the C-5R home third, splitting the works Jaguar team, while Cunningham/Spear drove a C-4R to seventh and the coupé (Morgan/Benett) finished tenth.

While the race was a triumph for Jaguar and Dunlop discs brakes, there is some truth in the idea that if the C-5R had been given its head, and the drivers not restricted by team orders, it might just have won.

After Le Mans, the team headed to the Reims 12 Hours and again took a respectable third, this time with Cunningham sharing a C-4R with Sherwood Johnston. The team's race was marred, though, by a heavy shunt to the C-5R when Fitch left the road, fortunately with only minor injuries, while lying second to Moss's winning Jaguar. Back home, the team successfully campaigned a number of SCCA races.

One C-4R is now owned by Bob Williams, who races it for fun, while the other two are in Miles Collier's collection.

Another new car, the C-6R, was scheduled for 1954 but it was not ready in time and Cunningham went to Le Mans with a couple of now venerable C-4Rs and a slightly modified Ferrari 340MM which sported a Cunningham body, but had one interesting innovation, liquid-cooled brakes.

Cunningham had tried to obtain Dunlop disc brakes, but when Jaguar heard of the approach it threatened to withdraw its business if Dunlop supplied a competitor. Dunlop complied, but it was a back-handed compliment to the Americans. A firm called Roy S. Sandford & Co of Oxford, Connecticut, had patented a drum brake system which was cooled both conventionally by air passing over the drums, and by pumping a mixture of water and ethylene glycol through the brake shoes. It was a fairly complicated system involving two pumps driving from the front of the camshafts, a five-gallon coolant tank and two heat exchangers and the team fitted it in a hurry and took it to Le Mans without proper testing. Unfortunately the system was too new, leaks developed, and braking proved to be significantly worse than with a conventional set up.

In the race the Ferrari retired fairly early with engine problems, caused by the extra strain which the brake pumps put on the timing gear, but the two older cars, though outclassed on speed, stayed the distance to finish third (Spear/Johnston) and fifth (Cunningham/Benett). Against good opposition, a C4-R won the Watkins Glen Sports Car Grand Prix.

Later the Ferrari was given conventional brakes and enjoyed a fairly successful competition career in the hands of Sherwood Johnston.

1955 saw Cunningham's last attempt to win Le Mans with one of his own cars. The C-6R appeared with a stroked 3-litre Offenhauser engine. Originally it was intended to use a Ferrari V-12 unit, but an argument between Cunningham and Ferrari over a broken rocker soured relations. It was an all-new chassis which inherited previous Cunningham thinking with a tubular chassis, a de Dion rear end, located by coil springs and parallel trailing arms, and independent front suspension by unequal wishbones which had twin dampers, one a lever arm type, one a telescopic unit. Drum brakes had to be used for Jaguar still had an agreement with Dunlop not to release its discs to the opposition.

Although the C-6R was lower and lighter than previous Cunninghams, it proved to be slower. The 'Offy' engine, which had to be converted from methanol to petrol, gave 272 bhp under ideal conditions, but when running hot the

The C-6R with a 3-litre Meyer-Drake engine was the last car to bear the Cunningham name. Driven at Le Mans 1955 by Cunningham/Johnston it retired with transmission troubles but later appeared as the C-6RD with a Jaguar engine. (T.C. March)

valve seats leaked and power dropped.

In the 1955 Sebring 12 Hours race, it retired after 54 laps with a shattered fly-wheel. At Le Mans it was no higher than 13th when it retired after six hours with a burned piston, by which time it had only top gear left. It was the last time that Cunningham entered one of his own cars at Le Mans, his other entry that year, a Jaguar D-type, indicating where his future as an entrant lay. The C-6R raced at Elkhart Lake, but retired with a leaky engine and, in 1957, it appeared at Sebring with a 3.8-litre Jaguar engine under the designation C-6RD. Cunningham was to share the car with Mike Hawthorn, but it was eliminated in practice with a cracked cylinder liner. Later it appeared occasionally in SCCA races.

Cunningham continued as a driver and entrant for some years, with Jaguars, Corvettes, Listers and Maseratis. He raced a 2-litre Maserati 'Birdcage' and in 1962, partnered by Roy Salvadori, finished fourth at Le Mans in a Lightweight E-type Jaguar. His final motor race was the 1966 Sebring event when he drove a Porsche 904 – at the age of 59.

Briggs Cunningham's greatest sporting achievement, however, was not behind the wheel of a car but as skipper of *Columbia*, which won the America's Cup in 1958. Though success at Le Mans eluded him, such was the style of the man and his team that they made a disproportionate impact and carved themselves a more honoured place in the history of the race than many an outfit which has actually won it.

Until late 1986, the team cars were housed in Briggs Cunningham's own museum and were kept in race-ready condition. The collection has now been acquired by Miles Collier, who drove for the team at Le Mans and so was part of the great Cunningham dream.

D.B.

Charles Deutsch and René Bonnet were two French enthusiasts who had once been promised a drive in a works car for the 1936 French GP (run for sports cars) and when the drive failed to materialize, set about making their own Citroën-based specials. Unfortunately they were not ready until 1939 so though the two friends were able to run in a few lesser events in France that year; the cars then had to stand idle for the next six.

In 1945, the French organized a race meeting in Paris, six weeks before VJ-Day. Both the Citroën Specials, one a 1,500 cc car, the other a 2-litre, competed in this Bois de Boulogne meeting and both were placed. Meanwhile a more advanced car was nearing completion.

Work on this had actually been started clandestinely in Occupied France during the war at some potential risk to the two enthusiasts. 75 bhp was claimed for the Citroën 11CV engine and suspension was independent all round, by torsion bars and wishbones at the front, and swing axles at the rear. Given the circumstances of its birth, the chassis specification alone was advanced, but what was truly out-standing was the body. It was a low, enveloping, aluminium shell resembling in profile the later Porsche 550.

That car had, in essence, the formula for all later D.B.s: low weight, low drag and a tuned production engine. Apart from the Germans, it was D.B. and other

French makers of small-capacity racers who pioneered aerodynamics as an aid to performance. They were on the right lines and in the early days at least were streets ahead of the British or Italians. The Brits tended to throw away surplus weight and fit cycle wings, and the Italians made 'em pretty and looked for more power.

In the partnership, Charles Deutsch was the theoretical engineer who had a natural instinct for aerodynamics, while René Bonnet complemented him admirably, being a pragmatic mechanical engineer. It was this combination of talents which was to make D.B. pre-eminent among French makers of small-capacity sports cars.

D.B. made a number of Citroën-based single-seaters and sports cars on a distinctive forked backbone chassis until, in 1948, Deutsch and Bonnet discovered Panhard. Panhard et Levassor had been founded as an engineering company in 1845 and began making cars (under licence from Daimler) in 1889. The following year a Frenchman called M. Vurpillod bought a Panhard-built car and so became the world's first private motorist. The company was as old as the industry and until World War II had a reputation as a maker of large, relatively expensive, cars. Unlike some other French makers, Panhard realized that post-war motoring conditions would require a different sort of motor car, mass produced and with an emphasis on efficiency and economy. Those French makers which did not realize this quickly went to the wall.

Jean-Albert Grégoire, one of the great innovators of the French motor industry and a pioneer of front-wheel drive, had been at work on an advanced lightweight saloon which made extensive use of aluminium and had fwd, an air-cooled flat-twin engine of 600 cc, hydraulic brakes, and independent front suspension by double transverse leaf springs with trailing arms locating the torsion bar-sprung rear beam axle. It was, claimed its designer, the first car in the world which would carry four people, achieve 60 mph, and return 70 mpg (under very special conditions). It appeared to have all the ingredients of a true 'People's Car' and licences were sold to companies in several overseas countries though few cars resulted.

Panhard took over Grégoire's concept and extended it so comprehensively that the agitated engineer was never able to extract royalties. Panhard designed a new 610 cc air-cooled flat-twin engine, and exhibited it as the 'Dyna' in 1946. These little cars, and their aerodynamic successor, the 'Dynavia', had excellent handling and power/weight ratio. While in Britain the 750 cc competition class meant Austin Seven specials, on the Continent it was a strongly contested category

This D.B. driven by Hery/Trouis finished 20th overall, and second in the 750cc class, at Le Mans 1955. (T.C. March)

based on such as Renault, Fiat and Goliath cars. Quite apart from sports cars, many races had classes for 'utility' cars and the little Panhard saloons performed excellently in them and took numerous class wins in races such as Le Mans and the Mille Miglia.

Moreover there was the handicap race at Le Mans, the Index of Performance, which carried equal prize money to the scratch race. While we often now regard Le Mans as a conventional race which happens to last 24 Hours, at which point an outright winner emerges, originally the event had been organized much more as a time trial and those who covered the minimum distance for their class were judged to have completed one leg of the three which would qualify them for the Trienniel Cup. That, at least, was the theory and, indeed, there was no 'Annual Distance Cup' (what we would now call the outright winner) until 1928, though now those who covered the most distance in the time in the years 1923–7 are referred to as the 'winners'.

When Panhard made the Dyna and Renault the 4CV, they were immediately seen as potential Index winners and appeared at Le Mans from the first post-war race in 1949 in conjunction with Gordini-modified Simcas in the early races. Sometimes these cars were modified but externally standard saloons, but as time went by they evolved into specials.

A number of small constructors turned to Panhard for the basis of competition and sporting road cars. Most are long forgotten: Veritas (better known for its B.M.W. 328-based cars), Monopole (makers of piston rings who built successful

Le Mans 1956 and Laureau/Armagnac won one of D.B.'s five victories in the Index of Performance. (Geoffrey Goddard)

The Index-winning 611cc Monopole-Panhard of R & P Chancel at Le Mans, 1953. (Geoffrey Goddard)

cars for Le Mans with direct sponsorship from Panhard), Rafale, Marathon (a rear-engined car based on the German Trippel coupé), Arista (pretty fibreglass-bodied coupés which stayed in production until 1963), Callista, and R.E.A.C. (the cream of the Moroccan motor industry, with a frankly odd-ball glassfibre body).

Of all the Panhard-based cars, however, it was to be D.B. which emerged pre-eminent. In 1949 the company built a 500 cc Panhard-based car complying with what was to become the International F3. It was an odd looking device with a huge ground clearance and the engine mounted to the fore of the front wheels, as on the Dyna. Suspension was by a transverse leaf spring and lower wishbones at the front with a beam rear axle which due to the car's light weight was suspended only by telescopic dampers.

About the only thing which can be said for it was that it was possibly the best French 500 cc F3 car, which was no distinction at all, and it had a more varied career than any other single-seater design. Undismayed by the fact that it was completely outclassed in F3, D.B. built 850 cc versions for a racing category on similar lines to Skip Barber's current Formula Saab (competitors paid a fee and drew a car), supercharged a 750 cc version, which made it a F1 car, and ran it in the 1955 Pau GP (it finished 16 laps down) and finally resurrected it for Formula Junior, in which it fared no better than in F3. It scored 'A' for effort and 'E' for achievement.

In 1951, D.B. put Panhard engines at each end of a chassis and came up with a

The 845cc Renault-powered V.P. which came last at Le Mans in 1956 or, if you prefer, 14th overall. This car typified the French approach at the time in that it had a tuned production engine, simple chassis, and good aerodynamics. (T.C. March)

1,500 cc four-wheel-drive car which was tested but not raced.

Concurrent with the first F3 car, D.B. had turned its attention to sports cars and in this class the results were somewhat different. While the single-seater had been outlandish, the sports cars were subtle. Many Panhard components were used, the suspension was pure Panhard except that only a single transverse leaf was used at the front, and a light tubular frame was constructed to carry them. As with the Citroën-engined D.B.s, the outstanding feature was the all-enveloping low-drag body.

Though D.B.s appeared at Le Mans from 1949 on, they were not initially successful and it was the Monopole-Panhards which proved most successful in the early years, winning the Index of Performance three years on the trot, 1950–52. D.B.s, however, were successful elsewhere. Araud won the 1950 Bol 'Or at Monthléry and Trouis and Gatsonides won their class in the 1951 Tourist Trophy. At Le Mans D.B. fielded an 850 cc car in order to compete in the 1,100 cc class but came up against Porsche's debut in the race in the same class.

In 1952 René Bonnet came seventh overall in the 1952 Sebring 12 Hours (still largely an SCCA club event) and the partners designed and built a rear-engined Renault-based car, but it did not race. Using a low-pressure supercharger Bonnet drove a D.B. Panhard to some International records at Monthléry.

At the 1952 Paris Salon, D.B. exhibited a road-going coupé based on a box-section chassis using Panhard Dyna suspension front and rear. Two forms of engine were offered, a normally aspirated unit which gave 38 bhp and a super-charged version which gave 55 bhp. These began to sell in small numbers, but the steel body was a little too heavy, though this was later remedied by the use of a glass-fibre shell. By 1955 engines of 1,000 cc and even 1,300 cc were offered (customers had a great deal of choice in choosing the final specification of their cars) and D.B. had developed the Panhard gearbox (originally a crash type) into an all-synchromesh unit.

While the cars gave a good account of themselves in French National racing and Bonnet returned to Sebring in 1953 and carried off the Index of Perform-ance, it was not until that year that the company achieved its first success at Le Mans when it won the 750 cc class. A works Panhard won the Index. This was an open 2-seater of 610 cc, the 'Wing-car Super Panther' with a body developed by Marcel Riffard which was shaped like the chord of an aeroplane's wing. At the same race Monopole sported an extraordinary shape, with massive overhang front and rear. It resembled the Cunningham 'Monstre' and had headlight covers like the spinners of a propeller-driven aircraft.

It was in 1954 that D.B. really made its mark on racing. After taking a maiden class win in the Mille Miglia no fewer than five D.B.s appeared at Le Mans and most were central-seaters though three of the cars had more powerful (and unre-liable) Renault engines with 5-speed gearboxes. These were particularly attract-ive little machines with tall tail fins and two had rear-mounted radiators. All three Renault-powered cars failed to make the finish (two had transmission troubles and the third shed a wheel), but Bonnet and Bayol brought home a Pan-hard car an excellent tenth overall to win the 750 cc class and the long-coveted Index of Performance.

Although it had only a sixth of the engine capacity of the winning 4.9-litre Fer-rari, it covered 2,020 miles to the winner's 2,880 miles and both D.B. Panhard cars finished. After its brief flirtation with Renault, thereafter like a cobbler to his last, D.B. stuck to Panhard components.

Among the French cars at Le Mans that year were the works-supported Mono-poles and Panhard's own 'Wing-car Super Panthers'; the B.G.-Renault which was based on the 4CV chassis and suspension but had a 1,063 cc engine and a GT body bearing some similarity to the later Costin Maserati 450S. The little firm of Constantin had decided not to run a modified Peugeot 203 saloon, as it had in past races, but built an open 2-seater with a bored-out Peugeot engine of 1,425 cc supercharged by a blower of Constantin's own design. Then there was the V.P.-Renault, a little open two-seater built on an ingenious tubular frame and powered by a Renault 4CV engine.

Few if any of these cars were ever seen outside France and some were seen only at Le Mans. The economic climate in France, which was still recovering from the ravages of war, did not permit the variety of types of car we enjoyed in Britain and, indeed, the French National racing scene was largely insular but within its confines it produced a rich variety of competition cars. That D.B. emerged as the pick of the crop was no hollow achievement for it had a lot of competition at home.

It was, however, in Ulster and the Tourist Trophy where D.B. had its greatest glory. Whereas at Le Mans the handicap win had been overshadowed by the Ferrari/Jaguar duel for the lead, the T.T. was a pure handicap race and Laureau and Armagnac emerged outright winners.

As they raced in 1954, D.B. Panhards had two twin-choke Solex carburettors (i.e. one twin choke per cylinder) so they would not have to use large-bore venturi, which would have adversely affected acceleration. In this trim they produced 45 bhp at 5,700 rpm, but the entire car weighed only 990 lb and, in 1954, was touching around 112 mph at Le Mans.

At Le Mans in 1955 the cars had conventional off-set seating and lovely teardrop bodies but the usual clockwork precision of the Panhard-engined cars was interrupted as only two D.B.s finished and a Porsche won the Index. Later in the year Laureau and Armagnac returned to Dundrod, where the T.T. was being run as a scratch race, and while an outright win was out of the question they did carry off the 750 cc class.

The following year it was business as usual and at Le Mans a 750 cc D.B. won both its class and the Index. 1957 saw class wins at Sebring and in the Mille Miglia, but at Le Mans the strong French contingent of small-capacity cars was roundly beaten by the 750 cc Lotus-Climax which took its class and the Index with a 1,100 cc Lotus finishing second in the Index.

Twin overhead camshaft cylinder heads were prepared for Le Mans the following year but this time a 750 cc OSCA took both class and Index honours.

With its last possible contender for outright honours, Gordini, now defunct the French were worried by their failure for two years running to win the Index, but D.B.s at least were going well elsewhere and the cars not only won the SCCA Class H Championship in 1958, 59, 60 and 61, but continued to be competitive until the mid-Sixties. On the whole, however, whatever interest there had been in the small-engined class began to wane and entries at Le Mans had been shrinking.

Monopole had disappeared and so had most other French special builders by 1959 when the small-car classes became less populated but more cosmopolitan. That year at Le Mans D.B.s took both the Index of Performance (Cornet/Cotton) and the new Index of Thermal Efficiency (Consten/Armagnac), a fuel consumption formula. For the record the winner of this new category averaged 86.4 mph for the 24 hours and returned better than 25 mpg. 1960 saw a class win in the Nürburgring 1,000 Km and another win in the Index at Le Mans and the following year saw D.B.'s fifth, and final, Index win.

A C.D. (Charles Deutsch) Panhard won again in 1962, but that brought to an end a remarkable run in which Panhard-engined cars had won 10 of the 13 Indices run between 1950 and 1962 with one of those wins being shared (Aston Martin DB2, 1950).

In 1961 the two partners split and went their separate ways. Charles Deutsch persevered with Panhard-based cars for a while, but René Bonnet turned to Renault power and produced the Djet coupé as well as some Renault-backed F2 cars and prototypes. The coupés had fibreglass bodies supplied by the giant Matra concern and when Renault withdrew its backing from René Bonnet in 1964 and his company fell into difficulties, it was saved by being taken over by Matra. Matra decided to open a racing division and so a new chapter in French motor racing began.

E.M.W.

E.M.W., Eisenacher Motoren-Werke, was born in the aftermath of World War II, being that part of B.M.W. which found itself in the Russian zone when hostilities ceased. Indeed, for some time its badge was identical to B.M.W.'s save that the coloured quarters within the roundel were red and not blue. The marque's brief competition career was shaped by the fact it was behind the Iron Curtain and also by the fact that its employees were of the great pre-war B.M.W. tradition.

Located in Eisenach, the factory was turned over to the production of hand carts in 1945, but when, two years later, the Russians considered moving all its heavy plant to Russia, the employees quickly built up some pre-war B.M.W.s from existing spares to make the point that it could be viable as a car producer. The point was made and production started on several types of pre-war B.M.W. cars and motor cycles. Though the cars looked the part, they had very low compression ratios, to cope with poor-quality fuel, and ended up pretty gutless. Production was low but a few were exported, mainly to Finland.

Later E.M.W. took over the making of a pre-war D.K.W., which was marketed as the I.F.A (Industrie-Vereinigung Volkseigner Fahrzeugwerke) and eventually developed into the Wartburg. Auto Union, D.K.W.'s parent company, was another firm which ended the war with factories in both East and West Germany.

Despite the constraints of making cars in a country controlled by Stalin, the workers at Eisenach were of the B.M.W. tradition and as early as 1949 work

The two E.M.W.s of Edgar Barth and Arthur Rosenhammer in the pits of the 1954 Eifelrennen at the Nürburgring.

Two of the four E.M.W.s entered in the 1955 Nürburgring 500 Km in which the cars of Rosenhammer/Barth and Paul Thiel finished third and fourth. E.M.W. constantly revised its cars' bodies and all were characterised by excellent aerodynamics. (LAT)

began on a B.M.W.-engined F2 car which apparently was never completed.

In 1951, an associated company, D.A.M.W., Deutsches Amt für Material- und Warenprufung, backed by the East German government, built three competition cars, an F2 model, a 1.5-litre sports and a 2-litre sports. All had engines based on the 1,991 cc, 6-cylinder, B.M.W. 328 engine. Quite apart from the internal politics of East Germany (Communism and motor racing are not natural bedfellows), wider politics anyway prevented these cars from being seen outside of Germany. One event which was permitted was the 1952 Avusrennen, where Arthur Rosenhammer won the 1,500 cc class ahead of Walter Glöcker's Porsche Special.

At the end of 1952, the D.A.M.W. project was handed over to E.M.W., which decided to develop a 1,500 cc sports-racer. E.M.W. discarded D.A.M.W.'s short-stroke B.M.W. engine and built a new d.o.h.c. unit which retained the in-line six layout (unusual for engines of that size at the time) and had the same cylinder dimensions (66 × 73 mm). It was more than just a short-stroke B.M.W. 328 with a new cylinder head for it also featured a roller bearing crankshaft, two plugs per cylinder, and with six motor cycle-type carburettors produced 130 bhp at 7,000 rpm By 1955 with three sidedraught twin-choke Webers it was giving a claimed 155 bhp.

Unfortunately, we have to take these claimed power outputs as an example of propaganda. Had they been true, no other 1,500 cc car in the world would have caught a sight of the cars on a speed circuit such as Avus. A more reasonable figure would be between 110–120 bhp. Similarly, a top speed of 155 mph was claimed at Avus in 1955, but subtract 20 mph and you'd be nearer the mark.

The E.M.W. chassis was simple enough, a rugged tube affair with double wishbones and torsion bars at the front and a de Dion rear axle sprung by torsion bars and located by an A-frame. What set the cars apart were the careful aerodynamics of their bodies.

In 1936 B.M.W. had achieved the astonishing drag coefficient of 0.22 on a Kamm-tailed coupé, this at a time when most cars had the aerodynamic qualities of a breeze block. While the general principles of aerodynamics were not lost on others, usually detail design was poor. At the time, a sound overall shape was often spoiled by odd lumps and protrusions into the air stream, but E.M.W. was faultless in this respect. It had been properly wind-tunnel tested and everything fitted flush.

Several distinct bodies were made. In 1952, the cars had the driver's cockpit enclosed. A year later and the cars had the lines of a typical sport-racer of five or six years later. When the cars appeared at Avus in 1954, they had enclosed front wheels and the overall line was sharply 'waisted' (and officially designated I.F.A./E.M.W.s). Behind the front wheels the body curved in to cover the narrow central section and then flared out again to sweep around the rear wheels. With the R3/55, of 1955, the line flowed more conventionally front to rear.

Body height was extremely low, much lower than the Porsche 550 for example, but whatever aerodynamic advantage this gave was offset by the fact that drivers sat high in the airstream and, in action, were probably slightly less efficient than the Porsche.

Politics, internal and external, unfortunately meant that its International competition programme was restricted to the Nürburgring and Avus. This, together with the fact that overseas drivers could not be placed under contract, and only Barth and Rosenhammer showed any sign of talent among East Germans, meant that the cars never stood an even chance.

The West saw the cars three times in 1955. In the Eifelrennen at the Nürburgring, Edgar Barth qualified his E.M.W. fourth fastest, beaten only by the works Mercedes-Benz 300SLRs of twice the capacity. Though the race did not attract other big-capacity works cars, there were respectable private Jaguars and Ferraris to say nothing of Porsches. Barth finally finished 6th overall with Paul Thiel's E.M.W. in 8th, the first two 1,500 cc cars home.

In the 1955 Nürburgring 500 Km, Barth and Rosenhammer finished third to Behra's Maserati 150S and von Frankenberg's Porsche. In the Avusrennen, von Frankenberg's Porsche led four E.M.W.s (Barth, Rosenhammer, Thiel and Egon Binner) in a tight group for most of the race. The E.M.W.s could match the Porsche for pace and, indeed, Barth set fastest lap before retiring, but could not quite get to grips with it. Von Frankenberg won at an average speed of 122.78 mph, six seconds ahead of Rosenhammer, Thiel and Binner.

By 1956 E.M.W.s were known as A.W.E.s and this car was driven in the Nürburgring 1000 Kms by Thiel/Binner but retired early in the race. At the end of the season the company withdrew from competition. (Corrado Millanta)

1955 may have been a severely restricted season, but it was a commendable one. The cars were quick on circuits as diverse in character as the Nürburgring and Avus and they were reliable too. What more could one ask for except the ability to move freely across Europe?

In 1956 the company name changed to A.W.E., Automobilwerk Eisenach, and two 1,500 cc E.M.W./A.W.E.s finished 1-2 (Rosenhammer and Barth) in the Coupe de Paris 2-litre sports car race at Monthléry. Writing in *Autosport*, 'Jabby' Crombac called the win 'convincing' and also commented that there was a 'peculiar smell coming out of their straight-through exhaust pipes' which suggests they may have been relying on a special brew. They were due to race in Britain, at the International Trophy Meeting, but never arrived.

In the Nürburgring 1,000 Km they proved slower than the works Porsches but quicker than any other 1½-litre car. Barth and Rosenhammer finished seventh, one lap down on the winning Moss/Behra Maserati 300S and on the same lap as the Brooks/Collins Aston Martin DB3S, which finished fifth. In the Coupe de Paris at Monthléry Barth was able to mix it with several Ferrari 750 Monzas but, uncharacteristically, retired with engine trouble.

The change of name had apparently ushered in a change of policy and competition was forgotten as the company concentrated on making increasingly appalling Wartburg saloon cars. It must have been a surprise to the racing department, for in late 1956, A.W.E. 'confirmed' it intended to build new cars for the 1½-litre F2 which was just starting.

The team cars were retained by the factory and two recently underwent restoration prior to being displayed in the Wartburg Museum.

Elva

Elva was a maker which so nearly became part of the motor racing establishment. In one sense it has no place in this directory for no serious Elva entry ever appeared in the WSCC. On the other hand, its cars were eligible, sold in quite large numbers, and achieved considerable success in the USA, particularly in the Mid-West. In the present context it can stand as an example of the many small British makers which glimpsed success but did not quite achieve it.

While for several years, Elva was Lotus's main rival in terms of cars sold, the philosophy of the marque's founder, Frank Nichols, was diametrically opposed to Colin Chapman's. While Chapman strove for success on the tracks and ran up to six works drivers, leaving his accountant, Fred Bushell, to pick up the pieces and keep the company going, Nichols was first and foremost a businessman who could not see a percentage in running in prestige events such as Le Mans. So long as he was selling cars, he was happy.

In the early Fifties, Nichols had built up a small garage business and decided he wanted to go racing. He commissioned Mike Chapman to build him a car and the result, the C.S.M., was a 1,172 cc Ford-powered, cycle-winged sports car built on similar lines to the Lotus Mk 6. It went sufficiently well to encourage Nichols to do better and, together with his mechanic 'Mac' Witts, he set about making an improved version, which was christened 'Elva' (from the French *elle và*, she goes).

'Mac' Witts was the true creator of the car and he, too, designed the overhead inlet valve conversion for Ford s.v. engines which Elva marketed. He did not, however, receive much credit for his work. Elva Mk I's space-frame followed the layout of the C.S.M. (the frame was *very* similar to the Lotus Mk 6, as Colin Chapman was the first to point out with some anger), but Standard Ten front suspension replaced the previous swing axles. A simple semi-enveloping aluminium body completed the plot.

These cars achieved some success in British club racing and perhaps two dozen were made in all. A Mk II model appeared in 1956 with de Dion rear suspension and a glass-fibre body made by Falcon Shells. Most Mk IIs were fitted with Coventry Climax FWA engines and a works-entered car driven by Archie Scott-Brown won a few club events, but that was no measure of the car, for Archie was a truly great driver who, had race organizers not been so obsessed by his physical deformities, would not have been available for club racing.

More significantly, a Mk II was bought by an American, Chuck Dietrich, who, as luck would have it, turned out to be a fine driver and his success brought in more orders. From then on Nichols concentrated on the lucrative American market, where he could sell cars to the strictly amateur SCCA drivers without worrying about running a works team with its attendant expense and erosion of profit margins.

A further update, the aluminium-bodied Elva Mk III appeared in 1957, destined to be the company's production racer the following year. Of all these cars, one stands out, the works Elva-A.J.B.

Archie Butterworth was the epitome of the eccentric boffin, a self-taught engineer/inventor with many patents to his name. He'd made his name in motor racing as the designer/driver of a crude but effective four-wheel-drive sprint car which used Jeep parts and an air-cooled Steyr V-8. He then designed his own flat-four air-cooled engine which was intended to provide capacities of between 1,500 cc and 2,500 cc by the simple expedient of changing the individually cast cylinder barrels and pistons.

Two of these engines, fitted with Steyr heads, had appeared in F2 in 1953 in the Aston-Butterworth cars. These were modified Coopers, but were not successful, partly due to being run by an amateur team, but given all circumstances, they did not disgrace themselves and even if they were not particularly reliable overall, the Butterworth contribution to the engine gave no problems, the bottom end was virtually indestructible.

69

Archie Scott-Brown at the wheel of 'Sabrina', the 1957 works Elva Mk III fitted with a flat-four air-cooled A.J.B. engine. The photograph shows Scott-Brown giving the car its only win, at Brands Hatch in October 1957. (NMM)

Cyril Kieft talked airily of a team of A.J.B.-engined 1,500 cc sports racers to take on Porsche and had Norton pistons and heads grafted on to an A.J.B. crank-case. It was run in a Kieft single-seater based on the firm's first, unsuccessful F3 car and in a sports chassis, but the works could never overcome cooling problems. The engine was sold on, enjoyed a long and varied competition career which included being run as a 1½-litre F1 engine (in Guy Eden's Cooper-Arden) and enjoying considerable success in a sprint motor-bike, and it still exists.

By 1957 Butterworth had produced the design he'd drawn years earlier. It had a d.o.h.c. head and the swing inlet valves had torsion bar springing. Conventional poppet exhaust valves were used and, ironically, these proved the unit's downfall. Butterworth specified large sodium-filled exhaust valves which had to be specially made and the subcontractor made a faulty batch with the result that the head frequently snapped off from the stem.

When the engine stayed together, the Elva was very rapid indeed and Scott-Brown did manage to win a minor race. Butterworth bought a Cooper F2 chassis and was in the process of mating it to one of his units for Scott-Brown to drive when the great little Scot was killed and that effectively ended his interest in motor racing. A sectioned A.J.B. engine is on display in the Donington Park Museum.

'Mac' Witts left Elva in 1957 and was replaced as designer by one of the mechanics, Keith Marsden, a self-taught engineer of considerable talent. Marsden's first design, the Mk IV, appeared the following year in readiness for full production in 1959. It was the first car of its class to appear with an independent rear suspension in which unsplined driveshafts served the function of the upper wishbones, though simultaneously Eric Broadley was building the Lola Mk I with the same layout.

With the Mk IV, Elva had finally made a Lotus-beater, for the 1959 Lotus 17 had a severe suspension problem, but unfortunately for Elva, it was no match for the new Lola save in SCCA events, where success more often than not depended on the individual driver. An improved, lower, version, the Mk V, followed it and meanwhile Elva was enjoying huge sales of its front-engined FJ car and its MGA-powered Courier road car. Then Nichols caught a cold when his American agent went bankrupt and Elva quickly followed.

The Courier project was sold to Trojan and Elva regrouped to enjoy some success with its Mk 6 and 7 rear-engined sports-racers in the early Sixties. Finally the company was taken over by Trojan and became the production base for the McLaren Can-Am cars.

Had Nichols discovered a special driver with whom to establish a relationship, and had he been less determinedly commercial, Elva would have enjoyed much more success.

Ferrari

To try to capture even only the sports racing side of Ferrari in a few pages puts one in mind of the song *That's Entertainment* and its summary of *Hamlet*: 'The ghost and the prince meet – and everyone ends in mincemeat.' It catches the raw outline but somehow misses the texture.

Throughout the entire period under review Ferrari was a force in sports car racing, indeed, the marque's reputation was largely founded on its sports cars for, during the whole of the 2½-litre FL, it enjoyed only spasmodic success apart from 1956, when it took over the Lancia D50 project.

Ferrari has always been a projection of its founder, Enzo Ferrari, who has run his company like a medieval Italian city-state with himself as the prince and all others as courtiers – and the courtiers have always included a measure of poisoners and stiletto merchants. Maranello has always been such a bed of intrigue that an outsider, especially an Anglo-Saxon, can only record what happened on the circuits and can only guess at some of its reasoning.

That said, Ferrari more than any other marque in motor racing history has engendered an aura of magic. Even when going through one of its periodic bleak periods, the non-attendance of the Ferrari team at a race has appeared to devalue the event. Collectors revere the cars more than any other, with the exception of Bugatti, and it is not difficult to see why, for even though they have frequently lagged far behind the engineering excellence of the Germans, and the ingenuity of the British constructors, they have always looked stunningly beautiful and most have worked well.

Enzo Ferrari was born in Modena in February 1898, the second son of an engineer. A conscript in the Italian army in World War I, he was set to work shoeing mules, and returned from the war in poor health. He was lucky enough to find a job driving reconditioned truck chassis to coach builders and started to cultivate motor racing people.

Eventually he landed a job as a test driver at Alfa Romeo and this set him on the way to a competition career. Ferrari was a good driver though somewhat short of being an 'ace' and after one win was presented with the 'rampant horse' emblem by the parents of the deceased World War I fighter pilot Francesco Baracca, whose squadron symbol it had been and who, like Ferrari, had been Modenese. Apart from his performances on the track, he became valuable to Alfa Romeo for his business acumen and his extensive network of contacts.

A win in the 1924 Coppa Acerbo brought with it the title Cavaliere and this was later upgraded to Commendatore, but after World War II all Fascist-bestowed titles were suspended and previous holders required to re-apply. Ferrari did not and so has been plain Signor Ferrari ever since.

Despite suffering a nervous breakdown which restricted his competition career, Ferrari continued to be useful to Alfa Romeo in many ways and in late 1929 he left to set up his own Scuderia Ferrari, which ran the Alfa Romeo works effort and prepared competition cars for customers.

When, despite all its efforts, Alfa Romeo found it had no answer at all for the might of the German teams in Grand Prix racing, it sacked its chief engineer, Vittorio Jano, and replaced him with the Spaniard Wilfredo Ricart. Ferrari and Ricart did not get along well and eventually the rift became such that Alfa Romeo severed its links with Ferrari in early 1939. As part of the severance agreement, Ferrari agreed not to run his Scuderia for four years.

Incidentally, Ferrari has claimed that the Alfa Romeo 158 was designed at his

Luigi Chinetti and Lord Selsdon's Tipo 166 at Silverstone in August 1950. Despite the huge crowd, this is a practice shot and the car was driven in the race by Dorino Serafini. (T.C. March)

instigation by the Alfa Romeo designer Giaocchino Colombo, who had been seconded to the Scuderia, and that he then sold the prototype and parts for four further cars to the company. These cars were successful in Voiturette racing in 1938 and 1939, and, postwar, dominated Grand Prix racing until the arrival of Ferrari's own 4½ litre cars in 1951. It is typical of the man that when his cars defeated Alfa Romeo he said, 'I killed my mother today.' It is almost a line from an opera or a minor Jacobean tragedy.

With his Scuderia dormant, Ferrari turned his workshops over to a new company, Societa Auto Avio Costruzione, Modena. Initially founded as a general engineering company, it was not long before a competition car was taking shape in its workshops. Designed by Alberto Massimino around Fiat parts, and developed by Enrico Nardi, it was a 1½-litre straight-eight and two were completed in time for the 1940 Mille Miglia. The drivers were the Marquis Lotario Rangoni Machiavelli (an appropriate name for a Ferrari driver) and a young motor cycle racer, Alberto Ascari; both cars retired. Ascari the son of Antonio Ascari, himself a great driver and a former racing rival of Ferrari, was later to win two World Championships for the team.

Ferrari began the war with a small workshop in Modena and ended it with a large one in nearby Maranello which employed 150 people making machine

Luigi Villoresi (partnered by Cassani) won the 1951 Mille Miglia with this 4.1 litre Tipo 340 America.

tools. When normality returned to Italy, Ferrari's thoughts turned again to making cars and he turned to his old friend Colombo to design it.

Colombo, who had designed for Alfa Romeo a blown flat-12 which never actually raced, decided on an advanced s.o.h.c. V-12 of 1,598 cc (55 × 52.5 mm) with hairpin valve springs which was designated Tipo 125 (125 cc being the capacity of each cylinder). With three down-draught twin-choke Webers, in competition trim, this gave a lusty 128 bhp and drove through a 5-speed gearbox.

The first engine was run in September 1946 and initial problems with its bearings were ultimately cured by the use of Vandervell 'Thin Wall' shells, which was to lead to Tony Vandervell's (Ferrari) 'Thin Wall Specials' and from thence to the Vanwall F1 car. In early 1947 the first complete Tipo 125 was ready for test driving. Its chassis was a cross-braced ladder-frame with two oval main tubes, with double wishbone and transverse leaf front suspension and a live rear axle and transverse leaf spring at the rear. The brake drums were cast from alloy.

From the start, Ferrari's reputation attracted the cream of drivers, but there was to be no 'fairy tale' debut. In their first race at Piacenza that May, Giuseppe Farina's car refused to start and Franco Cortese retired with fuel pump failure. Cortese, however, gave the new marque its first win at Rome later that month.

One of the first batch of three cars had a simple, cycle-winged, body, the other two had full-width shells. Later in 1947 two were converted to Tipo 159s with 1,902 cc (59 × 58 mm) engines which gave 125 bhp and over the winter all three cars became Tipo 166s with engines of 1,992 cc (60 × 58.8 mm) which gave 140 bhp. This became Ferrari's first 'production' car and stayed in the range until 1953. In supercharged 1,498 cc form, the engine formed the basis of Ferrari's first F1 car in 1948 and the Tipo 166 engine powered Ferrari's 1948 F2 car, which, supercharged, won many races in the South American 'Temporada' Formule Libre series between 1949 and 1952.

As with so many of Ferrari's cars, this initial model deserves a book to itself. Quite apart from the single-seater derivatives, there were a number of different bodies fitted to the sports cars, among them the Barchetta, which became the inspiration for the A.C. Ace. Then there are the different forms in which the sports cars were made. The Tipo 166 sports-racers were designated 'Mille Miglia', a road-going open car with a detuned 110 bhp engine was called the 'Inter', and then there was the prototype 'Sport' intended to sell in series with an 89 bhp engine. From the Tipi 125-159-166 came others, Tipi 195 (two versions), 212 (three versions) and 225. As if that was not enough there were two different wheelbases as well.

Then there comes the problem of telling how the cars fared in important races, for Ferrari was soon turning them out at a fine rate and most were raced – and often raced by top-line drivers. As early as 1950 no fewer than ten Ferrari 166s ran in the Targa Florio and this numerical superiority continued throughout the Fifties.

Regretfully, then, Ferrari's competition history, which should dominate this book as thoroughly as the marque dominated the sports-racing scene in the period, has to be dealt with more skimpily than any other maker.

It fell to Clemente Biondetti to give Ferrari its first important win, the Mille Miglia in 1948, and he followed that up with a win in the Tour of Sicily, and the Targa Florio – and repeated this treble the following year. Luigi Chinetti, who was to become Ferrari's North American importer, and Lord Selsdon won the 1948 Paris 12 Hours race at Monthléry and the following year the same pairing won the first postwar Le Mans. It was Chinetti's third victory at Le Mans, and he followed that by winning the Spa 24 Hours race with Jean Lucas.

This is the problem with Ferrari. In one paragraph we have just recorded two Targa Florio wins, two in the Mille Miglia and a win at Le Mans, and three other major victories – and we are still on the first design. It puts into focus the achievements of every other maker in this book. Simultaneously the same engine was carrying everything before it in F2, mopping up the South American Formula Libre series, and winning in F1 during 1949 when Alfa Romeo had been in retirement for a year.

Ferraris were soon to be everywhere. Ascari brought one over to Silverstone for the 1950 International Trophy meeting and waltzed away with the 2-litre

Immaculately dressed, in 1953 Giannino Marzotto won his second Mille Miglia with a Ferrari, in this case a Vignale-bodied Tipo 340MM. (Publifoto)

class. In America, Briggs Cunningham, Bill Kimberley and Bill Spear soon had them and built up an enviable reputation for the company across the Big Pond. Also in the States, a youngster called Phil Hill began to make his reputation at the wheel of a Tipo 166.

By 1950, though, the cars had passed their prime years of supremacy as other makers caught up, using larger engines. At Le Mans the Ferraris were challenged not only by the winning Talbots but also by entries from Allard and Jaguar. Stretched by the strong opposition the five Ferraris (a mixture of 2- and 2.3-litre cars) all gave up the ghost. If the young marque was to retain its position it had to have a larger engine and it was clear, anyway, in F1 that the only way Ferrari was going to beat the Alfa Romeo team it had to be with 4½-litre cars rather than supercharged 1½-litre models.

In 1949, Giaocchino Colombo left Ferrari to join Alfa Romeo (from whence to Maserati and Bugatti) and his replacement was Aurelio Lampredi. Lampredi, too, designed a V-12 for his F1 car and a glance at the raw specifications may suggest it was simply an enlargement. There is, of course, a great deal more to creating a larger engine than simply increasing all the dimensions, and though the Lampredi design followed the Ferrari house style in that it was a short-stroke unit with single overhead camshafts and hairpin springs, it was a wholly new engine. These long-block V-12s we may call Ferrari's second generation V-12. As a rough guide, engines up to three litres were derived from Colombo's engine, the larger units derive from Lampredi's successor though, of course, they underwent a great deal of development. Using Ferrari's capacity-related numbering system, V-12 engines up '250' derive from the original unit.

Ascari drove a F1 car with a 3.3-litre version of the Lampredi engine in the 1950 Belgian Grand Prix and by stages this rose to 4.5 litres at the end of the year. During 1951 the Ferrari F1 effort became increasingly stronger until, at Silverstone, Froilan Gonzalez defeated the Alfa Romeo team.

Simultaneously to the F1 car, Lampredi also laid down a related series of sports car engines. These were to appear in six different engine sizes under the numbers Tipi 275, 340 (three versions, 'America', 'Mexico' and 'Mille Miglia'), 342 (production car), 250 (two versions, 'Sport' and 'Mille Miglia'), 375 ('Mille Miglia', 'America' and 'Plus') and 410 ('Plus' and 'Superamerica').

Most of these cars had chassis similar to the Tipo 195, which followed the layout of the Tipo 166 but which had a foot longer wheelbase at 8 ft 2½ in and was generally stronger. Most Italian coachbuilders built bodies for these cars, but from 1954 on Ferrari reached agreement with Pininfarina which from then on supplied most shells with some being sub-contracted to Scaglietti. Other coachbuilders, especially Bertone, were also to produce one-offs or limited runs but Pininfarina has remained the base supplier ever since.

Apart from the plethora of engine sizes and bodies, the engines themselves varied enormously with different cylinder heads with one plug or two per pot, and variations in carburation and ignition. Some cars had 4-speed gearboxes, some had five speeds.

Two 275 Sports, driven by Ascari and Villoresi ran in the 1950 Mille Miglia and they both had 3,322 cc (72 × 68 mm) 220 bhp engines similar to the Grand Prix car but fitted in Tipo 166 chassis. The extra weight and power proved too great a strain on the components and both retired with broken gearboxes. It was the only race in which the 275S competed, but the day was saved by Giannino Marzotto's small 166, which went on to win.

From Ferrari's point of view, the Mille Miglia was the most important race of

Pit stop at Le Mans in 1953 for the fifth-placed Tipo 340MM driven by two of the four Marzotto brothers, Paolo and Giannino. (Louis Klementaski)

the year to win and between 1948 and 1957 only twice did another maker succeed in the event. There were other races which were more important from a commercial point of view, but nothing which gave greater satisfaction. For the rest of 1950 the larger-engined sports cars took a back seat to the single-seater programme.

The following year Villoresi won the Mille Miglia with a 340 'America' which had a 230 bhp engine of 4,101 cc (80 × 68 mm) and a greatly strengthened transmission. Piero Scotti's 212 came in second and Marzotto's 166 fourth. The showing encouraged Ferrari to enter Giovanni Bracco in a 340 in the Targa Florio, a race which tended to receive half-hearted support from Maranello except later when Championship points were at stake. Bracco's car retired and though private Ferraris finished second and third, Cortese won in his Frazer Nash 'Le Mans Replica'.

Four Tipo 340s were among the nine Ferraris to appear at Le Mans, where not only were they completely outstripped by Moss's Jaguar C-type but they also proved woefully unreliable. In the Carrera Panamericana there were 212 coupés for Taruffi/Chinetti and Ascari/Villoresi and they finished in that order though most of the opposition came from American production saloons, which did not pressure them.

For 1952 Ferrari concentrated on the Tipo 250 (2,953 cc, 73 × 58.8 mm) which, being smaller and lighter had far better road-holding than the 340s. The engine developed 220 bhp and fed through a 5-speed gearbox. Bracco drove one brilliantly in the Mille Miglia to beat the works Mercedes-Benz 300SLs after encountering tyre trouble, which at one point had relegated him to fifth. He became a national hero and the car was re-named the Tipo 250MM, and among detail revisions, power was increased to 240 bhp. Its engine became the *pattern* for the later Testa Rossa, 250GT and GTO models.

Ferrari missed the Targa Florio in which Lancia Aurelias scored a magnificent 1-2-3 but turned up in force at Le Mans. In the early stages of the race they ran well and Ascari set a new lap record, but only one car was destined to finish, in fifth place. It was beginning to appear that Ferrari could build cars which would last the Mille Miglia with the built-in advantage of an Italian driver but were completely out of their depth on a 'neutral' circuit such as Le Mans and that the 1949 win had been a freak result.

It is perhaps worth mentioning that the team had other fish to fry and in 1952 had not only won every single round of the GP World Championship but its drivers had filled the first three places in the final reckoning. For the Carrera Panamericana there were 4.1-litre 340 Mexico coupés for Villoresi, Chinetti and new World Champion, Alberto Ascari, but it was Bracco's 250MM which posed the greatest threat to the Mercedes-Benz team after early pacemaker Jean Behra crashed his Gordini. In the second stage Bracco led with Villoresi catching after early gearbox troubles, but then his clutch burned out. Chinetti was the best Ferrari finisher, in third place behind two Mercedes-Benz 300SLs.

With 1953 heralding the new World Sports Car Championship and the GP effort taking care of itself, Ferrari underwent a change of direction so far as sports cars were concerned. Until 1953 Ferrari had been Italy-centred, but afterwards it became much more Internationally minded. For the first time a non-Latin, Mike Hawthorn, became a leading member of the driver line-up. With the exception of Ascari, the old-stagers had reached mature years and though there were some promising young Italian drivers they were not quite ready for the big time. Then again, Ferrari road cars, though still made in small numbers, were increasingly selling abroad and Ferrari was keen to display its wares more regularly on the International stage.

For 1953 the team fielded two versions of its V-12 sports-racer, the Tipo 340 and the Tipo 375. The latter had an engine of 4,523 cc (84 × 68 mm) and while the chassis retained the established layout, its wheelbase was increased to 8 ft 6 in.

Sebring was missed, but in the Mille Miglia, Giannino Marzotto's private Tipo 340 duelled for the lead with Fangio's Alfa Romeo Disco Volante until a track rod broke on the Alfa and Fangio did well to finish at all, let alone in second less than 12 minutes behind the Ferrari. For Le Mans the works fielded a mixture of

Mike Hawthorn and Umberto Magliolo won the 1953 Pescara 12 Hours race in this 4.5 litre Tipo 375MM. (Autocar)

Umberto Magliolo at the wheel of a 4.9 litre Tipo 375 Plus during practice at Silverstone in May 1954. The car was driven in the race by Frolian Gonzalez. (Motor)

4.1- and 4.5-litre cars and the 375 coupé of Ascari/Villoresi held second for most of the race, and even led briefly, but retired with clutch failure after 19 hours. Ferrari honour was upheld by the Marzotto brothers, who finished fifth.

The Spa 24 Hours race was a round of the WSCC, but it was missed by both Jaguar and Aston Martin. Ferrari fielded a full team, but all retired save for the 375 coupé of Hawthorn/Farina, which ended the race a sick car but still 18 laps ahead of two private Jaguars. Again only one Ferrari finished in the next round, the Nürburgring 1,000 Km, but Ascari and Farina finished first in an open 375 after the Lancias had led but retired. No Ferraris went to the Tourist Trophy so Moss's fourth place with a sick Jaguar C-type put Jaguar joint top of the points table with only the Carrera Panamericana to run.

Jaguar scratched its single entry and, for some reason, Ferrari left its reputation in the hands of privateers in Mexico. The race resulted in a Lancia 1-2-3, but Mancini's Ferrari was just behind and clinched the first WSCC for Ferrari, though it could hardly be said to have been a distinguished win.

1954 began with the Buenos Aires 1,000 Km and Farina/Magliolo's 375MM won from the private 250MM of Schell/de Portago, the type's only notable success, after the other members of the Ferrari team eliminated themselves in a fierce struggle for second. For the Mille Miglia Ferrari fielded five examples of the 375 'Plus', which had an engine further enlarged to 4,954 cc by increasing the stroke from 68 to 74.5 mm, and an output of 330 bhp was claimed. Every one of them retired, leaving Ascari to win in a Lancia D24 with Vittorio Marzotto (brother of twice-winner Giannino) second in his private Tipo 500 Mondial, a car developed for privateers with the ex-F2 4-cylinder 1,984 cc (90 × 78 mm) engine which developed 160 bhp.

The position was redressed at Le Mans, where Ferrari faced the new Jaguar D-type. The two teams battled in the early stages, but eventually the race settled down to a duel between one car apiece, Gonzalez and Trintignant in their 375 'Plus' and Hamilton and Rolt in a D-type. The Ferrari held a two-lap lead until late in the race when it simply would not start after a routine pit stop. It finally fired with the Jaguar uncomfortably close, but in streaming wet conditions Gonzalez brought it home less than three miles ahead.

Even though the Jaguars were considerably less powerful than the 4.9 Ferraris, they still achieved higher speeds along the Mulsanne Straight. It never seemed to occur to Ferrari to seriously explore the art of aerodynamics or, for many years, to even consider disc brakes. Neither was the firm's chassis design ever very advanced. Maranello began with a superb engine and gearbox, built in traditional ways, and went on from there.

With Ferrari dominating the 2-litre F2 World Championship in 1952 and 1953 with a relatively simple design, it was a natural move to develop a winning formula into a sports car. Besides, Lampredi liked simplicity, so much so he de-

Le Mans 1954, and the Tipo 375 Plus, which Gonzalez/Trintignant were to drive to victory, receives the attention of the scrutineers. (Motor)

signed a 2½-litre twin for F1, which was one reason for his leaving Maranello. The first expression of this was the Tipo 735, which made a few unsuccessful appearances in 1953, but in 1954 it emerged as the Tipo 750 Monza. It had a 4-cylinder d.o.h.c. twin plug engine of 2,999.6 cc (103 × 90 mm) which gave 260 bhp at 6,500 rpm. The tubular frame featured transverse leaf spring and wishbone front suspension with an anti-roll bar, and de Dion rear axle suspended by a transverse leaf spring, and a 5-speed transaxle. It was, by all accounts, a brute to drive even after its first, positively vicious, handling characteristics had been tamed in 1955 by using the coil spring front suspension used on the 'Super Squalo' F1 car.

In the Supercortemaggiore GP at Monza, two 750s driven by Hawthorn/Maglioli and Gonzalez/Trintignant came first and second and Hawthorn/Trintignant finished second on handicap (first on distance) in the Tourist Trophy. The season ended with Ferrari taking its second WSCC win after Maglioli won the Carrera Panamericana in a 375 'Plus' after a race-long duel with Phil Hill's private 375MM. Despite a second success, however, Ferrari was in difficulties.

Apart from two fortunate wins it had had a thin time in F1 in 1954. It was not just that Mercedes-Benz had returned and set standards which were beyond the means of any other team, the first two races of the year (pre-Mercedes) had been won by Maserati. Ferrari had nothing in the pipeline either to deal with the competition in F1 or to cope with Mercedes-Benz when it came into sports car racing in 1955. Quite apart from Mercedes, Maserati was flexing its muscles and Jaguar was to seriously race its D-type.

Lampredi designed a new 6-cylinder engine for 1955, basically an extended version of the 4-cylinder F1 engine. It was a d.o.h.c. unit of 3,747 cc (94 × 90 mm) and gave 310 bhp which drove through a 5-speed transaxle. For the first time a Ferrari sports car had a space-frame chassis, though the suspension remained as before with coil springs and wishbones at the front and a de Dion rear axle suspended by a transverse leaf spring.

Designated the Tipo 118LM, and driven by Gonzalez and Trintignant, it battled for the lead of the first 1956 WSCC round, the Buenos Aires 1,000 Km, but

was blown off by a local 375 'Plus' driven by Valiente/Ibanez and later both works cars were disqualified for technical infringements. In a dull race, a second local Ferrari, the 375MM of Najurieta/Rivero, came home second. At Sebring, Mike Hawthorn and Phil Walters scored a narrow win in Briggs Cunningham's D-type from the private 3-litre Ferrari of Phil Hill and Carroll Shelby.

It was the calm before the storm for in the Mille Miglia, Mercedes-Benz scored a 1-2 after Eugenio Castellotti's Ferrari Tipo 121LM had led but retired. This was a 4,412 cc (102 × 90 mm) version of the Tipo118 LM and gave 360 bhp. As Castellotti demonstrated, it could be quick but was no match for the advanced Mercedes-Benz 300SLRs and was plagued by unreliability. Maglioli's 118LM finished third.

At Le Mans, Castellotti led for the first hour in his 121LM but retired with overheating, and its two sister cars, though they ran strongly in the early stages, were out by half-time. The Tourist Trophy saw another battle between the British and German firms with a Ferrari finishing down in sixth.

Still Ferrari led the Championship with 19 points with only one round, the Targa Florio, remaining. Mercedes-Benz and Jaguar tied for second with 16 points (only one car per round scored, so Mercedes-Benz received only 8 points for its 1-2-3 in the Tourist Trophy). Jaguar elected not to go to Sicily but Mercedes-Benz scored a 1-2 with Castellotti and Manzon bringing a 375MM home third.

At the end of the year Ferrari abandoned the 6-cylinder cars. Thus 1955 ended without a single works win and only the private 4.9 at Buenos Aires scored a victory at the highet level. Even then it was done against no works opposition save two Gordinis, which, by that time, did not represent a serious threat. Private cars did, however, win eleven International sports car races that year, though in most

Mike Hawthorn at the wheel of the 4-cylinder Tipo 750 Monza which he and Maurice Trintignant brought home second on handicap and first on scratch in the 1954 Tourist Trophy at Dundrod. (Louis Klementaski)

the fields were thin. In F1 Mercedes-Benz had swept the board save at Monaco when all retired allowing Trintignant's Ferrari to score a surprise win.

Ferrari was pleading financial hardship and threatening to withdraw from racing (Ferrari was always threatening to leave racing, sometimes adding for good measure that he intended to enter a monastery) when he was saved by an Italian consortium which handed over the Lancia D50 F1 project and guaranteed an annual subsidy for five years. With the Lancias came their designer, the great Vittorio Jano, and as Jano came in, Lampredi was sacked and went to Fiat. In 1957 Carlo Chiti was appointed chief engineer, but Jano remained as a consultant.

For 1956 Ferrari had the Tipo 860, which was a 'Monza' with its engine stroked to 3,431 cc (102 × 105 mm) and gave 310 bhp. Even with its improved suspension it still gave its drivers an uncomfortable time with an alarming tendency to understeer. It had first appeared in the 1955 Tourist Trophy and one was entered in the 1956 Buenos Aires 1,000 Km. Also entered were two Tipo 410 'Plus', which was an interim car which ran only in this one race. It had a twin-plug V-12 engine of 4,961 cc (88 × 68 mm) fitted to a Tipo 118LM frame.

During 1955 Ferrari raced the unreliable 6-cylinder Tipo 121. Eugenio Castellotti is seen during the Mille Miglia from which he retired after rear tyre blow-outs damaged the bodywork. (Publifoto)

In Buenos Aires, the 4.9-litre cars of Fangio/Castellotti and Collins/Musso controlled the race until both went out with broken differentials. From then on the Moss/Menditeguy Maserati 300S had the race in the bag, leading the Gendebien/Hill Tipo 860 home by two laps.

For Sebring Ferrari had a new car, the Tipo 290MM, and this reverted to the V-12 s.o.h.c. engine, this time with twin-plug heads and a capacity of 3,490 cc (73 × 69.5 mm) which produced 350 bhp. It was fitted to a chassis similar to the 6-cylinder cars but with a slightly shorter wheelbase. It was also the best sports-racer Ferrari had built for some seasons. For once Sebring attracted a very strong field indeed, but the 290MM always looked a likely winner. Driven by Fangio and Castellotti it spent most of the 12 hours in the lead and, despite being virtually brakeless in the closing stages, it out-lasted the opposition to win by two laps from its sister car driven by Musso and Schell.

It was no flash in the pan, for in the Mille Miglia Eugenio Castellotti drove like a man inspired in atrocious weather to win from Peter Collins in a Tipo 860 with three other Ferraris filling the next three places. It was to be Castellotti's finest hour, for the gifted Italian was killed early the following season before his talent had come to full maturity. The race was also Ferrari's best single result to date. With the F1 team, running 'Lancia-Ferraris', back on form it seemed as though Ferrari had turned the corner.

The Nürburgring 1,000 Km eventually came down to a duel between Fangio's 290MM and Moss's Maserati 300S. Fangio led with Moss biting into his advantage, then he had to bring his Ferrari in for fuel and Moss went by and continued to increase his lead to the end. Though the score read two wins each for Maserati and Ferrari, Maranello had clinched its third WSCC in four years.

Le Mans was restricted in 1956 to prototypes of 2½ litres and for the race Ferrari built a team of three Tipo 625LMs which used the old 4-cylinder d.o.h.c. F1 engine of 2,490 cc (94 × 90 mm) which produced 225 bhp and drove through a 4-speed gearbox. These cars, which appeared for the works only in the one race, had bodies by Touring and resembled those on the Tipo 500 Testa Rossa. From

For 1956 Ferrari reverted to V-12 engines and Fangio (seen here) and Castellotti drove this 3.4-litre Tipo 290MM to second place in the Nürburgring 1000 Km. (Leica-Studio Wörner)

the fifth hour on, the Gendebien/Trintignant car ran third and held the position to the end.

During 1956, Ferrari had produced an update of the (de Dion) 2-litre Tipo 500 'Mondial' which was designated 'Testa Rossa', for the cam cover of its 4-cylinder 190 bhp engine was finished in red. This is not to be confused with the later Tipo 250 (3-litre) 'Testa Rossa', for it was a fairly basic customer car with a ladder-frame and a live rear axle suspended on coil springs.

Despite the fact that Ferrari had clinched the Championship, both it and Maserati sent full teams to the final WSCC round, the Swedish GP. Having two sports car victories apiece and being fierce, equally matched, competitors in F1, both had a point to make. For Maserati, though, the race was a fiasco with all four team cars retiring and three 290MMs, led by Trintignant and Phil Hill, filling the first three places.

At the 1956 Swedish GP, Maserati's new 4½-litre 450S had been seen in practice and was a great potential threat. It underlined its menace when in the first race of 1957, the Buenos Aires 1,000 Km, where Moss and Fangio led easily in it until retiring with clutch troubles. This let into the lead the 290MM which had started off driven by Perdisa and Gregory but was then taken over by Castellotti and Musso when their own car failed. It won despite the best efforts of Moss, who had taken over the Behra/Menditeguy 300S.

Sebring brought the big Maserati's first win with Ferrari nowhere and for the Mille Miglia, Maranello responded with two new cars, the Tipo 315MM (3,780 cc, 76 × 69.5 mm, 380 bhp) and the Tipo 335 Sport (4,022 cc, 77 × 72 mm, 430 bhp). Alfonso de Portago, a remarkable all-round sportsman and Spanish nobleman, was leading in his works Tipo 335 on the last stage when a tyre burst. In the resulting crash he and his co-driver, Gunnar 'Ed' Nelson, were both killed along with a number of spectators, including children.

Peter Collins then took over the lead, but retired soon after with rear axle trouble and it was left to Pierro Taruffi to take his Tipo 315 across the line in first place. Having achieved his life-long ambition, the distinguished Roman then retired from racing. Ferraris also finished second and third, but it was a joyless win. The furore which followed de Portago's accident almost ended road racing in Europe (the Le Mans tragedy was still too fresh); it certainly finished the Mille Miglia, which thereafter was run as a closed-circuit speed trial.

In the Spa sports car race (won by Brooks in an Aston Martin DBR1/300), Ferrari entered a prototype for Olivier Gendebien, the Tipo 312LM. This had a twin overhead camshaft version of the 250 engine and it proved fast but unreliable. It was stored away for another day.

Neither of the Italian teams was prepared for what met them at the Nürburgring 1,000 Km, where Tony Brooks sailed into the lead in his new Aston Martin DBR1/3000 and, ably backed by Noel Cunningham-Reid, stayed there until the end to win by over four minutes from the Tipo 335 of Collins and Gendebien with the Tipo 315 of Hawthorn and Trintignant third. Almost unnoticed at the time was a new car entered by Temple Buell, a wealthy American private entrant who was allowed favours from Ferrari. Driven by Masten Gregory it ran well up, but his co-driver Morolli was not up to scratch and it did not figure in the results. It was the first 250 Testa Rossa.

Le Mans was back as a WSCC round, but all the Ferraris (and Maseratis) fell by the wayside save for the Ferrari of Stuart Lewis-Evans and Martino Severi, the works tester, which finished fifth, the only non-Jaguar in the top six. Among the Ferraris at Sarthe, however, was another Testa Rossa. It had a 3,117 cc (75 ×

By 1957 Ferrari was racing the larger-capacity 4.1-litre Tipo 335. Mike Hawthorn and Luigi Musso drove this car at Le Mans, but were eliminated by piston failure. (Louis Klementaski)

58.8 mm) version of the 250 engine in a new chassis and, driven by Gendebien and Trintignant, held third until it broke a piston. Although the engine raced only the once in a WSCC race, the chassis was to be the basis for the 1958 cars.

At the Swedish Grand Prix Hawthorn was sent out in his Tipo 335 to try to break the Maserati 450S opposition, but they survived him and Behra/Moss brought one home first with the Hill/Collins Tipo 315 second. The result left both Ferrari and Maserati with a chance of winning the WSCC with only the Venezuelan GP remaining.

The disaster which this race turned out to be for Maserati is told elsewhere. For the record the Tipi 335 of Collins/Hill and Musso/Hawthorn came home first and second ahead of the von Trips/Seidel Tipo 250 'Testa Rossa'. Thus Ferrari won its fourth WSCC, which was some recompense for failing to win a single World Championship Grand Prix race for the first time since 1950.

1958 began with a new set of ground rules. For one thing there was a 3-litre limit in the WSCC. For another, Maserati had left the scene. Jaguar had gone at the end of 1956, but had supported Ecurie Ecosse during 1957 and it remained to be seen whether the 3-litre version of the XK engine would work (it didn't). Thus Ferrari had the field to itself apart from Aston Martin and Aston Martin was not in the habit of attending every race.

Ferrari's weapon for 1958 was to be the 250 Testa Rossa and it was to be the most successful of all the front-engined Ferraris. It has become the sports-racing car which has caught the imagination more than any other, largely due to its stunning Scaglietti bodywork. Its reputation, however, has been exaggerated for it did not face stern opposition. It remained an old-fashioned design with drum brakes, a fairly rudimentary space-frame, styling rather than aerodynamics, and no advance at all in suspension. The *scientifically* designed Porsches gave it a hard time with just over half the engine size.

These are heretical remarks, but one can never take away from the car its many wins, its glorious sound and the magic of its style. For all its technical shortcomings it remains the essence of Ferrari in the Fifties and more than any other type embodies the indefinable magic of the marque.

The engine was another expression of the 60-degree V-12 s.o.h.c. unit first laid down by Colombo but successively developed by Lampredi and Carlo Chiti. With a capacity of 2,953 cc (73 × 58.8 mm), the 'classic' Ferrari dimensions used from the Tipo 250MM to the GTO, it delivered 300 bhp at 7,200 rpm and drove through a 5-speed transaxle. Its chassis was pure Tipo 290 with a slightly wider rear track, though the 'Venezuela' car had a live rear axle.

The cars began the year with a 1-2 in the Buenos Aires 1,000 Km though the Moss/Behra 1.6 Porsche was less than ten seconds behind. Another 1-2 was

Mike Hawthorn with a V-12 Testa Rossa at the Karussell in the 1958 Nürburgring 1000 Kms. Partnered by Peter Collins, he finished second. In the background is Jimmy Blumer's abandoned Lotus Eleven. (Leica-Studio Wörner)

scored at Sebring with again a Porsche in third, though for the first third of the race the Moss/Brooks Aston Martin led easily. In the Tanga Florio a 1.6 Porsche actually split the leading two Ferraris in the results and, until it broke its gearbox, the Moss/Brooks Aston Martin was the quickest car in the race.

Still, to finish first, you've first to finish, and everything was going swimmingly for Ferrari until the Nürburgring 1,000 Km. There Moss's Aston Martin stayed the distance and he drove almost the whole way to beat Ferrari into second and third.

Aston Martins were the quickest cars at Le Mans, too, but the works cars all retired, as did the 3-litre Jaguar D-types. The Gendebien/Hill Testa Rossa won through to the end from the Whitehead brothers' old DB3S and three Porsches. With the win went another WSCC.

Two interesting cars which appeared during the year were the Tipo 206/S Dino and the Tipo 296 Dino. The first was a 1,983 cc (77×71 mm) d.o.h.c. V-6 producing 225 bhp at 9,000 rpm. This was fitted to a live axle chassis and Peter Collins drove it to second place in a race at the Easter Monday Goodwood Meeting. It did race a couple of other times but was very much an experimental car.

The 296 Dino was a de Dion Testa Rossa-style chassis into which was fitted a 2,962 cc (85×87 mm) version of the d.o.h.c. V-6 'Dino' engine and gave 316 bhp at 7,800 rpm. Mike Hawthorn drove it in the *Daily Express* International Trophy meeting at Silverstone where it finished third. The car was never seen again in the same configuration and to judge by the way it handled, it is no wonder.

The 'Dino' series of engines was named for Ferrari's only son Alfredo, of which 'Dino' is a diminutive. Trained as an engineer, he was groomed by his father to take over the company, but tragically he was afflicted by muscular dystrophy to which he succumbed in 1956. According to Enzo Ferrari, Vittorio Jano spent hours by the dying youngster's sick bed discussing engines with him and Dino decided that the new unit should be a V-6. The grief-stricken father accepted the decision and credited his son with the engine's inspiration. Jano, however, was one of the greatest designers Italy has produced and was already responsible for the Lancia V-6 engine...

Anyway the Ferrari V-6 engines were named for Dino and they were to prove very successful. The unit first ran in a F2 car in 1957 and then became Ferrari's

F1 mainstay in 1958. Later they were to become the backbone of the sports cars. One thing which should be noted is that the 'Dino' models had a different method of type numbering. The first two numbers refer to overall capacity and the third to the number of cylinders, thus Tipo 196 equals 1.9 litres, 6 cylinders.

Having won the 1958 sports car Championship, Ferrari started to slide into another trough. In F1, Hawthorn had became World Champion, but it was not a great season for either driver or Ferrari. The marque won only two Grands Prix in the year, the same as Cooper and somewhat short of Vanwall's six. To the loss of Castellotti and Musso (killed in the 1958 French GP) were added Collins (killed in the 1958 German GP) and Hawthorn, who had retired at the end of the season and who died in a road crash soon afterwards.

Ferrari faced 1959 with only one top-line driver, Brooks, and his contract excluded some sports car races. By contrast Aston Martin had Moss and an improved car and Porsche was improving all the time. The Testa Rossa had had no dramatic development but its bodies were now made by the ex-Maserati builder, Medardo Fantuzzi.

The WSCC started with Sebring and a Ferrari 1-2 with a Porsche third, but in the Targa Florio the superior handling of the Porsches told. Five works and private cars hounded the Gurney/Behra Testa Rossa until it broke and Porsche scored a 1-2-3.

Only one Aston Martin was entered for the Nürburgring 1,000 Km, but with Moss doing the bulk of the driving and overcoming a handicap when his co-driver put the car in a ditch, Ferrari had to be content with second and third. There was no stopping Moss when he turned in one of his virtuoso performances.

Ferrari started favourites at Le Mans following times set in the April practice day and, at last, they had disc brakes just six years after Jaguar had demonstrated their superiority. The Testa Rossas, however, did not last long and, unusually, the Porsches all dropped out. Thus Aston Martin scored the win which had eluded it for so long but Maranello's face was saved by the performance of private 250GTs, one of which finished third and kept alive Ferrari's WSCC hopes.

The Championship was to be settled in the Tourist Trophy at Goodwood and

Phil Hill and Olivier Gendebien, one of the most successful sports car pairings ever, drove this Testa Rossa to victory in the 1959 Sebring 12 Hours.

Ferrari brought along a 196S Dino for Giorgio Scarlatti and Lodovico Scarfiotti. This was a 1,983 cc s.o.h.c. V-6 fitted to the 2-litre live axle chassis, but it did not last the distance. In the race Ferrari again encountered a stunning performance by Moss, who won for Aston Martin. Just as Aston Martins always went well at Goodwood, so Porsches seemed to like the place as well. Not even Tony Brooks at the wheel of a Testa Rossa could beat the 1.6 Porsche of von Trips and Bonnier for second place, though had it done so Ferrari would have tied the Championship.

As it was, Aston Martin took the title and became only the second to take it from Ferrari. As things turned out, Aston Martin was to be the last team to deprive Ferrari in the original WSCC.

With the title, Aston Martin retired and Ferrari faced only the semi-works Maserati Tipo 61s of the inexperienced Camoradi team and the increasingly irritating Porsches. 1960 was not a great year for sports car racing and Ferrari won more or less by having a power advantage, an experienced team, and turning up to all the races. Maranello has always been a bastion of conservatism which not only has never introduced a single advance in the design of racing cars but has also been slow to follow new advances. As a *Grand Constructeur* it has held aloof from the *Garagistes*. It had finished 1959 being humiliated by Cooper in F1 and was to face worse in 1960 when Lotus introduced its rear-engined 18.

Ferrari won the 1960 WSCC by the skin of its teeth. It won the opening round in Argentina after the sole Maserati Birdcage retired, but in the Argentine had a new model, the Tipo 246 Sport. This had a 'Dino' engine of 2,417 cc (85 × 71 mm) and gave around 240 bhp. It ran fourth until retiring with ignition problems.

At Sebring the team included a Tipo 196S and it went well until it, and the V-12 cars, failed. Maserati had a dreadful race and Porsche scored a 1-2 with the private Testa Rossa of Nethercutt and Lovely third, ten laps behind the Gendebien/Herrmann Porsche which had half its engine size.

For the Targa Florio Ferrari arranged its biggest possible arsenal. There were two Testa Rossas with a new independent rear suspension layout of coil springs and double wishbones, a new Dino 246, also with i.r.s., a Dino 246 with the old 2-litre-style (Tipo 500 Testa Rossa) chassis with live rear axle and a Tipo 196. The entire team seemed to do its best to wreck the cars and the only survivor, the von Trips/Hill Dino 246, came second sandwiched between two Porsches.

Moss and Gurney gave the Maserati Tipo 61 an overdue win in the Nürburgring 1,000 Km and the best Ferrari, a Testa Rossa, finished third behind the Maserati and a Porsche.

At Le Mans the opposition destroyed itself and the Testa Rossas of Gendebien/ Frère and Ricardo Rodriguez/André Pilette were able to take things easy to win from the Aston Martin DBR1 of Clark and Salvadori. Thus Ferrari took another WSCC, but only by the narrow margin of four points from Porsche, which was the moral victor of the year.

In the last year of the old WSCC Ferrari at last bowed to the inevitable and introduced a rear-engined car, the Tipo 246/SP (P for Prototype). This time the Rampant Horse had something to be excited over, for in F1 it was to be the dominant team though twice Moss demonstrated that genius could overcome horsepower. In sports car events it was to have more than the measure of Porsche even when the German team ran 2-litre engines. Alongside the new car were the faithful Testa Rossas and these had new, smoother, Fantuzzi bodies.

The Tipo 246/SP had a 2,417 cc (85 × 71 mm) d.o.h.c. V-6 giving 270 bhp

fitted into a fairly simple space-frame with coil spring and unequal length wish-bones front and rear. Even more astounding was that the body had actually been developed in a new wind tunnel Ing. Chiti had had installed at Maranello. After testing at Monza a lip was put on the tail to prevent lift, the idea coming from works tester Richie Ginther.

One of these cars was entered for Sebring, but retired with broken steering, though the rest of the race was a Testa Rossa benefit, Gendebien and Hill leading home four others. Two 246/SPs and a Testa Rossa appeared in the Targa Florio. Hill crashed a Dino on the first lap and it was left to von Trips and Gendebien to take on the Porsches. This they did successfully save for the 2-litre car driven by Moss which had victory in sight when its transmission broke four miles from the end. Von Trips had been laying second and he went on to take the flag and give the sports racing Dino its first victory.

In the Nürburgring 1,000 Km, which was run in very cold, wet, conditions, the Dinos suffered icing of the carburettors. This probably caused the sudden engine cut-out which befell Phil Hill in the leading car and caused him to crash. Then Moss's Porsche blew up and that left the dog-eared Maserati Tipo 61 of Gregory and Casner in the lead, which it held to the end, a lap clear of the Testa Rossa of the Rodriguez brothers and the Dino of Ginther and von Trips, which had been delayed by icing but which was running healthily at the end.

For Le Mans Ferrari played safe and fielded two Testa Rossas, a prototype 250GT, and one Dino. The Dino was troubled by water loss, but it led for a while and finally went out when lying second through running out of fuel. The trusty old V-12 cars finished first and second with a private 250GT third. Thus Ferrari won its seventh of the nine original Championships.

There was one other race that year, the Pescara Four Hours, to which a single works car was sent but crashed. Lorenzo Bandini and Lodovico Scarfiotti made amends for that by driving their Centro-Sud Testa Rossa to a trouble-free victory.

This necessarily brief résumé of Ferrari's sports-racing activities during the period of the first WSCC does not cover the many wins achieved by private owners. Though comparatively rare in Britain, Ferraris sold in large numbers in America and were not only hugely successful in SCCA events but bred a generation of first-rate drivers of the likes of Fitch, Hill, Ginther and Gurney. Then again, the road cars which were frequently thinly disguised racers were immensely successful in GT racing, particularly from about 1956 when Ferrari production began to take off.

Enzo Ferrari has always made a distinction between the *Grand Constructeur* and the *Garagiste*, or special builder, but when one looks at the profusion of models his company made during the Fifties one is drawn to the conclusion that there was something of the special builder about Ferrari. Those companies which set serious standards of engineering (Mercedes-Benz, Bristol, Porsche and Jaguar) did not have to constantly change their cars, they got them right from the start. Such companies identified their objectives and created cars capable of meeting them and used state-of-the-art engineering.

It was only late in our chosen period that Ferrari began to catch up in terms of design when Carlo Chiti began to instigate a more rational approach to building cars, but at the end of 1961 he, and a number of other key personnel, left to join Count Volpi's ill-starred A.T.S. team. In typical Ferrari fashion the defection was triggered by the constant interference by Ferrari's wife, Laura, in the running of the team. One cannot imagine such a thing happening at Porsche or Mercedes-Benz, but we began this story with suggesting that Maranello was run like a medieval Italian city-state.

Chiti, however, left a legacy which was extended by his successor Mauro Foghieri and under his guidance Ferrari continued to dominate sports car racing for years to come. It took the resources of the Ford Motor Company to knock Maranello from its pedestal.

Frazer Nash

Pre-war, A.F.N. Ltd both imported B.M.W.s and made its own Frazer Nash sports cars, which had a good reputation as club racers. When the war ended, one of the company's principals, H. J. Aldington, was a member of one of the teams which evaluated German technology and carried home selected items by way of war reparation. Aldington's trips resulted in him not only bringing back various B.M.W. designs, among them the 1,991 cc 6-cylinder 328 engine, but he also arranged the release from internment of Dr Fritz Fiedler, a leading B.M.W. design engineer.

A.F.N. and the Bristol Aircraft Company had come to an agreement during the war to combine to make and market a new car. This arrangement was short-lived but from it came a new deal. Bristol would take over the B.M.W. engine and A.F.N. would receive tuned FNS (Frazer Nash Special) versions, developed by Fiedler, for use in its own cars.

Fiedler's first creation for A.F.N. was the 'Grand Prix' which was styled after the streamlined B.M.W. 328 which had won the 1940 'Mille Miglia' (a 1,000-mile race over eight laps of a 125-mile circuit which was a Mille Miglia in name only). While the Germans had long appreciated the advantages of sound aerodynamics, the British were slow to latch on and from a purely marketing point of view it was felt that the body was too radical and out of keeping with the Frazer Nash tradition.

Accordingly when A.F.N. showed its first postwar production model, the 'High Speed', at the 1948 London Motor show it was a traditionally styled 2-seater with cycle wings, cutaway sides and an external exhaust system. As an aside, it is extraordinary how this style of car has become regarded as 'traditional'. It is nothing of the sort, it is merely old-fashioned and inefficient. Traditionally sports cars have been designed for performance and an important performance parameter is effective aerodynamics.

Peacock's Frazer Nash Le Mans Replica in the Production Sports Car race at Silverstone, May 1951. (T.C. March)

The 'High Speed's' chassis derived from B.M.W. practice with two large diameter (5¼-in) side tubes and 5-in. cross members. Front suspension was by a transverse leaf spring and lower wishbones (as was the B.M.W. 328) while at the rear longitudinal torsion bars (similar to the B.M.W. 326) sprung the live rear axle, which was located by an A-bracket.

B.M.W. rack-and-pinion steering was used, Borg-Warner supplied the 4-speed gearbox and, initially, the 2-litre Bristol engine gave 120 bhp. It was a compact car and weighed just over 1,500 lb.

Early in 1949, a 'High Speed' was bought by Count 'Johnny' Lurani's Scuderia Ambrosiana and Dorino Serifini drove it in the Tour of Sicily. He led until striking a kerb and deranging the steering. Franco Cortese drove it in the Targa Florio and was running well until a rock punctured his fuel tank.

Then in the first postwar Le Mans, in 1949, Norman Culpan entered his 'High Speed' for himself and H. J. Aldington and they came home a splendid third. Immediately the model was rechristened the 'Le Mans Replica'. Although only 60 cars were made they took many wins and Tony Crook, later the owner of Bristol Cars, was one of the leading contenders in the popular 2-litre class in Britain with his Le Mans Replica.

1950 saw the introduction of the 'Mille Miglia', basically a 'Le Mans Replica' with an enveloping body. Dickie Stoop and T.A.S.O. Mathieson used one to win the 2-litre class at Le Mans and finish ninth overall, but on the whole most preferred the earlier car. That year Norman Culpan's 'High Speed' finished third in the Manx Cup and Bob Gerard took his Le Mans Replica to third in the Tourist Trophy behind the Jaguar XK120s of Stirling Moss and Peter Whitehead.

In 1951 Franco Cortese won the Targa Florio in Count Lurani's 'Nash, came fourth in the Tour of Sicily and won the Enna GP. The Targa Florio win was remarkable especially in view of the number of Ferraris in the race, which included a works Tipo 340 for Giovanni Bracco. In the race Cortese had a stone jam his steering gear which led to an excursion from which he had to push his car back onto the road and then, in the later stages, he was running low on fuel and finally crossed the line with only the smell of petrol in his tank. Not many British cars ever did well in Sicily, no matter who was driving, and Cortese's victory in the Targa Florio was to be the only occasion a British car won the race.

Still in 1951, Stirling Moss drove Sid Greene's 'Le Mans Replica' to victory in the British Empire Trophy, held on the Isle of Man, with Bob Gerard's similar car second.

What is telling about Frazer Nash's competition successes is that the vast majority were achieved by private owners. The cars were ideal for the privateer,

The Frazer Nash Le Mans fixed head coupé driven by Ken Wharton on its debut at Silverstone, May 1953. (T.C. March)

being strong, simple, and very reliable. Twenty-four hours of Le Mans presented no fears for a well-prepared Bristol engine, while the considerable Sicilian successes speak not only of excellent handling but of engineering integrity.

A Mk II version of the 'Le Mans' was introduced in 1952. This had a 132 bhp engine, lower frontal area, the shedding of over 100 lb in weight and a de Dion rear axle (still sprung by torsion bars) was available. Bolt-on steel wheels replaced the centre-lock alloys.

In 1952 Harry Grey and Larry Kulok took a 'Nash to victory in the first Sebring 12 Hours, though this was really a glorified club event. Tony Crook finished third in the Monaco GP (run for sports cars) and Bob Gerard and David Clarke finished fourth in the Goodwood Nine Hours. In the Targa Florio, Cortese ran a strong fourth behind three works Lancia Aurelias until he hit a hard object and lost a wheel on the last lap. Other cars finished tenth at Le Mans and seventh in the Reims 12 Hours race.

Dickie Stoop and Tony Gaze drove this Frazer Nash Sebring at Le Mans in 1956 but were eliminated by an accident. (LAT)

While Frazer Nashes remained competitive in British events for several seasons afterwards, 1952 was the last time the cars made an impact at International level, though one finished 13th at Le Mans in 1953.

The works also made, in 1952, three Formula Two cars based on sports chassis. Ken Wharton drove one for the works and appeared in several World Championship races, finishing fourth in the Swiss GP (two laps down) and qualifying seventh for the Belgian GP, though nearly half a minute off the pace. It was soon clear that the car was outclassed in F2 and was not even a match for the Cooper-Bristols, and the project faded at the end of the year. Two cars sold to privateers had undistinguished careers.

Frazer Nash continued to make road cars in small numbers, a Bristol-engined model with a striking enveloping body, the 'Sebring' was offered from 1954 but only three were made. One, driven by Dickie Stoop, enjoyed some success in British club racing and it was his driving of the works Sebring which led to Tony Brooks being invited by Aston Martin to test for a works drive.

A coupé powered by B.M.W.'s 2,580 cc V-8, the 'Continental', was offered from 1956, but only a couple were sold, though it, and the Sebring, theoretically remained in production until 1964. 'Production' is not quite the right word for Frazer Nashes were like bespoke suits, rather the company was willing to build cars to order for some time after it had actually stopped making cars.

By the late Fifties Frazer Nash cars, though beautifully made, were too expensive to attract many buyers and offered nothing that could not be bought cheaper elsewhere. The cheaper Bristol-powered A.C. Ace took much of the company's potential market. Thereafter A.F.N. Ltd imported Porsche cars into Britain until Porsche bought back the franchise in 1986, though A.F.N. continues as an important distributor.

A total of 95 post-war Frazer Nashes were built and many are enjoying a new lease of life in Historic racing. With Le Mans Replicas being relatively simple to make and attracting very high prices, not every Frazer Nash now in existence saw the inside of the A.F.N. works.

Gilby

When he was 16, Sid Greene was knocked down by a bus and lost an arm. As so often happens when a man is disabled, the handicap did not hinder him, rather it spurred him to do better. During the war he flew as a pilot and both before and after it he raced cars. He also built up a successful business, Gilby Engineering.

When he retired from racing in 1953, he became an entrant, and his best-known relationship was with Roy Salvadori, who raced a variety of Gilby-entered cars, including a Maserati 250F. In the back of Greene's mind, though, was the dream that one day he would build his own F1 car and his son, Keith, would drive it.

Keith Greene's driving career was progressing smoothly when, in 1959, he was bought a Lotus 17 which had a severe inherent suspension problem. Meanwhile Len Terry, the first designer Colin Chapman employed, had been making his own Terrier 1172 cars as a part-time occupation. When these proved more successful in racing than the Lotus Seven, Chapman sacked him.

Terry was then taken on the strength of the Gilby team, initially to sort out the Lotus by designing a new front suspension layout. It was then a short step to making a Gilby car. It had a light, strong, space-frame, with a front-mounted Coventry Climax FWA, driving via a 4-speed Austin A35 gearbox (with Lotus gears) and a BMC differential housed in a bespoke Gilby casing. Front suspension was by coil springs and double wishbones while the rear followed Lola Mk I practice with articulated, but not splined, drive-shafts acting as the top wishbones. The aluminium body, built by Williams & Pritchard, was inspired by an Abarth record-breaker at the front and the Costin Lister-Jaguar at the rear.

It raced seriously only in 1960, then only in British national events, and Keith Greene anyway was not a top-flight driver, though he later became a top-flight team manager. When Greene Jnr had other commitments, Peter Arundell took over the wheel, and in a meeting at Snetterton, in appalling weather, Arundell won the Formule Libre race and finished second to a Lister-Jaguar in the unlimited sports car race. That showing and a fine second in the 1,500 cc class at the British Grand Prix Meeting, also with Arundell driving, demonstrated that in the right hands the car was on a par with the Lola Mk I.

Designed by Len Terry, the Gilby-Climax was built for Keith Greene and in his hands, and those of Peter Arundell, achieved a fair degree of success in 1960. Here the car is seen in the hands of a later owner at Brands Hatch in March 1962. (NMM)

In its one season of serious competition it started 15 times, took five wins, two seconds and four thirds and then passed into other, amateur, hands while Gilby went on to build its own F1 car. Now the Gilby sports car is owned by Frenchman Lionel Aglave, who races it in Historic events with a 1,100 cc Ford Cosworth MAE engine, which was originally fitted in the early Sixties.

On the surface the Gilby was merely a moderately successful club racing special, but in the broader history of motor racing, it had a significance which none at the time could have seen. Until its appearance, new racing cars had been made by factories or derived from specials with a man making a car for his own use and others requesting replicas. Len Terry was the first of what was to become a steady stream of British designers who began by working for a constructor and then going on to offer their services to others. His subsequent career would include spells at B.R.M., Eagle, and Lotus again.

It was to be this stream of design talent, employed and shaped by the likes of Chapman and Broadley, which was to ultimately establish Britain as the dominant force in single-seater motor racing.

Gordini

Amédée Gordini was an Italian who, pre-war, established a name for himself as a tuner and driver of Fiat cars. Indeed, in the days when engine tuning was regarded as something of a black art and 'tuning wizards' did not apparently apply science but, rather, 'breathed' on engines, Gordini was nicknamed 'The Sorcerer'. His exploits came to the attention of Sté Industrielle de Mécanique et Carrosserie Automobile (Simca), which had been set up in France in 1934 to build Fiats under licence, and Simca offered him financial support to promote its name by using its products as the basis for his racing.

By the time war broke out, the relationship was well established and Gordini-developed Simca saloons and sports cars were regular competitors at Le Mans from 1937 onwards. No fewer than ten Simcas appeared in 1938 and one won not only the 750 cc class but also the Index of Performance. A 1,100 cc Simca had also led its class before crashing. In 1939 the 1,100 cc Simca of Gordini/Scaron, a car remarkable for its low height and slippery shape, finished tenth overall and won both the Index and the Biennial Cup.

This arrangement continued after the war and led to a number of Simca-Gordini single-seater racing cars built in Gordini's workshop in Paris. They used a number of production components, including the suspension, and engines came in various sizes and forms, including a blown 1,430 cc unit which qualified for Formula 1. Though these cars could be very competitive on tight circuits, for they were small, light and nimble, the production-based engine proved fragile. Robert Manzon's car, however, held together for long enough to finish fourth in the French GP behind two Alfa Romeos and a Ferrari.

Fangio was among the drivers of these cars in 1947 and, indeed, continued to make odd appearances in Gordinis even after he had become World Champion. One of these little racers found its way to Argentina, where a German-born garage owner, Carl Delfosse, converted it to a mid-engined, central-seat sports car with a pretty aerodynamic body. Fitted with a Porsche 547 engine it actually finished third in the 1,500 cc class in the 1955 Buenos Aires 1,000 Km, though the race was largely an amateur event.

When Simca backed Gordini in the building of a new 4-cylinder d.o.h.c. engine for Formula Two it stipulated a capacity limit of 1½ litres, for it had in mind the possibility of turning it into a production engine and the French excise structure was such that a 2-litre engine was undesirable. It is no wonder the car did not shine at International level and, at the end of 1951, Simca severed its links with Gordini.

Thus began the six-year history of the Gordini marque, which was characterized by excellent design limited by severe financial strictures. Gordini had a fairly large establishment to maintain, and around fifty employees to care for, so he began his career as an independent facing bankruptcy. The wonder is not that Gordini cars did not make a greater impact in International motor racing but that the company survived at all.

Gordini's first design as an independent was an F2 car fitted with what was basically a dry-sumped 2-litre 6-cylinder version of the 'four' he had designed for Simca. With 'square' cylinder dimensions (75 × 75 mm) and three twin-choke Weber carburettors, it gave a decent 155 bhp. It was fitted into a lightweight ladder-frame chassis with torsion bar suspension all round and a live back axle. This suspension, which Gordini was to use on all his cars was, at the front, a rhombus formed from single links with the longitudinal torsion bars located in

1500cc Simca-Gordini of Veyron/Monneret at Le Mans in 1951. It retired because of a broken distributor. (Geoffrey Goddard)

the top of a cast cradle on which the suspension links were pivoted. It may have given away 25 bhp to the Ferrari 500 but, at 990 lb, it was 220 lb lighter.

Driven mainly by Jean Behra and Robert Manzon, the F2 Gordinis scored some excellent results in 1952. Outstanding among several places in World Championship Grands Prix were Behra's third at Berne and Manzon's third at Spa, both beaten only by two works Ferraris. Behra's Swiss GP result is even more remarkable when one considers that due to his car's late completion he drove it from Paris to Berne on trade plates to arrive just in time to practice.

Non-Championship race wins included Aix-les-Bains (Behra); Caen (Maurice Trintignant); and Manzon's win in his heat in the International Trophy. Behra came second to Hawthorn's Cooper-Bristol in his heat, but neither he nor Manzon finished the Final. The highlight of the year, however, came in the Reims GP.

This was effectively a full Grand Prix which was not included in the World Championship. It was a three hour race which attracted all the major works teams and Behra completely outstripped the works Ferraris of Ascari, Villoresi and Farina to win by a mile. It was a feat which should not be diminished because of the technicality that it did not count for the Championship.

The same basic car was adapted for sports car racing running with either 2-litre or 2.3-litre engines. At the beginning of the year Gordini announced he was prepared to sell up to ten cars a year for road use and offered them in either 'Berlinette' or open form. Unfortunately, at prices ranging between £2,500 and £4,000, they were expensive, you could buy a Jaguar C-type at an ex-tax price of £1,495, and there were few takers.

At Le Mans, the Behra/Manzon 2.3-litre car went into the lead after the re-bodied Jaguar C-types all overheated and retired in the early stages. It led until half-time, ahead of the works Mercedes-Benz 300SLs and, of course, Pierre Levegh's Talbot. Early on the Sunday morning, however, it retired when a brake shoe came loose.

In the Monaco Grand Prix (for sports cars) Manzon won the 2-litre event and then, in a 2.3 Gordini, led the main race in the early stages but was eliminated in the multiple accident which wiped out a fair proportion of the field. It was by any standards an outstanding performance because to take the lead he first had to pass Moss's Jaguar C-type and there was strong works representation in the race. This he followed with an outright win in September, in the Coupe du Salon at Monthléry. Success on two such disparate circuits indicates that the Gordini left little to be desired in either handling or power and further confirmation of this came in the Carrera Panamericana, when Behra won the first stage only to go down a ravine in the second.

Money continued to be very tight and Gordini nearly folded during the winter of 1952–3. As a result components remained in use long after they should have been scrapped. The inevitable unreliability which followed this expedient reflected unjustly on the soundness of Gordini's work, but still, in the World Championship, Trintignant managed fifth places at Spa and Monza, won the non-Championship Chimay GP and led home Harry Schell and Jean Behra for a Gordini 1-2-3 in the Cadours GP.

So far as sports cars were concerned, 1953 saw a new 2,982 cc (78 × 78 mm) straight-eight which was basically double the 1,496 cc engine Gordini had designed for Simca. With four twin-choke Webers it gave 235 bhp and drove, for the first time, through a 5-speed gearbox. With an all-up weight of 12½ cwt the car had the then outstanding power/weight ratio of 390 bhp per ton. The chassis followed previous lines, but, as on his 1948 Simca-based sports cars, Gordini specified a central seating position.

Its early testing showed it in need of a good deal of development, not least to get it to steer in a straight line. In designing the new car, Gordini had been forced by circumstance to cut corners in that he incorporated all his new thinking in the drawings, for he had not the luxury of testing his ideas one stage at a time.

For Le Mans, then, there were two of the earlier models, though both were re-bodied and one had a full 2½-litre engine. Driven by Maurice Trintignant and Harry Schell this ran in the first ten throughout the race and finished a fine fifth, and first in the 3-litre class, behind three Jaguar C-types and a Cunningham which all had substantially larger engines.

With a 2.3, Trintignant won at Nîmes while the Italian Franco Bordoni, who had bought a similar car, had a very successful time with it. Bordoni began by beating a 3-litre Ferrari to win the Coupe de Vitesse at Monthléry and followed that with wins in the Tuscany Cup and the Trullo d'Oro and second places at Senigallia and in the Sicilian Gold Cup. They were all Italian national races, true, but racing in Italy was pretty serious and Bordoni emerged as an Italian Champion in 1953.

A French driver called Rinen bought a 2-litre car and won at Bressuire, and the same car, driven by Loyer, won at Agen and in the Coupe du Salon at Monthléry. Another 2-litre car went to André Guelfi of Morocco, who scored wins at Agadir and Marrakesh (popular venues for some Europeans with a taste for the exotic) and also took a class win in the Coupe du Salon.

Behra finally had the 3-litre car for the Tour de France which masqueraded as a rally but put a great deal of emphasis on the special stages, with the result that it attracted racing drivers and high-performances cars. Behra won eight of the nine special stages and easily took the 'speed' event.

1954 started with Behra taking the 3-litre to Morocco to finish a good second to Farina's 4.9 Ferrari at Agadir, while Guelfi brought his car home second in the 2-litre class. Also at the meeting was a new 1,100 cc (75 × 66 mm) sports car driven by Mme Bousquet, who, with Mlle Thirion, also drove it in the Mille Miglia, where they came second in class, and at Le Mans. It was similar to the 1½-litre car and the engine delivered a claimed 80 bhp, but at nearly 11 cwt it was a little adipose for the power available.

Meanwhile, in Paris, Gordini's financial position was even worse than before but he was still preparing a new F1 car for the 2½-litre formula. The chassis was a lightly modified version of the previous F2 car and the engine was the same as the one which had powered the fifth-placed car at Le Mans in 1954. Gordini's income came solely from motor racing so the cars appeared everywhere they could pick up good starting money.

In World Championship terms, the single F1 car was rewarded with two sixth places, in Argentina (Élie Bayol) and Belgium (André Pilette), but as soon as Mercedes-Benz entered the fray, the little team was pushed down the order and out of the points. Still, Behra managed a couple of minor wins at Cadours and Pau, where he beat Trintignant's Ferrari, and he took several good places in other non-Championship races. Much of Gordini's F1 success, such as it was, was due to Behra, for the cars were now embarrassed by the power of their engines, which stressed the chassis, live rear end and all, beyond reasonable limits.

The F1 effort stretched the little team's resources, but Le Mans remained a 'must'. The 3-litre car had been further developed and featured Messier disc brakes, but during preparation the hard-pressed crew overlooked the fitting of a servo motor and the result was a disaster with the car proving very slow and retiring. All was not lost for Gordini, however, as the Jacky Pollet/André Guelfi 2½-litre car came home sixth overall and first in the 3-litre class.

In the Reims 12 Hours race, the works 3-litre car ran into trouble when it rammed the back of the Rolt/Hamilton Jaguar D-type and holed its radiator. It was small consolation that the 1,100 cc car, given a 1½-litre engine, finished third in the 1,600 cc class.

In 1956 Gordini tested a new 4 cylinder 1500cc engine, intended for F2, in this old sports model. It is seen at Silverstone in July 1956 where André Pilette drove it unsuccessfully in the Formula 2 race. (NMM)

Franco Bordoni had taken delivery of a new 3-litre car and had a terrific time with it, winning five races outright and taking several good places. A second Tour de France fell to the marque. Jacky Pollet won in his 2½-litre car and at Monthléry Behra won the Coupe du Salon.

It was Behra's last drive for the team, for he could not resist an offer from Maserati, for whom he had a distinguished career in sports and F1 cars though without ever winning a World Championship Grand Prix. Had he done so it would have been a popular win, for the Frenchman was widely admired for his courage and verve.

Without his star, but retaining the services of Robert Manzon, a good driver who is barely remembered today, Gordini completed the building of a new straight-eight GP car which, while it had a useful 245 bhp, was heavier than all the competition save for the Mercedes-Benz W196, which had power to spare to cope with its weight. It completely went against Gordini's normal practice and was never a success.

Gordini's sports car effort suffered as the team struggled to make the F1 car competitive, but ever optimistic, Gordini laid down a new 1½-litre engine with an eye on the forthcoming Formula 2. This engine derived from the 1951 unit, but was claimed to give up to 142 bhp in competition trim. A road car, using a version giving 110 bhp was also mooted and, indeed, Gordini went so far as to publish a leaflet giving details.

One of these units was fitted into an old 1,100 cc sports car and Loyer/Rinen raced it in the 1,000 Km of Paris race at Monthléry. It came home a creditable eighth overall (the race was won by a Maserati 300S) and second in class behind a Porsche. In the same race the Manzon/Guelfi Gordini battled for third with a gaggle of Ferrari 750 Monzas, an A.W.E. and the 2-litre Gordini of Hermano da Silva Ramos. Neither of these cars finished, da Silva Ramos spun on some oil and the 3-litre car retired with engine trouble.

Three Gordinis appeared at Le Mans, a 2.5-litre for Manzon/Guiché, Guelfi's 2-litre, which he shared with da Silva Ramos, and the 1½-litre car for Rinen and Milhoux. The small-engined car did not shine, but the 2-litre car was the fastest in its class and the 2.5 was running in fifth place and leading the Index of Performance in the early stages, but it slowed and retired with no oil pressure at midnight. Neither of the other cars finished.

The 1½-litre car also appeared in the British GP meeting, and elsewhere, but it failed to please Gordini and when he finally unveiled plans for a new front-engined F2 car, it had a 6-cylinder engine. It was not built, but is interesting in so far that while retaining torsion bar springing, front suspension would be by trailing arms while the rear would have been independent with inboard drum brakes. Since the design was both front-engined and retained the traditional tubular chassis it is probably just as well it was not completed for it would have been unlikely to have been competitive with such as the Cooper-Climax.

During 1956 Gordini made increasingly spasmodic appearances at races both in sports cars and F1. He must have been wondering whether the continuous struggle was worthwhile, but in the background was an offer from Renault. Early in 1957 it was announced that he was working on a performance version of the new Renault Dauphine. Gordini struggled on until early 1957 until after the Naples GP he folded his team and went to work full-time for Renault, transforming a succession of its road cars. Two private Gordinis ran at Le Mans that year but neither finished.

It was a sad day for French motor racing for one of the greatest national traditions in the sport folded with Gordini though it has to be said that a country which does not support its sole maker does not deserve a team to carry its colours on the track. It was to be more than ten years before a French car was again to compete in F1, the Matra-Cosworth which Jackie Stewart drove in 1968.

Gordini continued to work for Renault and in 1968 unveiled a 3-litre V-8 F1 engine which was never raced. Gordini's name has been kept alive in the Renault range, and it was pleasant to see his name on the Renault turbocharged F1 engines. It was justice because for so long 'The Sorcerer' had kept the blue of France to the fore of formula and sports car racing.

H.W.M.

Soon after the end of World War II, George Abecassis and John Heath found themselves trading in cars and competing for the same customers. It made better sense to combine and so they set up H.W. (Hersham and Walton) Motors in Walton-on-Thames. Abecassis had been a successful driver both before and after the war (he won the last race in Britain in 1939 and the first in 1946) and had spent the intervening years flying SOE agents into occupied Europe until he was shot down and captured in 1944.

It was highly dangerous flying, unarmed and at low altitude, but George revelled in the danger and afterwards hoped that the Western Allies would strike Russia so he could re-live the most exciting experiences he'd known. His driving reflected that attitude.

John Heath, by contrast, was a tall, aristocratic man of fixed views. He had trained as an engineer and spent the war working at Lagonda in the experimental engineering department. It is not maligning his memory, though, to suggest that his inflexible personality and his lack of attention to detail (he never used a new part when a second-hand one was available) told against him and it would be more true to describe him as a mechanic with unusual flair. Heath's ability to take a pile of parts and make of them a saleable car was a decided asset to the business.

With the flamboyant Abecassis cutting a dash on the race tracks, Heath decided he would like to go racing as well, although, according to George, his heart was not really in it. In 1946 he began competing with a sports Alta in which he had some success. Another Alta followed and for 1948 he decided to build up his own car from a 2-litre Alta engine and an experimental Alta chassis frame which had been gather dust in the workshop of Geoffrey Taylor, the constructor of Altas. On this Heath put a handsome, fully enveloping body somewhat resembling the German Veritas.

Called the Alta-H.W., the car proved quick if fragile, and the partners drove it in several races abroad. While on the Continent they discovered that race organizers paid very good starting money and this set them thinking.

The upshot was the H.W.-Alta, a dual-purpose sports/F2 car. The first car's 2-litre Alta engine was fitted to a new tubular ladder-frame and drove through an E.N.V./Wilson pre-selector gearbox which had ideal ratios and a very quick change. The rack-and-pinion steering came from a Citroën Light Fifteen (H.W. Motors held a Citroën agency), the transverse leaf spring and lower wishbone

George Abecassis at the wheel of the first H.W.M.-Jaguar on his way to third place in the Unlimited Sports Car race at Goodwood, September 1954. (LAT)

front suspension was fabricated around Standard-Triumph uprights and the live rear axle, located by a torque tube and suspended on ¼-elliptical springs (à la Bugatti), was an old Lagonda Rapide unit which had been lying around the workshop.

It may have been a 'Bitza' but the package worked. It can hardly be said to have caused a sensation, but running in F2 form it inherited a lucky win in the Manx Cup and in the (sports car) French GP at Comminges, Heath finished an excellent second to Charles Pozzi's Delahaye. It was just the sort of result which could be translated into good starting money the following season.

The car itself had been under-powered, over-weight, and not altogether reliable, but it did have excellent handling and its deficient areas could be worked on.

For 1950 Geoffrey Taylor provided a new 2-litre Alta engine which retained the d.o.h.c. head of previous units but had a much shorter stroke (83 × 90 mm compared to 79 × 100 mm) and though with 115 bhp the engine was not a lot more powerful than the earlier unit, it was fairly reliable.

For his part, Heath designed a new independent rear suspension with a transverse leaf spring and lower wishbones with the E.N.V. differential attached to the chassis. Armstrong-Siddeley pre-selector gearboxes were chosen because of availability (like the E.N.V. they were made to Wilson patents) and neat aluminium bodies were made by Leacroft, with the option of adding headlights and cycle wings and becoming instant sports cars. Apparently there was some idea of running at Le Mans, but in the event they were almost always run as F2 cars.

In the style of many at the time Heath did not go in for detailed drawing but cut and welded one chassis and, when it was to his satisfaction, had the others made up like it. Four cars were built for 1950, three for the works and one for Maurice Baring, an amateur racer who happened to be a friend of the partners. Heath and Stirling Moss were to be the regular drivers with the third car being used by Abecassis, when he wasn't minding the store, or by any local hero who could be persuaded to rent a drive.

Now called H.W.M., the team led the gypsy life around Europe. Apart from an occasional tendency to lose wheels through broken half-shafts, the cars proved reliable. They were still over-weight and under-powered but on tight circuits their excellent handling came into its own. The Belgian jazz band leader Johnny Claes won the Grand Prix des Frontières at Chimay, though against weak opposition, but on other occasions Moss and a newcomer, Lance Macklin, performed heroically.

In the Rome GP, Moss slip-streamed the works Ferraris until losing a wheel but, incredibly, he set fastest lap. In the Coupe des Petites Cylindrées at Reims, the team finished third (Moss), fourth (Heath) and fifth (Macklin) behind Alberto Ascari's Ferrari and the Simca of André Simon. Moss took third at Bari behind two F1 Alfa Romeos and in the process beat Villoresi's Ferrari and Bira's Maserati, an astonishing feat. Macklin took second to Cortese's Ferrari at Naples, and Moss and Macklin came second and third at Mettet behind Robert Manzon's Simca. At Perigueux Moss finished third to the Simcas of Manzon and Simon and at Castle Combe won a F2 race against poor opposition.

It was a respectable season and one which returned the financial investment with good interest. For the British racing public, still feeling the humiliation of the B.R.M. disaster, it was something to cheer about. H.W.M. was the first British works team to do the European tour, it had come back with heads held high and that 1950 season consolidated Moss's growing reputation.

The cars were sold and one, bought by Oscar Moore, was run in sports trim and eventually fitted with a Jaguar engine and another finished up in America as a Chevrolet-engined sports car, 'The Stovebolt Special'. New cars were made for 1951, but since these were single-seaters they have not even a tenuous position in this book. It was another year of the gypsy existence on the Continent which was to continue with a final season in 1953. During that three-year period, despite much more power from the Alta engine, the team was overtaken by others. Both the Cooper-Bristol and Connaught Type A F2 cars proved to be quicker and to have better handling (if anything, Heath's revisions to the H.W.M.'s chassis were to its detriment). In F2 H.W.M. was in a steady decline and never recaptured the excitement or success of 1950.

A large part of the trouble was that Heath was a bloody-minded individual who refused to accept that his agricultural chassis could be made lighter without losing their excellent handling, and who refused to accept that it might not be a bad idea to change engines, possibly taking on the Bristol unit. George Abecassis recalls that his partner would never, ever, accept a suggestion which he did not believe was his own idea.

Heath was keen to continue to battle in the new 2½-litre F1 which came into force in 1954, but Connaught had come to an exclusive arrangement with Alta for the supply of engines and the promised Coventry Climax FPE 'Godiva' engine was not released. H.W.M. entered a few F1 races with a new single-seater using a stretched Alta F2 engine, but it was outclassed. From then on H.W.M. concentrated exclusively on Jaguar-engined sports cars.

During 1951 George Abecassis cobbled together a single-seater around a discarded prototype chassis and he used it in a miserably wet meeting at Boreham. He ended the race stuck in fourth (top) gear and thoroughly nonplussed except he had the sudden idea that the car would make a fine sports cars. This feeling grew into a certainty when, fitted with a Jaguar engine for 1952, Oscar Moore's car performed extremely well in British club events. It proved to have better acceleration than a Jaguar C-type though its cycle-winged body limited its top speed.

H.W.M. took the prototype single-seater chassis which Abecassis had driven at Boreham and extended it with outriggers and on to this frame was fixed a fairly simple enveloping body built by Leacroft. Front suspension was the transverse leaf spring and lower wishbone layout of the original 'dual-purpose' cars, while at the rear was a de Dion axle suspended by torsion bars and a Halibrand

quick-change final drive.

Into the equation entered the Jaguar XK engine to which Heath had fitted three double-choke Weber carburettors. According to Abecassis, H.W.M. passed on this tweak to the Jaguar works and obtained a Jaguar agency as a result. Engine specialist Harry Weslake made new camshafts for the engine, which was soon producing 240 bhp.

Registered HWM 1, the car was debuted by Abecassis at Shelsley Walsh in mid-1953, where it came second in class. In the Reims 12 Hours Abecassis, partnered by Paul Frère who had often been a member of the F2 team, was running in third place at about half distance when a bracket holding the de Dion rear axle broke.

Abecassis raced the car with some success in British club races and in its next important race, the Goodwood Nine Hours, he made fastest practice lap, four seconds quicker than the Jaguar C-types present. In the race itself he held third ahead of all the works Aston Martins (one of which won) until tyre trouble slowed him and a broken timing chain sidelined him.

Abecassis entered the 1954 Mille Miglia with the car (Denis Jenkinson rode as passenger and wrote memorably of the experience), but retired after 200 miles with a broken damper. At the International Trophy Meeting at Silverstone in May George brought it home second to Gonzalez's 4.9-litre Ferrari in the very wet sports car race, ahead of all the works Jaguars and Aston Martins.

In the Swedish Hedemora meeting Abecassis came second to another big Ferrari (George often raced in Sweden and thoroughly enjoyed the Swedes' winter racing on ice) and he crashed on the last lap while lying second (with Tony Gaze) in the Hyères 12 Hours race.

A second H.W.M.-Jaguar (VPA 8) was built with coil spring and wishbone front suspension and a de Dion rear axle on ¼-elliptical springs (similar to the Lancia D24). It appeared in the Reims 12 Hours race in the hands of Tony Gaze and Graham Whitehead and finished seventh. With this car Gaze won a minor race at Crystal Palace shortly afterwards and in the Tourist Trophy, Abecassis and Mayers in HWM 1, came home 14th on handicap, fourth on scratch.

Later Abecassis led the Karlskoga Kannonloppet in Sweden, but lost concentration on the last corner and finished up well off the road. 1954 was the last year when an H.W.M. made any significant impact in International racing.

Another car on the lines of Tony Gaze's was made for an amateur driver from the Midlands, while a fourth was made up by another amateur from a pile of parts and fitted with a Cadillac engine.

A lighter car (XPE 2) with minor suspension revisions and a new curved ladder-frame was made for 1956. It had an attractive body styled by Abecassis but its aerodynamics were rudimentary and this at a time when every other British maker had woken up to the importance of low drag.

It made its debut at Silverstone and ran well before retiring with overheating, though later in the year, in the Goodwood Nine Hours, Lance Macklin and Bill Smith brought it home fourth. In between times there were numerous appearances, and some successes, in British club and National events culminating with Abecassis beating Rosier's Ferrari in a 20-lap race at Castle Combe with Noel Cunningham-Reid bringing HWM 1 home third.

Tony Gaze, an Australian, took his car home that winter (or summer) and had a good time with it, taking two wins and two thirds, before selling it to Lex Davison.

Improved cars with Jaguar D-type engines were fielded in 1956 and with one Abecassis finished second to Moss's Aston Martin DB3S at the Easter Monday Goodwood Meeting. HWM 1 had been sold to Ray Fielding, a skilled hill-climber who re-registered it YPG 3, while the original number plate passed on to a new works car. A cycle-winged H.W.M.-Jaguar was built for Phil Scragg, who excelled in hill-climbs and sprints.

Then Heath decided to drive one in the Mille Miglia to fulfil a long-standing personal ambition. George Abecassis says, 'I tested his car and found the steering far too under-geared, it felt like an American saloon. I told John he would have trouble with it, but, as usual, that made him more determined to go ahead. He got into a slide on the course and could not correct it; there was no way he could with that steering.'

Two days later Heath died as a result of the crash. He had not been an easy man to deal with but his contribution to British motor racing in the early Fifties had been enormous. At a time when British thinking was parochial, it had been Heath and his team which had blazed a trail across Europe. While BRM, which was supposed to blaze the way for Britain, floundered in a morass of incompetent organization and engineering, H.W.M. with a fraction of the money, actually built cars, got them to races, and competed with honour. There had been no major successes in terms of race wins but it had been a massive contribution to the growth of British motor racing, not least because it aided the brilliant careers of Stirling Moss and Peter Collins.

On Heath's death, Abecassis retired from racing to run the business they had founded. Entries of H.W.M.-Jaguars had always been spasmodic and they so continued with the cars becoming increasingly uncompetitive. Les Leston and Nel Cunningham-Reid drove one in the 1956 Reims 12 Hours race and lay sixth after the first hour when the engine ran its bearings.

The works continued to enter cars until the end of 1957, the season when the much lighter and better handling Lister-Jaguar appeared and carried all before it. Later in private hands the works cars took a fair number of awards in British club events, but their owners knew there was no point in entering serious events.

Most H.W.M.s made still exist though many have had varied careers. One of the 1951 single-seaters, for example, was converted to a sports car, another was sold Down Under and given a Jaguar engine. In 1960–61 Abecassis had a road-going coupé built from spares in the workshop which had an attractive body created from his own sketches. This is now in the Philippe Renault collection.

H.W.M. made its mark in the days when, in Formula and sports car racing respectively, a well-furbished special could be competitive, but they were never more than specials. They were way behind the time in terms of aerodynamics and chassis design, no H.W.M. ever had disc brakes for example, and were always overweight. While the competition advanced, H.W.M. stood still and the early promise of both the Formula and sports cars faded.

The sports cars were not helped, either, by the fact that they frequently used second-hand parts or inadequate proprietary components, so it is no wonder that the typical scenario for an H.W.M.-Jaguar in a long-distance race was 'ran well until retirement'. Then again, they were not raced by top-class drivers for the team was trying to cover its costs and the budget did not extend to high retainers.

Their drivers, however, remember them with affection as being enormous fun to drive, but in the final analysis the position of H.W.M. in British motor racing history is secure. Its contribution to the sport was much greater than the sum of its results.

Jaguar

William Lyons began making motor cycle sidecars in 1922 and within four years had turned his attention to building bodies on a number of proprietary chassis. Though untrained, Lyons was a brilliant natural stylist (who influenced the shape of all Jaguars until his death in 1984) and was soon selling respectable numbers of special bodies. In 1928 he moved his company, Swallow Sidecars, from Blackpool to Coventry and three years later unveiled his first car, the SS1, based on a Standard chassis.

Lyons took as his philosophy the idea that cars sold on their looks and it was as cheap to build a handsome car as it was an ugly one – and the SS1 reflected that belief. When it was first shown the SS1 had no price tag but the public was invited to guess how much it cost. It looked like a £1,000 car but actually cost just £310 and established a tradition of offering outstanding style for a fraction of what the opposition asked.

While this was appreciated by the buying public, which immediately beat a path to Lyon's door, the cars were treated with disdain in some circles and 'Wardour Street Bentley' was just one of the labels used by some of those who could afford a real Bentley. They were considered flash, the sort of car which might be driven by a bookmaker or someone in show business. Despite this snobbishness, the company prospered and by the time war broke out was an established make. Production had risen from 1,354 cars in 1932, the company's first full year and itself an astonishingly successful launch, to 5,378 in 1939.

It was an incredible achievement for a firm starting in the worst days of the Depression at a time when many established makers were closing their doors. In 1945, the company re-registered as Jaguar Cars Ltd, for the initials 'SS' had unfortunate connotations, and a popular pre-war model was named the 'Jaguar'. Swallow Sidecars was sold and later, as part of the Tube Investments group, made the TR2-based Swallow Doretti sports car which was killed off when Jaguar threatened TI with withdrawal of its considerable business if the group

One of the original C-types raced at Le Mans in 1951 seen under construction in the Jaguar competition department. (Jaguar Cars Ltd)

continued to market a rival sports car.

During World War II the factory was turned over to war production, but as the tide turned in the Allies' favour, Lyons and his engineering team, among whom were William Heynes, Claude Bailey and Walter Hassan, began to think of new cars for the post-war world. One night a week everyone had compulsory fire-watching duties and as German attacks became less frequent these duties turned into planning meetings.

Pre-war SS had used extensively modified Standard engines but there was now an opportunity to start from scratch. All manner of proposals were considered and several small units reached the prototype stage, but Lyons was thinking big and finally chose a long-stroke, seven-bearing, 3.4-litre d.o.h.c. straight six, code-named 'XK'. It was something of a gamble, for it was not known whether the postwar market would stand so large an engine or whether the company

Peter Whitehead at the wheel of the Jaguar C-type with which he and Peter Walker won the 1951 Le Mans 24 Hours. (Louis Klementaski)

could make a unit of such advanced specification at its traditional keen price. In the event it stayed in production for close on forty years and powered five Le Mans winners.

Another promising engine, the XK100, a 2-litre d.o.h.c. four remained 'warm' for some years and one 146 bhp version was installed in 'Goldie' Gardner's record-breaking special in 1948. On the Jabbeke highway in Belgium, it powered the car to 176.96 mph, but it never quite achieved sufficient levels of refinement for it to go into series production.

The new engine was intended for use in a new large saloon, the Jaguar Mk VII, which was due for production in 1950 but in the meantime Lyons decided to build a run of 200 sports cars both as an image-building exercise and to obtain feed-back about the new engine from owners. Lyons himself styled the body which, since it was to be built in small numbers, was made of aluminium on an ash frame.

The box-section chassis (basically a shortened version of the one proposed for the Mk VII saloon) had torsion bar and double wishbone front suspension, a live rear axle suspended on semi-elliptical springs, and a 4-speed gearbox which featured synchromesh on the top three gears. The 3,442 cc (83 × 106 mm) XK engine with twin SU carburettors produced an honest 160 bhp, to give a claimed top speed of over 120 mph, hence the name 'XK120'.

Surprisingly enough, Jaguar was able to keep the exciting new car a complete secret until unveiling it at the 1948 London Motor Show. To say it created a sensation is to understate the case. It was, quite simply, the most beautiful car in the world and that at a time when anything with wheels would find a buyer. Its claimed top speed was so extraordinary that it was widely doubted until the following year when the works tester, Ron Sutton, took a car to Jabbeke, regularly exceeded 130 mph and recorded a best of 132.6 mph. A motor manufacturer had, for once, been 12 mph too modest in its claims!

As for the price, £998 excluding purchase tax, that appeared so low as to be a leg-pull, but again it was true, unbelieveable but true. Purchase tax bumped the

Panicked by the pace of the Mercedes-Benz 300SLs Jaguar built 'low drag' bodies for Le Mans 1952. Unfortunately the cars suffered overheating and all retired early in the race. Pictured is Stirling Moss who was eliminated in the second hour with a broken con-rod. (Louis Klementaski)

Stirling Moss drove this works C-type, XKC037, at the Silverstone meeting in May 1953. He was off-form after a practice crash and finished seventh. (T.C. March)

price up to £1,273 (still a snip), but had the basic price been £2 more, double-rate tax would have been levied, something which seriously damaged the prospects of many established makers of quality cars.

Needless to say orders flooded in, particularly from America. At a time of 'Export or Die', the original limited production run went by the board (240 aluminium-bodied cars were made) and work proceeded on a steel-bodied version. It delayed volume production by a year but allowed ultimate sales of 12,078, until replaced by the XK140 in 1954, with most going abroad.

To allay any lingering doubts about the car, Jaguar entered a team of three in the 1949 One Hour Production Sports Car Race at Silverstone. One, driven by 'B. Bira', suffered a puncture while leading while Leslie Johnson and Peter Walker brought the other two home for a decisive 1-2.

Five special development cars were supplied to selected drivers for racing in 1950 and the lessons learned from this exercise led to a 180 bhp optional engine in 1951. A sixth works-prepared car, NUB 120, was rallied by Ian Appleyard (William Lyon's son-in-law), who, in 1950, won the first of five successive Coupes des Alpes in Jaguars.

Clemente Biondetti briefly led the Targa Florio in his works XK120 but retired with a broken con-rod. Four of the five 'racers' ran in the Mille Miglia and Leslie Johnson brought his home fifth with Biondetti eighth despite a broken rear spring.

Three cars went to Le Mans as a recce. Lyons was well aware of the publicity value of the race which, uniquely, emphasized the car rather than driver. Bentley's five wins in the Twenties were still remembered and the maker of the 'Wardour Street Bentley' knew he had the ingredients of a successful machine.

Leslie Johnson and Bert Hadley ran as high as second at half-distance but supplementing their brakes by using the gearbox (brakes were not the XK120's best feature) caused the clutch centre to pull out in the 22nd hour. The other two cars finished 12th and 15th.

Tommy Wisdom, a journalist who was also a successful driver and one of the recipients of the special cars, believed in the potential of a 20-year-old youngster called Stirling Moss who had been refused a car by Jaguar on the grounds that he lacked experience. Backing his belief with action, he entered Moss in the 1950 Tourist Trophy at Dundrod. The race was run in a downpour and Moss emerged a decisive winner. It was to be the first of seven TT victories for Moss, who remains the only driver to have won a classic race so many times.

Moss's great win clinched the decision to go racing seriously and the lessons learned in that first season were taken to heart. In November, at Pebble Beach, Phil Hill gave Jaguar its first important American victory in a car which he and Richie Ginther had bored out to 3.8 litres. Both were to become Grand Prix winners and Hill, America's first World Champion.

Shortly before the 1951 race, Jaguar unveiled its Le Mans challenger. Officially designated the XK120C (Competition), it quickly became known as the C-type. Its sleek body was designed by Malcolm Sayer, an ex-aircraft aerodynamicist and the man to whom Frank Costin, popularly supposed the great pioneer of the science in Britain, is quick to pay tribute. Under the skin was a 210 bhp (even on the poor-quality fuel available) engine with modified cams, lighter flywheel, bigger valves, improved porting, and larger carburettors which fitted into a properly triangulated space-frame with stressed bulkheads and channel steel bottom members.

Front suspension was similar to the standard car and used some production components while the live rear axle was located by radius arms and an A-bracket and sprung a single transverse torsion bar and hydraulic dampers. The car's dry weight of 2,070 lb was close to the Aston Martin DB3.

The C-type was designed specifically to win on the fast, smooth, Le Mans circuit and it rarely shone on twisty or bumpy tracks. Two of the three cars retired as a result of broken oil pipes, that of Moss and Fairman holding a clear lead at the time. The third car of Peter Whitehead and Peter Walker ran without trouble and won by nine laps from the Talbot of Meyrat and Mairesse. The winning car established a new distance record (2,244 miles) and Moss set a new lap record at 105.232 mph.

Moss won his second Tourist Trophy in September, with fellow team-members Peter Walker and Tony Rolt second and fourth; he took a win at Goodwood the same month; and rounded off a brilliant season for Jaguar by co-driving, with Leslie Johnson, an XK120 coupé at Monthléry which averaged over 107 mph for 24 hours. To complement the Le Mans victory, production XK120s proved successful in rallies and production sports car races and Johnny Claes not only won the tough Liège-Rome-Liège rally but became the first driver to do so with a clean sheet.

Le Mans was the target for 1952, but a single car for Moss was entered in the Mille Miglia and, a portent, this was equipped with Dunlop disc brakes. Stirling was in third place with 150 miles to go when he made an error and crashed. In the Monaco GP (run for sports cars) Moss was holding second to Manzon's Gordini when both came across the multiple pile-up. Moss restarted but was disqualified for receiving outside assistance. C-types were starting to reach privateers and Wisdom finished sixth in his.

The performance of the new Mercedes-Benz 300SL coupés then panicked Jaguar into making a stupid error. New, longer, bodies were made with smaller radiators and in practice the cars overheated. Hasty modifications did not cure the problem and caused the retirement of all three cars within four hours. It was an own goal of classic proportions. The irony was that the 300SLs were not as quick as thought (Levegh's old Talbot proved that) and had Jaguar entered unchanged cars it would, as like as not, have walked the race.

Moss then took Wisdom's C-type to Reims and won the 224-mile sports car GP and Ian Stewart (older brother of Jackie) won the Jersey Road Race in Ecurie Ecosse's car. In the International meeting at Boreham, Moss and Duncan Hamilton scored a Jaguar 1-2 against the works Aston Martins. Aston Martin had its revenge in the Goodwood Nine Hours when one by one the three leading Jaguars hit trouble and only the car of Moss/Walker finished, fifth, after a long time in the pits changing the broken A-bracket.

C-types were offered in 'production' form at £1,495 plus tax and 47 of these were made which, with six works cars (three in 1951 and three in 1953) makes a total of 53. It was the ultimate road car of its day (and a bargain at that) and Fangio, Farina and Ascari all bought examples for road use.

Customer cars were successful in British club racing at the end of 1952 and continued the following year. The private cars of Sherwood Johnston/Robert Wilder and Harry Gray/Bob Gegen represented the marque at Sebring in 1953 and came third and fourth behind a Cunningham and an Aston Martin.

Three cars were entered in the Mille Miglia, which was not the C-type's natural habitat, and none finished, but in the Hyères 12 Hours, Peter Whitehead and Tom Cole won in Whitehead's private car.

Jaguar returned to Le Mans in June in good order having tested extensively. The new works cars were lighter and, with triple twin-choke Webers, more powerful. The vulnerable rear end had been strengthened and, in place of the A-bracket, there were twin trailing arms and a Panhard rod. Most significantly, the team cars were fitted with Dunlop disc brakes. Disc brakes were nothing new to racing, they had first appeared at Indianapolis in 1940 and were anyway well established in aviation, but it was Jaguar's great victory at Le Mans in 1953 which was to do more than anything else to advance their cause.

Three works cars started and three finished, in first (Rolt/Hamilton), second (Moss/Walker after trouble with a dirty fuel filter) and, split by a Cunningham, fourth (Whitehead/Stewart). To make matters complete, a private Belgian entry finished a trouble-free ninth.

Moss and Whitehead were loaned a works C-type for the Reims 12 Hours race, and won. Private cars finished second and third in the Spa 24 Hours race. The Goodwood Nine Hours race proved again Jaguar's bogey; for some reason they suffered oil surge and two works cars retired with damaged engines while the third had inexplicable brake trouble and could only manage third behind two Aston Martins and ahead of two private C-types.

Ecurie Ecosse sent cars to the Nürburgring 1,000 Km, like the Spa race a round of the WSCC, and with the demise of the works Lancia team, Ian Stewart and Roy Salvadori finished a strong second to the works 4.5-litre Ferrari of Ascari and Farina, and won the Production Sports Car category.

There was not to be another Jaguar success in the Tourist Trophy for the abrasive road surface put unusual strains on the transmission and only one car, that of Moss and Walker, finished. Even then its gearbox had nearly gone and it limped across the line in third (on distance, it was a handicap race) behind two Aston Martins but with a Frazer Nash ahead on handicap.

With one race remaining in the WSCC, the Carrera Panamericana, and aided by Ecurie Ecosse's splendid performance, Jaguar headed the points table, but scratched its single entry. Ferrari too, did not send a team, but a privateer's fourth place behind Lancia's splendid 1-2-3 gave Ferrari the title. Jaguar would never again be so close to winning the Championship and its decision not to send one car, let alone a full team, was unfortunate. Possibly Jaguar was sensitive to its huge American market and knew that on past performances in races such as the Mille Miglia, its cars had little chance of finishing.

The lightweight works cars were sold to Ecurie Ecosse which, among minor race successes, took fourth in the Buenos Aires 1,000 Km, and second and third in the Barcelona sports car race later in the year. Duncan Hamilton, who was sold the car the works had prepared for the Carrera Panamericana, won the Coupe de Paris at Monthléry while a private C-type (Swaters/Laurent) came fourth at Le Mans.

So far as the works was concerned, the C-type's career ended at the end of 1953 because work was nearly complete on its successor, the D-type. Again, it was a car designed primarily for Le Mans, but whereas the earlier car had been merely at the fore of chassis and body design, the D broke new ground. First of all there was Malcolm Sayer's body shell which was stunning to the eye and aerodynamically efficient, a hard trick to pull off.

Then the central section of the car, made from magnesium alloy, was a

Jaguar's third Le Mans victory came in the tragic 1955 race when Mike Hawthorn and Ivor Bueb won in their new long-nosed version after Mercedes-Benz withdrew its cars. The performance of Bueb (seen here) was particularly commendable for the event was his first long distance race. (Louis Klementaski)

stressed, semi-monococque structure surrounding a tubular frame which ran forward from just behind the seats to the front of the car. At the rear there was still a live rear axle, twin radius arms with a transverse torsion bar, telescopic dampers and an A-bracket, while the torsion bar and double wishbone front suspension from earlier cars was retained. Detail attention to the engine paid off with increased power, initially 245 bhp, and this had dry sump lubrication. Disc brakes were standard and so were alloy Dunlop wheels with knock-off hub caps.

It was a compact car, too, with a wheelbase of 7 ft 6 in. and a scuttle height of only 31½ in. and, at 1,900 lb, significantly lighter than the C-type. It was also a car whose style immediately caught the imagination. It had the voluptuous lines of Jaguar's production cars and so was recognizably a Jaguar and yet it was also an advanced motor car in its own right.

D-types made their debut at Le Mans in 1954 and immediately proved to be very quick in a straight line, with Moss's car timed at 173 mph on the Mulsanne straight, quicker than the 4.9-litre Ferraris with nearly 100 bhp more. With such speeds available, and little help from wind resistance, their disc brakes did not prove such an advantage and the Ferraris' drum system, aided by the cars' higher drag, actually coped better in the early stages. The race came down to three Ferraris versus three Jaguars. Two of the Italian cars went out with transmission problems and so did one of the Jaguars, with a second retiring with brake problems.

With the race two-thirds run, most of it in the rain, the remaining D-type of Rolt/Hamilton was two laps behind the Ferrari of Gonzalez/Trintignant and was ordered to try to catch the leading car, which proved equal to fending off the attack. With ninety minutes remaining the Ferrari called in for its last pit stop and as Gonzalez prepared to go out, he found the engine would not fire.

The minutes ticked by as the Ferrari's lead was eroded. Had he so wished, 'Lofty' England, Jaguar's team manager, could have protested his rival, for there were certainly more than the permitted number of mechanics working on the car, but he knew it was the excitement of the crisis and not deliberate rule-breaking so held his peace; instead he called in Rolt and sent out Hamilton, the faster wet-weather driver.

When the flag fell at 4 pm, it called to an end one of the great duels in the history of the race with the Ferrari emerging triumphant by 2½ miles on the road. Ferrari thoroughly deserved its win, but Jaguar was not disgraced.

A two-car works team next appeared at the usually important, non-Championship, Reims 12 Hours race, but for once the opposition was not of the first order and though the car of Ken Wharton and Peter Whitehead won, it was small consolation for Le Mans. The private Ecurie Nationale Belge C-type of Swaters/Laurent, fresh from its fourth at Le Mans, finished third with the two results being, in purely qualitative terms, perhaps the best Jaguar performance of the year.

Jaguar returned to Dundrod to take part in only its second (and last) of the six WSCC rounds that year. For some obscure reason the Tourist Trophy was still run as a handicap while being included in a World series which was otherwise run on a scratch basis. To beat the handicapper two D-types were entered with short-stroke 2,482 cc engines and, in passing, it was hoped to learn something of the new unit, which was scheduled for production in the 2.4 saloon eighteen months in the future.

The TT was an anti-climatic end to a brief, but promising, season, but the 2.4-litre car of Wharton and Whitehead did finish fifth, though, as is always the case in a handicap race, nobody was quite sure what that meant or, even, particularly cared.

Late in 1954 Jaguar listed the D-type as a production car at an ex-tax price of £1,895. It's a figure which nowadays is enough to make the eyes water, but even at the time it was dirt cheap compared with what else you could buy for the same money.

The magnesium alloy of the original monocoque was replaced by a non-stressed aluminium tub to make repairs easier. For 1955, the works cars had longer noses and a new cylinder head which increased power to 285 bhp, but it was a privately owned car that scored the firm's first important win of the year.

No Jaguars appeared at the opening WSCC round in Buenos Aires, but at Seb-

Ron Flockhart at the start of the 1957 Mille Miglia in an Ecurie Ecosse D-type. He was running third when forced to retire with a loose fuel tank. (Publifoto)

ring Briggs Cunningham's D-type, driven by Mike Hawthorn and Walt Hangsen, had a two-lap lead late in the race when it made a succession of pit stops to sort out fouled plugs. This confused the race organization, which mistakenly showed the chequered flag to the Ferrari of Shelby and Hill. It took eight days to reverse the decision, by which time the pleasure had eroded.

The team's main effort was, as always, Le Mans, so apart from a single car for Hawthorn at the International Trophy Meeting (he led but retired with a broken water hose) it was not until June that the works cars appeared and when they did so it was with 'long nose' bodywork which has since become accepted as the definitive style of the several D-type variations. Ranged against the green cars were strong teams from Ferrari and Mercedes-Benz, fresh from a debut 1-2 in the Mille Miglia.

The opening stages of the race saw a wonderful duel between Hawthorn and Fangio, both driving as if in a ten-lap sprint. For the first hour or so the duel was for second place, but after Castellotti's Ferrari retired it was for the lead. On the Mulsanne Straight the Jaguar was faster, but the 300SLR regained ground through the bends. At about 6.30 pm Hawthorn made for the pits, appeared to change his mind and moved out in front of Macklin's Austin-Healey. Macklin braked and Levegh's Mercedes glanced it, swerved across the road into a bank and then flew high in the air and into the crowd. Levegh and more than eighty spectators perished.

At Oulton Park in April 1957 Henry Taylor with the Murkett Brothers' D-type leads the works H.W.M.-Jaguar of Duncan Hamilton. This D-type was later raced with great success by Jim Clark for Border Reivers.

Hawthorn's co-driver, Ivor Bueb, who was having his first major race, had the unenviable job of taking over the car immediately after the crash and after eight hours the Jaguar was the meat in a Mercedes-Benz sandwich but two laps behind the Fangio/Moss car. The race had not been stopped for fear of interrupting the vital rescue work going on in the in-field, but at 1.45 am the orders came from Stuttgart to withdraw the 300SLRs.

Of the three works Jaguars, only the Hawthorn/Bueb car survived to the end and it won. No win at Le Mans is ever inconsiderable but this one had a hollow ring to it. A subsequent inquiry exonerated Hawthorn, but public opinion did not. In truth the one memorable aspect of the victory was the way in which the inexperienced Bueb rose to the occasion under the worse possible circumstances.

In the aftermath of the tragedy several races were cancelled, there was talk of severe restrictions on road racing, and Switzerland completely banned racing, though hill-climbs were allowed to continue.

At the British GP meeting, Hawthorn's D-type was soundly trounced by four works Aston Martins, but Écurie Ecosse cars came in 1-2 at the International Snetterton meeting and the same team scored a good second in the Goodwood Nine Hours with Desmond Titterington and Ninian Sanderson sharing the wheel.

Despite the fact that Jaguar still had a chance to win the WSCC, only one works car (Hawthorn/Titterington) appeared in the Tourist Trophy to resume battle with Mercedes-Benz and, at last, the race was run from scratch and not as a handicap. Again there was a thrilling battle for the lead, but by the last lap Hawthorn was in a secure second place when the engine seized and allowed Mercedes to score a 1-2-3, though the Jaguar had in fact covered more laps than the third Mercedes.

It was perhaps wise not to enter the Targa Florio, for the cars would not have shone, and work was directed instead on preparing for the following season. Lucas fuel injection was tried and a car was built with a de Dion rear axle.

Once again the British teams missed the opening Buenos Aires round of the WSCC, but at Sebring Hawthorn and Titterington led until half-time when their car suffered brake failure. One of Cunningham's cars (Sweikert/Ensley) finished third.

The Mille Miglia was given a miss, but the works cars made their first visit to the Nürburgring 1,000 Km, where, predictably, they proved something of a handful. None of the cars distinguished themselves, or even finished, but Hawthorn/Titterington held fourth after being delayed with a leaking fuel tank (a common D-type problem) when a half-shaft broke and it lost a wheel.

The Reims 12 Hours race resulted in a works Jaguar 1-2-3 with an Ecurie Ecosse D-type fourth, but there had been only fifteen starters so, outside of the inevitable advertisements trumpeting the success, there was not much excitement about the victory. Normally Reims followed Le Mans, but work was still in hand on numerous safety measure at Sarthe so it was not until the end of July that the race was run. Fuel and engine capacity limits were imposed. Prototype cars were limited to 2½ litres as a supposed safety measure, but even at 3.8 litres a D-type counted as a production sports car. These restrictions meant that the race did not count for the WSCC, but Le Mans was still Le Mans.

It was to be a Jaguar triumph but a disaster for the works. On the seventh lap Paul Frère spun one car at the Esses and a second, driven by Jack Fairman, spun to avoid it and was rammed by 'Fon' de Portago's Ferrari. After only four hours, the third car (Hawthorn/Bueb) spent an hour in the pits having its fuel injection system repaired.

Privateers saved the day with the Ecurie Ecosse car of Ron Flockhart/Ninian Sanderson winning from the Moss/Collins Aston Martin with the Ecurie Nationale Belge entry of Swaters/Rousselle fourth. After their lengthy delay, Hawthorn and Bueb finished sixth.

Jaguar then decided to retire from active racing, the 1956 team cars were sold to Ecurie Ecosse and with them went works assistance. In early 1957 came the announcement of the XKSS, a road-equipped version of the D-type with open cockpit, large screen, hood and other creature comforts. It had been in 'production' (actually it was a ploy to use up D-type parts) for just a month when a serious fire ravaged the factory. These cars were never seen in major races, though one did win two Macau Grands Prix.

In all, production was 71 D-types and 16 XKSSs. At least two D-types were converted to XKSS specification and several XKSSs have been converted into D-types. With several outfits making rivet-for-rivet D-type copies, some people have 'forgotten' that they have bought a modern copy and seem under the impression that they own genuine factory-built D-types. One notorious car claims a genuine history on the grounds that it was built up round a real front subframe which was scrapped after a severe crash.

The economics of the exercise are, at the time of writing, that a first-class copy costs around £40,000, but the record paid for a genuine car is £300,000. The difference in value is determined by the chassis plate and supposed history. If you can reproduce an entire car, you can reproduce a chassis plate. Less highly valued, but simpler to build, new Jaguar C-types are also appearing.

1957 was to be the last year of success for Jaguar, and despite the firm's fortunes resting on privateers, it was perhaps the greatest year of the D-type. Ecurie Ecosse was a little more prolific in their appearances than the works had been and entered most of the seven WSCC rounds. Ninian Sanderson and Robert Mieres finished fourth behind two works Ferraris and a Maserati in the Buenos Aires 1,000 Km and, at Sebring, Hawthorn and Bueb took a Briggs Cunningham car to third behind two Maseratis.

Ecurie Ecosse entered a car for Ron Flockhart in the Mille Miglia and he confounded expectations by being in third place when forced to retire with a loose fuel tank. Henry Taylor, driving the Murkett Brothers' car, finished third behind two works Aston Martins in the Production Sports Car Race at Spa. As usual the cars did not go well at the Nürburgring 1,000 Km, but at least both Ecurie Ecosse cars finished, albeit in 8th and 20th places.

Le Mans was restored to the WSCC in 1957 and the five D-types entered faced stiff opposition, particularly from Ferrari and the 4½-litre Maseratis. After setting a blistering pace, the opposition fell by the wayside and the result was a

Jaguar steam roller: 1, Flockhart/Bueb (Ecurie Ecosse 3.8-litre injected); 2, Sanderson/Lawrence (Ecurie Ecosse 3.4-litre); 3, Lucas/'Jean-Marie' ('Los Amigos' 3.4 litre 'production'); 4, Rousselle/Frère (Ecurie National Belge 3.4-litre 'production'); 6, Hamilton/Gregory (ex-works 3.8-litre). Only the Ferrari of Severi/Lewis-Evans prevented the result being a complete whitewash.

It was perhaps the greatest performance by a marque ever seen in a single Le Mans and, of course, it brought the tally of wins achieved by the 'Wardour Street Bentley' to five, the same as the real Bentley.

Straight from Le Mans, the Ecurie Ecosse cars went to Monza for the 'Two Worlds' 500-mile race, where USAC roadsters were to meet the Europeans. The race was boycotted by all the Europeans except Ecurie Ecosse, who had three cars entered. It was a hopeless, but wonderful, gesture by the Scottish team and, thanks to reliability, the three Jaguars finished fourth, fifth and sixth a long way behind, true, but still running.

In the Championship Swedish Grand Prix, the Ecurie Ecosse D-type of Jock Lawrence and Archie Scott-Brown (in his first race on the Continent) was in third place when an oil pipe broke, spraying the driver, 'Jock' Lawrence, in the face and causing him to crash. Other D-types finished fifth and eighth.

So far as serious International competition was concerned, 1957 was the last year of the D-type, though cars continued to perform well in minor events for several seasons more. Indeed, in 1958, a novice driver called Jim Clark made quite a reputation in the ex-Murkett Brothers' car. For 1958 the WSCC had a 3-litre upper limit and Jaguar produced a short-stroke (83 × 92 mm) version which, on improved fuel, gave a respectable 254 bhp.

Unfortunately the works dropped a clanger with this for the con-rods were expected to move through impossible angles and they frequently broke. A much better solution would have been to bore and stroke Jaguar's 2.4-litre production unit and this was done in 1960. D-types, even when new, had only performed well at Sebring, Reims and Le Mans, but they were now four years old and already the lighter Lister-Jaguar and the smaller-engined Aston Martin DBR1 had proved their superiors. It is kinder to draw a veil over the succession of failures which comprise the D-type's remaining years in International racing, though cars ran at Le Mans until 1960.

At Le Mans in 1960 Briggs Cunningham entered a 'private' D-type which was actually a works prototype and was somewhere between the D and the E. The chassis was similar to a D-type, but from the scuttle back the frame and aluminium body were integral and had large, stressed, box sections riveted in. Suspension was independent all round with the familiar wishbone and torsion bar front end and at the rear, non-splined drive-shafts and lower wishbones and twin coil spring and damper units. The rear disc brakes were placed inboard.

The engine was a 3-litre (85 × 88 mm) injected unit which gave nearly 295 bhp, but though the car proved quick, with a best lap in practice faster than Masten Gregory's official fastest lap in the race, it retired in the race with a broken piston, and with its demise Jaguar's sports-racing history ended for over 20 years.

At the Geneva Show in 1961 the new E-type was unveiled to reaction similar to the original SS1 and the XK120....

Kieft

Cyril Kieft was a high-flying young manager in the British steel industry when, shortly after the end of World War II, it was nationalized. Casting around for an outlet for his considerable energy, he turned to motor racing in which he'd had a brief and undistinguished career as an amateur driver.

Supported by a small forging and casting business, Kieft made and marketed a simple ladder-framed F3 car which proved too heavy and ill-handling to be competitive, though, thanks to the skill and courage of hill-climber Mike Christie, a

D.J. Calvert at the wheel of his central-seater 2-litre Kieft-Bristol at Goodwood in April 1954. In the foreground is Bert Rodgers' ex-Tony Crook Cooper-Bristol known as 'Mucky Pup'. (NMM)

1,000 cc J.A.P.-powered version achieved some success on the hills. Then the opportunity came to buy and reproduce a F3 car designed by Ray Martin, John A. Cooper (of *The Autocar*) and Dean Delamont when the project ran short of funds. With Stirling Moss at the wheel this car, with all-independent suspension using rubber bands, was immediately successful and attracted a number of customers.

Unfortunately the Kieft-manufactured cars were very poorly made and the only one to achieve unusual success was a works car driven by Don Parker, who insisted on building, and modifying, it himself. This 'Kieft' (it might really have been called a 'Parker Special') was a front-runner in F3 for several reasons and gave the company a reputation which it did not deserve.

Having tasted success, Kieft became ambitious and contemporary magazines were constantly reporting his latest exciting project, which usually came to nothing, for Kieft was long on press announcements and short on achievement. Among the pronouncements were a F2 car (which was never made) and a team of 1,500 cc sports cars to take on Porsche. These were to use the air-cooled A.J.B. flat-four engine (see Elva) but although Kieft built a unit using the A.J.B. bottom end and Norton cylinders and ran it in both a sports and a modified F3 chassis, the company could never overcome overheating problems, though others using the A.J.B. engine did so.

From the end of 1951 Kieft employed an aircraft engineer, Gordon Bedson, as his designer. Bedson's previous racing car experience was confined to the F3 Mackson which Alan Brown, a leading F3 driver and close friend of Bedson, thought so bad that he aborted the testing of it.

For 1953 Kieft announced a 3-seater, sports-racer, the idea being that sitting the driver in the middle would give superior weight distribution. Eight were made, with either M.G. or Bristol engines, and despite being in the hands of some talented amateur drivers, they rarely showed in the results. They were heavy, poorly made, and had mediocre handling.

Still, 'The Monkey Stable' (a team of amateur drivers which employed a professional team manager) managed a 1-2 in a low-key sports car race in Lisbon and a Bristol-engined car won the poorly supported 2-litre class in the 1954 Sebring 12 Hours.

An F1 design was completed with the intention of using the Coventry Climax 'Godiva' V-8 2½-litre engine, but when Climax did not release the unit the project was still-born, though the car, a spare chassis, and all eight 'Godivas' still exist. A one-off large sports car with a 5½-litre V-8 De Soto engine was built for an American amateur, Erwin Goldschmidt, and this car still exists in the States.

A small sports car which, in typical Kieft fashion, was originally going to be made in a batch of 25 with 4-cylinder 500 cc Turner engines (one example of which was used in a Kieft F3 car and proved pathetically underpowered), was eventually made and it was interesting for two reasons. The first was that it had a single-piece glass-fibre body, perhaps the first example of a one-piece moulding for cars, the second was the first use of the 1,100 cc Coventry Climax FWA engine in a car.

Coventry Climax had designed the FW (Feather Weight) engine for the Ministry of Defence for use as a fire pump engine. It was light, powerful and reliable, and its relative cheapness and ready availability was to spawn a host of light British sports cars and create a class of racing which became the equivalent of F3 today, the category for ambitious young drivers with their eyes on better things. When sold for use in cars, and nearly 1,000 were made, the engine was desig-

nated FWA (Feather Weight Automotive).

This car appeared at Le Mans in 1954, retiring after 10 hours with a broken differential. Two were entered in the Tourist Trophy at Dundrod, one retired with collapsed front suspension and the other went on to win its class, which was poorly supported, the Kieft being the only finisher.

These cars had a wide and robust ladder-frame chassis with independent suspension all round, at the front by coil springs and double wishbones, at the rear by a transverse leaf spring and double wishbones. The chassis was unnecessarily wide and heavy and was the sort of frame an amateur special builder might have made.

In what had otherwise been a poor year for British motor racing, Kieft's achievement in winning two classes in WSCC races (Sebring and the TT) turned out to be the highlight of the year even though neither could be called a distinguished win. In recognition of the 'success' Kieft was granted a stand at the Earls Court Motor Show and displayed two ill-finished examples of the 1,100 cc car, one in road trim ostensibly offered as a sports car.

The show car (LDA 5), now owned by Duncan Rabagliati, who uses it on the road, must have been a last-minute thought. Even a man of average height finds it hard to drive because the ill-designed dashboard makes it very difficult to take the right foot from the throttle pedal and activate the brakes. Passenger leg room is severely limited and the boot is completely filled when the spare wheel is in place. It is not surprising that the 'road' car attracted no buyers.

With the steel industry returning to private hands, Kieft returned to it at the end of 1954, selling the car business to fellow Welshman, Berwyn Baxter. At Le Mans in 1955, LDA 5 was fitted with a 1,5000 cc Turner engine and ran without distinction until it retired with transmission troubles. The firm faded at the end of the year, though later the assets were bought by a company called Burmans which made a few Formula Junior cars called 'Kiefts'. They were a decent effort, but no match for the best opposition.

It is believed that three central-seater cars exist today. One is owned by Julian Mujab (LDA 6) in Britain and Benjamin Bragg IV has another in the States. Both are Bristol-powered and a third, now only a chassis, is in Belgium. Goldschmidt's one-off is still in America. There is, too, LDA 5 (which is similar to the Climax-powered cars but has an aluminium body) and one of the five glass-fibre 1,100 cc cars is in the Midland Motor Museum in Bridgnorth.

Lagonda

Lagonda has had a chequered history, indeed, the marque disappeared altogether between 1964 and 1975. Pre-war it had a fine reputation as a maker of quality sporting cars and a Lagonda 4½-litre Rapide won Le Mans in 1935, albeit rather luckily. W. O. Bentley was employed as chief designer that year and the V-12 engine he created for the firm was probably his automotive masterpiece.

In 1947 Lagonda was taken over by the David Brown group, largely to acquire a Bentley-designed 2.3-litre d.o.h.c. engine for Aston Martin which Brown had also bought. In various forms this engine was to sustain the production ranges of both Lagonda for some years and power the Aston Martin DB3 and DB3S sports-racers. Unfortunately, since it could be stretched to no more than 3 litres, in what was an unlimited capacity class of racing, it always had a disadvantage, though the Aston's chassis was sometimes able to overcome the handicap.

It was decided, therefore, to create a new Lagonda 4½-litre V-12 engine, giving a minimum of 350 bhp in racing trim, which would not only have more power than the opposition but would form the basis of a new generation of advanced Lagonda road cars which would become flagships for the Aston Martin-Lagonda range of road cars. Thus went the theory, but the reality turned out rather differently.

Professor Robert Eberan von Eberhorst, who, prewar, had been involved with Ferdinand Porsche and the Auto Union Grand Prix team had joined Aston Martin from E.R.A. at the end of 1950 and among his design briefs was the cre-

The V-12 Lagonda DP115 driven at Le Mans in 1954 by Eric Thompson and Dennis Poore. It was eliminated after Thompson crashed, possibly due to steering failure, but never looked like being competitive. (Louis Klementaski)

ation of the new engine. Work on the project progressed slowly and in 1952 William G. Watson was hired to take over the Lagonda engine under von Eberhorst's direction.

Watson, a gifted but restless engineer, followed the general layout of the existing Aston Martin-Lagonda LB6 6-cylinder engine but gave his unit oversquare (82.55 × 69.85 mm) cylinder dimensions and light alloy heads, two plugs per cylinder and dry sump lubrication. He followed LB6 practice in giving his design a barrel-type crankcase, with seven main bearings instead of the 6-cylinder's four, and in the interests of lightness specified that the crankcase be of aluminium instead of cast-iron as on the LB6. This was to be the unit's downfall.

When an LB6 unit became hot, the aluminium diaphragms which carried the main bearings expanded faster than the cast-iron crankcase, took up any clearance which occurred, and so kept the engine sealed. With the crankcase and diaphragms made from the same metal, this process did not occur and consequently oil pressure dropped as initial testing soon showed.

Instead of taking the sensible course of action and redesigning the engine, it was decided to try to bypass the problem. Despite its high profile, Aston Martin-Lagonda was a tiny company with limited resources and had made, in its own terms, a considerable investment and desperately needed the new engine. So in order to overcome a fundamental design fault, the engines were built with virtually no bearing clearance with the result that, on cold mornings, they refused to turn. To solve this the cooling system was filled with hot water before the engine was fired. It was a solution more becoming a back-street used car dealer than a serious manufacturer.

Designed to run at 7,500 rpm, the engine could not go over 6,000 rpm because of its inherent weakness, at which point it produced 312 bhp, which was considerably below expectations. Thus long-term plans to increase the bore to 87 mm, giving a capacity of 4,983 cc and a theoretical output approaching 400 bhp were never implemented.

In 1954 the engine was fitted to an old-fashioned ladder-frame chassis which followed the general lines and suspension layout of the Aston Martin DB3S with the wheelbase extended to 8 ft 4 in., a 2 in. wider track, and everything correspondingly beefier. Design Project 115 weighed an adipose 2,516 lb. Its body followed the same broad lines as the Aston Martin DB3S and, despite its increased size, retained the handsome lines of that car though aerodynamically it was dated.

From the start the Lagonda was fated. David Brown himself was at the wheel when the first car (DP115/1) ran at Aston's proving ground at Chalgrove and the car rewarded him by catching fire, fortunately without injury to the driver or too much damage to the car.

A few weeks later, it made its debut at the Silverstone International Trophy Meeting and Reg Parnell managed to bring it home in fifth place, running marginally quicker than the works DB3S cars but not looking as though it had any answer to the speed of the Jaguar C-types which were about to become obsolete.

At Le Mans the prototype was entrusted to Eric Thompson and Dennis Poore, but its top speed (148.27 mph) was actually slower than the smaller Aston Martins (149.94 mph) and they were up to 16 mph slower than the best opposition. Thompson crashed after 25 laps possibly due to a key shearing in the steering arm. The most that could be said for it was that it was leading its sister Aston Martins at the time.

In a curtain-raiser to the British Grand Prix, the order was reversed with

Le Mans 1955 saw Reg Parnell and Dennis Poore drive a Lagonda DP166 which had an improved chassis (later used for the Ason Martin DBR2) but retained the seriously flawed V-12 engine. It retired from fuel loss due to an official not properly sealing the petrol filler. (T.C. March)

Astons taking the first three places and Parnell bringing a new Lagonda (DP115/2) home fourth. The Great White Hope was showing distinct signs of being a White Elephant.

The following year, Watson and Ted Cutting produced a space-frame around a rigid central backbone section and disc brakes and this was named Design Project 166. Two DP166 Lagondas were entered for Le Mans, but in view of the engine's continuing unreliability, one was scratched. The one which raced was only marginally faster than the Astons and it retired after six hours when in ninth place. In fairness, it was not the car's fault that it retired. The Plombeur, an official assigned to supervise refuelling stops, failed to seal the fuel cap properly with the result that petrol splashed out in the corners causing the car to splutter to a halt.

It was never raced again. At the end of the year the whole unhappy project was quietly buried.

Both DP115 (ladder-frame) cars were put into order, starred in the film *Checkpoint* and were later sold. Currently they are both owned by Maurice Leo. The two DP166 space-frames were retained by the works and later they were to become the basis of the 3.7-litre Aston Martin DBR2s and the performance of those cars indicated there was at least little wrong with the chassis. One Lagonda body finished up in a scrap yard from whence it was rescued and fitted to a ladder-frame Tojeiro.

The Lagonda was an aberration in Aston Martin's history. The company made its share of mistakes but none was so fundamentally incompetent as the V-12 engine. With the engine's failure, plans for a range of advanced Lagonda road cars were shelved and the marque has never since made the sort of car once promised by a competition-bred V-12.

Lancia

Lancia is a little like Alfa Romeo in that it is hard to equate the company's current image with the niche it once had, though happily that position is currently changing in the wake of vastly improved production cars and considerable rally successes. Whereas Alfa Romeo had always been a maker of rather grand cars, Lancia was noted for technical excellence and innovation. It was the first manufacturer, for example, to dispense with a separate chassis and use 'integral' construction, and that was in 1922 on the Lambda, which also had independent front suspension, a V-4 engine and four-wheel brakes.

Though Vincenzo Lancia had been a noted driver for Fiat in the early years of the century, after he founded Fabrica Automobili Lancia e Cia in 1906 he had always kept racing at arm's length. Like a reformed alcoholic, he knew only too well that one could not go racing half-heartedly and once involved Lancia would soon be involved in heavy expenditure. This policy changed in the Fifties when Lancia, headed by Vincenzo's son, Gianni, embarked on an ambitious programme which was to embrace F1 and, ultimately, Fangio's fourth World Championship.

Overseeing the programme was Vittorio Jano who remains perhaps the greatest car designer Italy has ever produced. His early career (1911–23) was with Fiat, which was then successfully involved in motor racing. From Fiat he moved to Alfa Romeo, where he was responsible for a number of important designs including the P2 and P3 racing cars, which were both outstanding in their respective periods, and the 8C-2300 sports car which won Le Mans four years in succession (1931–34).

His towering reputation did not protect him when his 4½-litre V-12 Alfa Romeo 12C-37 proved unable to match Mercedes-Benz and Auto Union (it was during the Mussolini period) and he was replaced by Wilfredo Ricart, whose political opinions were approved by Il Duce. Ricart was no more successful, for Alfa Romeo simply did not have the same resources as the German firms.

Jano was immediately snapped up by Lancia and 1949 saw his Aurelia saloon, which had all independent suspension, inboard rear brakes, a rear-mounted 4-speed gearbox and a 60-degree V-6 o.h.v. engine of 1,750 cc. It was perhaps the most advanced production car of its day and superbly fitted for competition use.

A GT version (B20) was introduced in 1951 with a slightly shorter wheelbase, a 75 bhp 2-litre engine and a body styled by Pininfarina. For a modified production saloon, it was outstanding and it enjoyed numerous successes in International racing and rallying. So far as racing is concerned, these included the 2-litre GT class in the 1950 Mille Miglia, second overall in 1951 and third overall in 1952. Also in 1952, Lancia Aurelias finished 1-2-3 overall in the Targa Florio and in the 1951 Le Mans, Lancia's first-ever entry finished 12th and won the 2-litre class. The following year, Lancias finished sixth and eighth and scored 1-2 in the 2-litre class.

The majority of manufacturers listed in this book could not match that record with bespoke sports-racing cars, but those successes were achieved with modified saloons.

With Jano on the staff and the company enjoying its competition success, it was only a short step to a fully-fledged racer, the D20, which appeared in 1953. Its engine was a development of the Aurelia's, not in the metal for it was longer, but in inspiration. It retained the staggered V-6 layout with 4-bearing crankshaft, but it was of 2,962 cc (86 × 85 mm) and chain-driven d.o.h.c. heads replaced the

At Le Mans in 1953 Lancia became the last works team to field a full team of supercharged sports cars. Here one of the D20 coupés pits during the race. (Louis Klementaski)

standard push-rod system. There were two plugs per cylinder and three down-draught twin-choke Weber carburettors. Initially it gave 217 bhp but, with development, this rose to 245 bhp.

Under its Farina-styled coupé body was a space-frame, with trailing arms and a transverse leaf spring at the front and a similar system at the rear but with friction dampers. These could be adjusted by a system of levers leading to chains in the roof of the cockpit. As on the Aurelia the gearbox was mounted in front of the final drive and not only were the inboard rear brakes retained but, unusually, the front drums were inboard too.

A five-car team was entered for the 1953 Mille Miglia but were not up to the Ferraris and Alfa Romeos, though Bonetto/Peruzzi did bring one home a distant third. Two weeks later the Targa Florio brought a better result with Piero Taruffi leading until he crashed and his team-mate, Umberto Magioli, winning from two works Maseratis.

For Le Mans Lancia took a curious decision. It reduced engine capacity to 2,683 cc, lowered the engines' compression ratios and added belt-driven Roots-type superchargers. It was a curious decision because it was not intended to increase power as Aston Martin was to do the following year (only 3 bhp was added) but to improve the shape of the power curve, which is not the overriding consideration at Le Mans.

The experiment is a historical curiosity in that it was the last time a major constructor ran a full team of supercharged cars in a classic race, but it was a failure. The Lancias were about 15 mph slower down the Mulsanne Straight than the Jaguar C-types, never ran near the front, and all retired. The team also discovered the problems associated with running coupés for, given the state at the

The D20 driven by Robert Manzon and Louis Chiron which retired from the 1953 Le Mans race due to engine failure. (Louis Klementaski)

time of car aerodynamics as applied to ducting, the drivers found them unbearably hot, the windscreen prone to misting and windscreen wipers of the time could not guarantee visibility.

An open version, designated D23, was quickly made and the cars soon began to score good results in second league events. Taruffi finished second to Marzotto's Ferrari in the Dolomite Gold Cup, Bonetto finished second to Villoresi's Ferrari in the Inter-Europa Cup at Monza and Bonetto won the Lisbon GP from Moss's Jaguar C-type.

For the Nürburgring 1,000 Km in August, Lancia produced its fourth variant of the year. The racing department must have been working around the clock for it had quickly responded to the lessons learned from a handful of races and came up with the D24. While it retained the basic chassis and body design, its wheelbase was reduced by eight inches to 7 ft 10½ in. and the shape subtly cleaned up.

The great Alberto Ascari at the start of the 1954 Mille Miglia in his Lancia D24 with which he won. (Publifoto)

A de Dion rear axle replaced the independent set-up and this was suspended by ¼-elliptical springs located by radius arms. The gearbox was in unit with the final drive in the same casting and the engine had been increased to 3,284 cc (88 × 90 mm), giving 265 bhp.

Between April and August, in its first season of serious racing, Lancia had fielded three distinct engines, three body styles, two transmissions and two chassis. It was an incredible effort and one which puts some other makers into perspective.

Two D24s and a D23 were entered at the Nürburgring and Fangio was in the team. The opposition was thin; but the cars were able to match the speed of the pace-setter, a lone Ferrari. Fangio's car retired with a broken fuel pump and after their first pit stops neither of the other cars would start for their batteries had boiled dry and substitutes were forbidden.

Four cars were entered for the Supercortemaggiore Grand Prix and they proved fast but fragile and all four retired, allowing Fangio to score the only victory for the Alfa Romeo Disco Volante.

After such a poor showing the final race of the year redressed the balance. Five cars were entered in the Carrera Panamericana and they had 3.1-litre (88 × 85 mm) engines which gave 230 bhp. The cars ran faultlessly and dominated the race and Fangio led Taruffi and Castellotti home for a 1-2-3. The triumph was marred by the death of Felice Bonetto, who, spurred by a long-standing rivalry with Taruffi, lost control of his car in a Mexican village, struck a lamp post and was killed.

Jano meanwhile was pressing ahead with a new design for the 2½-litre F1 which was to come into force at the beginning of 1954 and Lancia pulled off a coup by signing the reigning World Champion, Alberto Ascari. Ascari's reputation has faded with the years but he was one of the greatest drivers who has ever lived. Fangio actually nominated him as the greatest. He had had several successful seasons with Ferrari which took him to two World Championships and, between 1952 and 1953, nine successive Grand Prix wins, a run which has never been equalled.

Ascari had no great confidence in Ferrari's plans for the new formula, believing that they were too conservative to be competitive against the likes of Mercedes-Benz. By contrast, Lancia had an exciting new design on the stocks, had proved in its first season of racing that it was capable of developing it and, moreover, was prepared to pay him a salary worthy of a World Champion. By contrast, Ferrari took the view that it was an honour to drive one of his cars and was tight on the purse strings.

It was not expected that the F1 car would begin the season but it was hoped it would appear in time to contest most of the Championship. It was soon apparent that this was an optimistic estimate as early problems were soon apparent. With a top-line team of drivers to keep employed, it was decided to soldier on with the sports cars.

Deciding not to go to Buenos Aires, 1954 began for Lancia with the Sebring 12 Hours and the team fielded four 3.3-litre D24s. There was not a great deal of opposition to stretch the team, but the quickest of its cars were soon out. After eleven hours Piero Taruffi and Robert Mazon led easily when the engine seized. This allowed Stirling Moss and Bill Lloyd in Briggs Cunningham's 1.5-litre OSCA to score a remarkable win. Lancia's fourth car, driven by the amateurs, Rubirosa and Valenzano, finished a lacklustre second five laps down.

Back on home ground, Taruffi won the Tour of Sicily in a D24 and four cars

Piero Taruffi led much of the 1954 Mille Miglia before retiring and is seen here in his Lancia D24 at Ravenna. (Publifoto)

were entered in the Mille Miglia. Originally Ascari was not going to drive, his contract had an exclusion clause, but when his friend and mentor, Luigi Villoresi, was injured in a practice accident he stepped into the breach. Taruffi, whose overriding ambition was to win the race, set a cracking pace in his Lancia, but crashed. Ascari then took the lead and, though pressed hard by two Ferraris which did not last the distance, finished first.

Two cars were entered in the Targa Florio which, while it still had not received WSCC status, was still a considerable race. Castellotti's car retired after hitting a kerb and damaging its steering, but Taruffi went on to complete Lancia's hat-trick.

Le Mans was given a miss, partly due to Lancia realizing that its car would perhaps not last the distance, partly due to seeing the new Jaguar D-type, and a team was entered instead in the Oporto Grand Prix. There was not a great deal of opposition so the 1-2 of Villoresi and Castellotti did not amount to much.

For the Tourist Trophy, though, a new car, the D25, was prepared. For some odd reason, considering the race was a handicap, Lancia produced a larger, 3,750 cc (93 × 92 mm) engine while Jaguar, in an attempt to beat the handicap, built smaller engines. The D25 also differed from its predecessors with a reduced wheelbase of 7 ft 6 in. and outboard brakes.

Both D25s retired, but while the D24s finished second and third on distance they were unplaced on handicap. That race virtually ended Lancia's career in sports car races, for the D50 F1 car was ready to race, though later Villoresi won the purely national Siracusa GP in a D24. The WSCC final score for 1954 was: 1st, Ferrari 38 pts; 2nd, Lancia 20 pts; 3rd, Jaguar 10 pts.

One D24 was sold to President Perón of Argentina and when the dictator was deposed it was bought by one Camilo Gay, who reduced the engine to 3 litres and entered it in the 1958 Buenos Aires 1,000 Km. During practice he damaged it against a concrete post, and though it was repaired in time it was not allowed to start.

The D50 F1 car finally appeared in the final round of the 1954 World Championship, the Spanish GP, and it bristled with innovations. Externally the most striking feature were the pontoon fuel tanks on each side between the wheels, but the great step forward was the fact that the V-8 engine was a stressed member. At

127

In the 1954 Tourist Trophy this 3.7 litre Lancia D25 was driven by Alberto Ascari and Luigi Villoresi, but retired. (Motor)

Barcelona it showed great pace, but it succumbed to teething troubles. So Ascari finished 1954 without a single F1 finish to his name.

The following year the car was starting to show promise when Ascari was killed in an inexplicable accident at Monza while driving Castellotti's Ferrari 750 during a mid-week test session. The death of Italy's greatest postwar driver (then and now) was shattering and, worse, Automobili Lancia was in desperate financial straits due partly to the cost of the competition programme. The Lancia family sold their interests to an outside combine which immediately curtailed the F1 programme.

Ferrari was going through a lean period and threatening to withdraw from racing. This would have been a blow to the Italian motor industry as a whole for Ferrari successes sold Italian cars no matter who made them. In an extraordinary deal, Fiat promised a measure of financial support for a five-year period and the new owners of Lancia handed over the complete D50 project. Vittorio Jano joined Ferrari as a consultant, and the cars proved themselves in 1956 with five wins from seven WSCC rounds. Jano continued with the team and was responsible for the line of V-6 engines which bore the name of Ferrari's son, Dino.

History has not treated Lancia kindly and so often the company does not receive due credit for having instigated the D50; rather, the 1956 successes are perceived as Ferrari's. Lancia's competition career at the top level was brief but distinguished. Its cars were handsome, fast, and handled well, and Lancia's competition department showed an astonishing ability to respond and progress very quickly. Unfortunately in motor racing short reaction times come expensively and that was partly responsible for bringing the company uncomfortably close to bankruptcy.

Lister

Brian Lister had been enjoying some moderate success as a driver in minor events with, first, a Cooper-M.G. and then a Tojeiro fitted with a highly tuned 1,100 cc J.A.P V-twin engine, when he turned up at a sprint meeting near his native Cambridge and was soundly beaten by someone driving a standard M.G. TD. That put his driving into perspective and he invited the man who had beaten him to drive his car while he entered and prepared it. Thus was born one of the great partnerships in British motor racing.

The man in the M.G. was a Scot, Archie Scott-Brown, who had been born physically deformed. He had ill-formed short legs which terminated in tiny feet and his right arm was withered and short and terminated in a vestigial palm and thumb. Despite these disadvantages Archie drove himself to be an all-round sportsman who fenced and played cricket, soccer and snooker. He was physically disadvantaged but in no way handicapped, though his career was to be dogged by the refusal of race organizers to accept his entries.

By sheer guts and determination Archie could on occasion beat even Stirling Moss in a Le Mans start, and Moss was the acknowledged master. On his day he could out-drive anyone, for he was a driver of whom that over-used word 'great' could justly be applied. Further, he was a man of huge generosity of spirit who had not an enemy in the world.

When he took over the driving of the Tojeiro-J.A.P. he proved unbeatable, while the beast lasted, and at the end of 1953 Brian Lister laid plans to build his own car. Brian worked for the family firm, George Lister & Sons, an established precision engineering company and he approached his father with the proposal. The upshot was that he was given a grant of £1,500 to see if he could make his point.

He laid down a ladder-frame chassis which would form the basis of all but one of the Lister sports cars. Two 3-inch tubes formed the lozenge-shaped frame with three similar tubes forming the cross-bracing. Front suspension was by equal length wishbones and coil springs while at the rear was a de Dion axle suspended by coil springs and located by twin radius arms and a central sliding block. The rear Girling brakes, with Alfin drums, were mounted inboard. A tuned 1,500 cc M.G. XPAG engine and a simple all-enveloping aluminium body completed the plot.

After some successes in minor events, the Lister appeared for its first important race, the British Empire Trophy at Oulton Park. There the organizers woke up to Archie's deformities and promptly banned him. Fortunately his driving during practice had caught the attention of several important people, including Earl

Archie Scott-Brown with the Lister-Maserati at Oulton Park in April 1956 in the third year of a wonderful but tragically short partnership between Brian Lister and the great little Scot. Here, as at many races during the year Archie was plagued by engine problems. (T.C. March)

Howe and Gregor Grant, the editor of *Autosport*. They campaigned on Archie's behalf while others drove the Lister. By the time Archie's licence was restored it had become clear that the car was too heavy for the M.G. engine.

Brian managed to prise more money from his father for a second car, this time with a 142 bhp Bristol engine tuned by Don Moore, who, like Lister, Scott-Brown and John Tojeiro, operated in the Cambridge area. It followed the pattern of the first car except that larger brakes were employed.

It was ready in time for the British Grand Prix meeting, where, in the Unlimited Sports Car race, Archie drove it to a fine fifth, beaten only by works Aston Martins and Lagonda. The race was televised and back home Brian's father was so astounded by the number of times the name 'Lister' was mentioned that thereafter the racing project received wholehearted support.

For the rest of that season, Archie and the Lister were front runners in the 2-litre class in Britain against opposition which included Roy Salvadori in Sid Greene's Maserati A6GCS. Archie ended the season with a tally of three wins and five seconds in the Bristol car and five wins and eight seconds in the M.G. car, which was then re-engined and re-bodied and sold as a Lister-Bristol.

Lister had received overtures for replicas and for 1955 sold five new cars plus the prototype. Five had Bristol engines, while the sixth had a Rover unit, and all had a new body developed by Thom Lucas using models in a wind tunnel. Given the state of wind-tunnel technology at the time, at least so far as it was applied to cars, the body was probably little improvement on the original, but at least it showed Lister's heart was in the right place. Brakes were further up-rated from 11 in. to 12 in. drums, and minor changes were made to suspension and steering geometry.

The works car retained the original slab-sided body and in it Archie had a wonderful season taking 13 wins, four seconds and two thirds. Particularly sweet was a return to the British Empire Trophy. The final was run on handicap and Archie came through to win from Kenneth McAlpine's Connaught AL/SR and a 2½-litre Aston Martin DB3S driven by Reg Parnell.

Though the Bristol engine was strong and powerful, it was extremely tall (29 in.), which led to a large frontal area. To overcome this, for 1956 Lister turned to the 2-litre Maserati A6GCS engine and the resultant car was extremely low, just 27 in. to the top of the scuttle. The chassis followed established lines but Girling disc brakes replaced the former drum system.

Unfortunately, the Maserati engine was ill-made and unreliable and all that Lister and Scott-Brown had to show for their efforts were three wins and two seconds. The Bristol-engined cars were still going strong, however, and took a

dozen wins during the year. At the same time Archie's career expanded in other directions. He led the Connaught F1 team at home, made his first foray abroad driving a D-type in the Swedish GP, and turned out at the wheel of a wide range of other cars, including a D.K.W. saloon and the works Elva-Climax.

A customer asked Brian to sell him a chassis in which he intended to install a Jaguar engine. Initially against the idea, for he felt his frame would be inadequate for so much power, Lister was eventually persuaded. From there it was a short step to making a bespoke Lister-Jaguar.

The chassis followed previous practice, but Dunlop alloy disc wheels replaced the previous wires, the car had a 2 in. wider rear track, and the engine was a 3.4 (later 3.8) dry sump D-type unit prepared by Don Moore. It was registered MVE 303.

Its debut at Snetterton was inauspicious, for the clutch failed, but thereafter Archie and the Lister was the combination to beat in British sports car racing. The Lister's chassis was not terribly rigid, but Archie's driving style consisted of

For the final of the 1958 British Empire Trophy Archie Scott-Brown took over Bruce Halford's Lister-Jaguar and finished third behind two works Aston Martins. (T.C. March)

driving around a circuit in a series of blood-curdling slides and a diagram of his lines round a circuit shows that his car was rarely travelling in a straight line. His racing was still restricted to Britain, but he frequently came up against the Ecurie Ecosse Jaguars and the works Aston Martins, and he invariably beat them.

Apart from the initial failure at Snetterton and an occasion when he suffered mechanical problems and could only manage second, Archie won race after race until finally beaten by Roy Salvadori in a 3.7-litre Aston Martin DBR2 at the International Trophy meeting at Silverstone in September. Later it was found that the Lister's rear spring had settled and the de Dion tube was hitting its bump stops. In that state Archie still managed to beat the rest of the four-strong Aston Martin works team.

At the end of the season MVE 303's record was: 14 races, 11 wins, two seconds and a retirement. Archie took the car Down Under for the winter season and meanwhile Lister coped with a flood of orders for his car. Briggs Cunningham ordered three, two to be fitted with 3-litre Jaguar engines (there was a 3-litre limit in the WSCC in 1958) and one to have a Chevrolet engine. 1958 cars had bodies of a new style which have since been known as the 'Knobbly' Listers to distinguish them from the later Costin-bodied cars, and these were made in both magnesium alloy and aluminium. One of the ten Lister-Bristols had been crashed and when it was re-built its new owner Tom Kyffin, installed a Jaguar engine and this car was later raced successfully by Bruce Halford and Jim Clark.

The 1958 cars had numerous detail modifications, the most noticeable of which was a wheelbase of 7 ft 6¾ in. (1¾ in. longer than MVE 303), wider front and rear tracks and an overall length some 6 in. longer. Exact production figures are unavailable because the works records were lost during a move to new premises and because the cars are simple and now fetching high prices there are perhaps more now than were made in Cambridge.

In March, Archie flew to Sebring to drive one of Briggs Cunningham's 3-litre Lister-Jaguars. Four laps into the race and the car slowed suddenly causing Olivier Gendebien's Ferrari Testa Rossa to mount its back, leave tyre marks on Archie's helmet, and end up with a wheel in the passenger compartment. A piston had holed, though whether that caused the accident or happened as a result of it is not known. In view of the hapless season the 3-litre Jaguar engine had in 1958, the former seems most likely. In creating a short-stroke engine, Jaguar made the con-rods go through impossible angles and they invariably failed, though generally with broken con-rods.

For 1958 Scott-Brown had a new works car, VPP 9, which suffered some early season breakages due to the increased cornering power of the new Dunlop R5 tyres. At the Aintree 200 meeting, Archie beat, just, the works Aston Martin of Stirling Moss and Masten Gregory's new Ecurie Ecosse Lister. On his day Gregory could compete with anyone and that day came during the International Trophy meeting. The Ecurie Ecosse Lister had some aerodynamic tweaks but they do not account for the fact that Gregory won by over half a minute. Archie could not believe that he had actually been out-driven; it had never happened before even though he had been competing against the likes of Moss and Brooks.

The two men met again at the Spa sports car race and so far as Archie was concerned he had a point to make. The two Listers swapped the lead all the way around the circuit, leading works cars from Aston Martin and Ferrari, when one of Spa's notorious isolated showers caught him out. His car left the track at the same point where Richard Seaman had crashed during the 1939 Belgian GP when he was trying to make a point by attempting to out-drive Caracciola in the

At the 1958 May Silverstone meeting Masten Gregory in the Ecurie Ecosse Lister scored an emphatic, surprise, victory over Scott-Brown's works car. Archie was to die a few weeks later when trying to redress the balance at Spa. (T.C. March)

wet. The Lister caught fire, the magnesium alloy body burning furiously. Archie was mortally burned and died next day.

Brian Lister wanted to give up at that point, but had responsibilities to his customers. A gentleman of the old school, he took his responsibilities seriously and was unusual among constructors of the day in that he scrupulously kept his customers informed about latest developments, particularly where safety was involved.

Three Listers ran at Le Mans and two retired with various engine problems while the third had a virtual engine re-build during the race and limped home in 15th place. A special off-set single-seat was built for Ecurie Ecosse for the 'Two Worlds 500' race at Monza but it proved slower than the team's D-type.

Eventually the works fielded cars again and the drivers were Ivor Bueb, Ross Jensen and Stirling Moss, and all won races in Britain. The cars did not, however, face International competition and even the other WSCC event the cars entered, the Tourist Trophy at Goodwood, was virtually a British national race in the big-capacity class. No Listers finished following a spate of kingpin failures probably due to being stretched beyond their limits by a combination of the new Dunlops and the nature of the Goodwood track.

Unlike some, Brian Lister had the sense to know his limits as a designer. Twice he had designed front-engined F2 cars and in neither case were they successful. The first was an ungainly device which Lister had sawn up before it was completed, the second was a low-slung, very pretty car with the engine off-set to the left to allow the prop-shaft to pass alongside the driver and not beneath him as was the norm in front-engined single-seaters. Archie Scott-Brown was not impressed by having the whirring bar mere inches from him and, besides, the car never worked properly because the left-hand drive-shaft in the de Dion rear suspension necessarily finished up impossibly short. Archie drove the car a couple of times without success and the car was sold on and was last heard of in America.

Having realized he was a special builder who had happened to strike a winning formula and was unlikely to do so again, Brian employed Frank Costin as Lister's chief engineer with a brief to take the company forward. Costin is a brilliant designer but a maverick. His interest in any design ends with his satisfying himself that he has got it right regardless of production or marketing considerations. In his wake he has left a host of innovations and exasperated business partners. His

133

partnership with Lister was no exception. It was not a marriage made in Heaven.

First of all Costin designed a bulbous aerodynamic body which drivers on the whole disliked because it was difficult to place in corners and which Brian Lister regrets because it took away from the car its essential character. He has since said he wished he had designed a smaller successor to the 'Knobbly' along the lines of his Lister-Maserati.

These cars were sold with Jaguar and Chevrolet engines and most of the latter went to America, where they failed to take racing by its ears. Some Chevrolet-engined cars were sold in Britain, but though the package looked promising they were unsuccessful until converted to Jaguar power.

Stirling Moss and Ivor Bueb shared Briggs Cunningham's 'Costin' Lister-Jaguar at Sebring and were in contention for the lead when, in his anxiety to leave the pits after one of the fuelling stops, Moss drove back into the race with the tanks still light and ran out of fuel. It is possible the car might otherwise have won. Be that as it may, no Lister was ever again to come so close to a WSCC victory.

As 1959 continued, Listers began to be outpaced in Britain by the new F1-based Cooper Monaco sports cars. Ecurie Ecosse and Jonathan Sieff both entered cars in the Nürburgring 1,000 Km, but the Ecosse car had a half-shaft U/J go after six laps and Mike Taylor crashed the Sieff car.

For Le Mans Frank Costin had the idea of fitting an 'insect deflector' on the bonnet which was actually a cockpit-activated air brake seeking a loop-hole in the regulations. Tests proved inconclusive (Lister says it didn't work, Costin maintains it did) and the car did not race with it. At Le Mans the Costin Lister, even with an aerodynamic tonneau cover, proved slower than the 3-litre D-types. After nine hours the No 1 Lister, driven by Bueb and Halford, lay fourth and rising and then the engine let go.

At Le Mans in 1959 the works Costin-bodied Lister-Jaguar of Ivor Bueb and Bruce Halford leads the D.B. of Alejandro de Tomaso and Colin Davis. The Lister retired with engine problems, a common occurrence with the 3-litre version of the Jaguar XK engine. (Geoffrey Goddard)

Shortly afterwards both drivers were severely injured in a F2 race at Clermont-Ferrand and poor Ivor Bueb succumbed to his injuries. For Brian Lister the fun had gone out of racing when Archie died and his relationship with Costin had not restored his enthusiasm. As soon as he heard of Ivor's death he closed down his team.

An enthusiastic amateur, Jim Diggory, bought the space-frame Costin had designed and had it built up. It performed quite well in British club events though the rear end was never properly sorted and the 'lightweight' car was actually 100 lb heavier. Eventually it passed through other hands and, fitted with a Costin body made into a coupé appeared at Le Mans in 1963 and the Nürburgring 1,000 Km in 1964. It failed to finish in either.

Lister-Jaguars exemplify the best traditions of British special building and were certainly the most successful of the Jaguar-engined cars even though they rarely competed at the highest levels of racing. Despite 'improvements', however, Lister never again reached the heights it enjoyed in 1957 when the sublime Archie Scott-Brown drove it sideways to victory after victory.

Lola MK I

Eric Broadley began racing in 1954, sharing the 750 Special of his cousin, Graham. Two years later he began work on his first car, a 1,172 cc Ford Special, which he and Graham raced with great success in 1957, ironically in races counting for the Colin Chapman Trophy. It was the first car to bear the Lola name, but after it was sold at the end of the season, its new owner re-christened it 'Lolita'. Thus Broadley's *second car* was the Lola Mk I.

Encouraged by his first effort, and harbouring ideas of being a top-flight racing driver, Broadley began work on an altogether more ambitious project, a Coventry Climax-powered sports-racer for the 1,100 cc sports car class. That was then the recognized class for driver with serious ambitions, a rough equivalent of Formula 3 today, which was then dominated by the Lotus Eleven.

The decision to build an 1,100 cc car was an audacious one, for it was certainly going to be little cheaper than buying a Lotus. Broadley had been trained as an architect so had experience of stressing structures, but his car design experience amounted to one club racing special while Chapman had been building cars for ten years. Along the way Lotus had wiped out strong opposition in small-capacity sports car racing and had recruited the very best young driving talent into its works team.

At the time he started on his new car, Broadley was working as a quantity surveyor for a building firm. His spare time was spent on his car, helped by Graham, working in a lock-up garage behind the family tailoring firm in Bromley, and a garage-owning friend, Rob Rushbrook (now Lola's works manager and a Lola director), allowed him the use of his plant in the evenings.

Given the circumstances of its building, it would not have been surprising if the little car had been derivative in its design or crude in its execution. It was neither, rather it was a beautifully detailed, original little car with a very stiff, brazed, space-frame and an attractive aluminium body made by Maurice Gomm. It was typical, for example, that the differential casing was cast from Elektron using

The Lola was the sensation of the British 1959 season and dominated the 1100cc class. Here works driver Peter Ashdown is on his way to second place behind Alan Stacey's 1500cc Lotus Fifteen at Oulton Park, April 1959. (T.C. March)

wooden moulds that Eric had carved and varnished.

The independent rear suspension used non-splined drive-shafts as part of the upper wishbones which has been called an original idea but was really a case of Broadley thinking in parallel to Elva and Lotus.

The prototype Lola took nine months to complete and it was not until the August of 1958 that Broadley turned up with his car at a fairly important meeting at Brands Hatch. During practice, the Lola became the first sports car regardless of size to lap the circuit in under a minute, which alone was enough to raise eyebrows, but then Broadley won his heat by no less than 24 seconds, equalling the class lap record in the process. In the final he was rammed from behind at the start and later black-flagged for erratic driving in his attempt to make up lost ground.

Undeterred, he joined the grid for the 1,500 cc sports car race and, starting from the back of the grid, came through to finish a fine fourth. It was, so said a contemporary report, 'a sensational debut'. There were not many races left that year, but in those he entered, Broadley underlined the car's potential. Despite his ambitions as a driver, Eric had little form and so the car itself was taken seriously. It is not surprising that he was soon pressured to build replicas.

Testing at Brands Hatch during the close season, Eric invited Peter Ashdown, who was there to test an Elva, to try the car and Ashdown's performance was such that Broadley realized that perhaps he wasn't going to the World Champion after all. Ashdown was engaged as the works driver.

The prototype car was sold to Peter Gammon and the first customer car went to Mike Taylor. At Snetterton on Good Friday, 1959, Ashdown led Taylor across the line but was penalized for jumping the start, so the positions were reversed. Then it was down to Goodwood for the popular and prestigious Easter Monday meeting.

The three Lolas sat in the first three places on the grid, swapped places throughout the race, left the opposition for dead, and came home in the order: Ashdown, Gammon and Taylor. The Lotus Eleven, which had had a stranglehold on the class, was suddenly history. That initial display of superiority was no flash in the pan, for Lolas went on to dominate the 1,100 cc sports car class for several seasons.

Lola's first continental excursion was to the Nürburgring and the 1959 1,000 Km. Ashdown qualified the little car eighth overall and led his class by a country mile until Broadley took over and put it into a ditch on lap 16. In the meantime

Ashdown had taken a full minute off the class lap record. Ashdown won a well-supported race at Clermont-Ferrand and rounded off the year with sixth overall and an easy first in class in the Tourist Trophy.

The following year, co-driving with a Swiss amateur, Charles Vogoele, Ashdown undertook a full WSCC season. The pair retired at Le Mans and were pipped for second in class at the Nürburgring, but won everything else. For three successive seasons, 1959, 1960 and 1961, Ashdown and his Lola won the *Autosport* Championship, one of the most important British national series.

1959 was the last year of prime importance for the 1,100 cc sports car class, for attention switched to Formula Junior, and Lola's new models for the next few seasons were for FJ, though the Mk I continued in production. In all, 36 Mk Is were built, 35 of which were powered by Coventry Climax's 1,098 cc FWA engine, the other having a 1,500 cc unit.

Lola has since gone on to build over 2,000 racing cars and is the world's longest-established maker whose business is solely the production of customer racing cars. It has also nurtured the talents of a number of young designers, starting with Tony Southgate in 1960, who have gone on to carve out individual careers for themselves and so has had a wider influence on the growth of the British racing car industry.

Despite success in many categories, notably Indycar racing, none of Lola's subsequent designs has ever been so clearly superior to the opposition as its first car. Pound for pound, it was among the finest sports-racers of the postwar era.

Lotus

As time recedes it is possible to see the genius of Colin Chapman in better perspective. Quite apart from the fact that he was the most innovative chassis designer the sport has seen, he did more than anyone else to pave the way to British dominance of the motor racing industry.

His charisma attracted an extraordinary wealth of talent to his modest workshop in North London, and it included Keith Duckworth and the Costin brothers. The drivers whom he signed to run works-supported cars, at a time when it was really financial folly, included some of the finest young British prospects of the late Fifties and early Sixties. Chapman's fostering of their careers did much to ensure a British domination in terms of numbers of Grand Prix drivers in the early Sixties.

By subcontracting to meet customer demand, Chapman was instrumental in laying the foundation of the motor racing supply industry which is unmatched in the world. By employing a succession of bright young designers, starting with Len Terry, he helped create the pool of design talent which still keeps Britain at the fore.

Chapman was responsible for the chassis design of the Vanwall, Britain's first successful Grand Prix car, and he sorted out the ill-handling BRM P25. When all the small national racing car constructors met for the first time in an International category, Formula Junior, Chapman's Lotuses were so far ahead of the foreign opposition that they dealt a blow to the Italian, French and German industries which virtually wiped them out, leaving Britain in a league by itself. His use of tuned Ford engines brought that giant, previously in Britain the maker of dull cars, into the sport and aided the development of Cosworth Engineering, which undertook the development of the Ford-based engines Lotus used.

Brilliant, impetuous, original, a man in a hurry, he earned respect rather than love. He remains the most important individual of postwar motor racing and that includes Enzo Ferrari. While Ferrari astutely gathered around himself fine engineers to whom he gave inspiration, Chapman strove to push back the limits of design – and the regulations which governed them.

He made what are, in retrospect, silly mistakes such as insisting on a front-engined F1 car (the Lotus 16) when Cooper had already shown that a mid-engined layout was the right way to go. One can understand, if not applaud, his doggedness, for he knew that Cooper had hit upon its winning formula by chance and Cooper cars were designed by blacksmiths, not engineers, so they could not be right even when they were winning.

So far as Britain is concerned, he showed what was possible and inspired followers like Eric Broadley. It's always easier to believe something is possible when it's been done by someone in your own back yard. In the wake of Ferrari there has been no such renaissance in Italian motor racing.

Colin Chapman with the Mk 9 Lotus-Climax at Le Mans, 1955. He was disqualified for rejoining the race without authority having extracted his car from a sand bank.
(Geoffrey Goddard)

Like most small constructors Lotus was bound by the engines which were readily available (Fiat in Italy, Panhard and Renault in France, M.G. and Bristol in Britain) and Chapman therefore looked to gain advantages in his chassis. Since British racing largely consisted of short sprints on smooth ex-World War II airfield circuits, he was able to plough a different furrow to European makers, whose cars had to withstand the rigours of genuine road circuits. Consequently Lotuses did not often succeed on the Continent save at smooth tracks like Le Mans and Reims. Their handling was superior but they tended not to last the distance.

After building a number of successful specials, Chapman's first production car was the Mk 6, which was offered in kit form in late 1952. It was small, low and light, with a rigid space-frame and simple aluminium body which together weighed only 120 lb.

Many Ford components were used, including the axles, the front being a beam unit split to give i.f.s. and the live rear axle was securely located by a Panhard rod. Originally intended as an all-purpose car for the amateur, which at the time meant that trials would be included, its initially high ground clearance was later lowered and, depending on the engine used and the skill of the driver, it could be a successful club racer. In 1954, for example, Peter Gammon entered 17 races and took 14 wins, two seconds and a third. About 100 Mk 6s were sold between 1953 and 1955.

In early 1954 Chapman began work on a new car, the Mk 8, which for the first time would be a Lotus with an all-enveloping body. He had been introduced to Frank Costin, an aerodynamicist with de Havilland, who was fired by the problem of applying aerodynamics to cars. The result of the collaboration was a low car of startling appearance and an all-up weight of less than 10 cwt, which retained swing axle i.f.s. but used a de Dion rear axle, a transverse coil spring and telescopic dampers.

Although Lotus's modified M.G. XPAG engine gave only 85 bhp, the car's combination of light weight and low drag allowed it to reach 125 mph and it immediately established itself as the fastest 1,500 cc car in the country. Its speed was not initially matched by its reliability and part of the reason must have been that Chapman still held down a day job and devoted himself to the business of Lotus only in the evenings and at weekends. He had his band of helpers, but the

man was designing, overseeing production cars and race preparation, and fitting in a full driving programme all on a part-time basis. Something had to suffer.

The first production cars reached their buyers in mid-season and two of the six built are of interest. One was John Coombs's car into which he fitted a Connaught/Lea-Francis engine, making it the quickest 1,500 cc car in the country. The other, later in the season, was Dick Steed's, which became the first Lotus powered by Coventry Climax, in this case a 1,100 cc FWA engine. The combination 'Lotus-Climax' was to become a dominant force in world racing over the next eleven years.

Despite teething troubles, Chapman had a successful year and in the Mk 8 the highlight was a curtain-raiser for the British GP at Silverstone. There Chapman trounced Hans Herrmann's works Porsche 550, the first time one of the new small British makers had taken on and beaten top continental opposition.

For 1955 Chapman planned two new cars, the Mk 9 and Mk 10, and he and Mike Costin took the decision to leave their jobs to work for Lotus full time. The Mk 9 was based on the Mk 8 but was shorter, stiffer, and intended mainly for the Coventry Climax FWA engine, though Chapman continued with an M.G. unit. Its de Dion rear axle was suspended on coil springs and Frank Costin evolved a new shape for it, notable for its high tail fins.

For 2-litre racing, there was the Mk 10, based on the Mk 9 chassis but stronger and heavier. Its body followed the lines of the Mk 8 but with a prominent bulge in the bonnet. Most of the seven customers specified Bristol engines, though one had a Connaught, and the actor James Dean intended fitting an Offenhauser unit to his but he died before it was ready.

Lotus Mk 10s enjoyed only moderate success and then only in Britain. Archie Scott-Brown's Lister-Bristol was more than a match for them and Cliff Davis regretted swapping his successful Tojeiro-Bristol for one.

1955 was the year which saw a sudden growth in 1,100 cc sports car racing for Coventry Climax had built an engine which was powerful, reliable, light, relatively inexpensive and readily available. An 1,100 cc Climax-powered Mk 9 was quicker to 60 mph than its M.G.-powered sister and was only marginally slower. Over the next few years the class was to develop into the rough equivalent of F3 today, the class for the serious young driver.

It was to be, however, Cooper's year, but Mk 9s still took lots of wins in

Britain Peter Ashdown won a 1,500 cc sports car race in Sweden. Two ran at Sebring, but both retired and, for the first time, a Lotus ran at Le Mans.

Chapman shared the driving with Ron Flockhart and though they initially led the 1,100 cc class, a slipping clutch slowed them and they were disqualified after Chapman had a minor brush with a sand bank and had reversed out against the flow of traffic. All the Mk 9s retired in both the Goodwood Nine Hours and the Tourist Trophy, but not before they had demonstrated their pace.

Quite a number were sold, including some abroad, but even though they did not score any important wins, they looked exciting and there was building up around Chapman and his crew a sense of excitement, of possibilities. Lotus attracted *fans*.

Though the Mk 6 remained in production, Chapman concentrated on just one new model for 1956, the Eleven. Its space-frame followed the principles of the Mk 9 but was lighter, front suspension remained by swing axles, and Frank Costin deisgned a new, neater, body and the car was available in three basic types.

The Eleven 'Sports' was fitted with an 1,172 cc Ford engine and 3-speed gearbox, live rear axle and drum brakes. It had a full-width windscreen and a hood could be specified. The 'Club' was similar but had a Coventry Climax FWA engine angled ten degrees from vertical, a 4-speed BMC gearbox with special ratios, and was intended as a road car-cum-occasional racer. For competition work there was the 'Le Mans' with Girling disc brakes, a de Dion back axle and the option of a flared headrest and wrap-around windscreen. Buyers had the choice of 1,100 cc (FWA) or 1,500 cc (FWB) Coventry Climax engines.

In terms of performance the first Eleven was not a big advance and a well-driven Mk 9 was not overshadowed by the newcomer, as Peter Ashdown demonstrated on many occasions, but Lotus had caught the imagination. The Eleven was not greatly superior to the 'bobtail' Cooper, but they finished up in the right hands and by sheer weight of numbers put Lotus ahead.

Chapman, himself a driver of quality, had a highly successful season, beating Mike Hawthorn in Ivor Bueb's Lotus on several occasions. A Lotus mechanic called Graham Hill was allowed a drive in April at Brands Hatch and he won the 1,200 cc race and finished second to Bicknell's larger-engined car in the 1,500 cc race, setting a new lap record in the process.

Bicknell finished third overall in the Oporto Cup in Portugal and at Rouen, in the Coupe Delamare Debouteville meeting against good opposition, Chapman won from Harry Schell, both in 1,500 cc Elevens, with Cliff Allison third and an easy winner of the 1,100 cc class. At Sables d'Olonne, David Piper and Bob Hicks scored a Lotus 1-2 in their private 1,100 cc cars.

Three cars were entered at Le Mans, two 1,100 cc versions and one with a s.o.h.c. Coventry Climax 1,500 cc unit. Two retired, but the third, driven by Reg Bicknell and Peter Jopp won the 1,100 cc class and finished fourth in the Index of Performance.

Late in the year, an 1,100 cc Eleven fitted with a bubble canopy went to Monza and came away with six International records and achieved a speed of 143 mph for a flying lap. During 1956 Elevens scored a total of 148 wins and the following March Chapman and his US importer, Jay Chamberlain, won the 1,100 cc class at Sebring.

Most Elevens were sold with Coventry Climax engines, but Mike Anthony fitted a 2-litre Bristol engine in one and Brian Naylor had a 1,500 cc Maserati unit in his. An 1,100 cc Stanguellini engine was imported for another car, but it was quickly discovered that Stanguellini's claimed power output erred on the side of the optimistic.

For 1957, the Eleven was given double wishbone front suspension and called 'Series Two'. A d.o.h.c. 1,500 cc Coventry Climax engine (FPF) was offered and Brian Naylor fitted a 2-litre Maserati engine into a new car.

The Lotus steamroller continued and the company established a virtual monopoly of the small-capacity classes. Mackay Fraser ran a works 1,500 cc car in the Spa sports car GP, winning his class by a full lap and finishing 7th overall while Naylor took the 2-litre class.

The highlight of Lotus's first ten years came at Le Mans. There three works cars were entered along with two privateers. Peter Ashdown and Alan Stacey were to drive an 1,100 cc car, but when the 1,500 cc twin cam (FPF) Climax engine of the Mackay Fraser/Jay Chamberlain entry dropped a valve in practice it was considered expedient for the two Americans to take over the 1,100 cc car.

Cliff Allison and Keith Hall's car had an experimental 750 cc (FWC) Climax engine in which the stroke had been reduced from 66 mm to 45 mm and here the intention was to try to beat the French Renault- and Panhard-based cars for the Index of Performance, though Coventry Climax held no great hopes for its reliability. Only one example of this little engine was made and its entire competition history was just three races, but it never missed a beat. Maximum output was 59 bhp at 8,000 rpm and there was little power below 6,000 rpm, but then that was not important at Le Mans.

The team cars all complied to the new Appendix C regulations which called for full-width windscreens and Costin designed these to curve back, which, in conjunction with a raised rear body panel, made the cars almost into coupés.

The four Elevens which started the race all performed impeccably. Allison and Hall brought the 750 cc car home first in class, first in the Index of Performance and 14th overall. Fraser and, Chamberlain won the 1,100 cc class, came second in the Index and finished ninth. The two private entries came home 14th and 16th overall, and second and fourth in the 1,100 cc class. It was a magnificent achievement and though Britain had plenty to cheer with Jaguars finishing 1, 2, 3, 4 and 6, the performance by Lotus was felt by many to be of equal merit.

After Le Mans Lotus returned to Rouen, where Allison easily won the 750 cc class and Ron Flockhart and Jay Chamberlain came first and second in the 1,500 cc race. The following weekend was the Reims 12 Hours, but Chamberlain crashed in practice and Allison had a brush with the law which landed him in clink and Chapman was so busy attending to the pair of them that the cars were not presented to the *parc fermé* in time and were disqualified.

Mackay Fraser drove a 1,500 cc Eleven in the following day's F2 race and was going well when he skidded on some oil, crashed, and died from his injuries.

Later in the season more records were attempted at Monza with the 750 cc car and an 1,100, both supercharged. Both engines suffered piston failure before serious work got under way.

Unchanged, the Eleven stayed in production until the end of 1958, adding many more hundreds of victories to its score. Team Lotus returned in force to Le Mans with four works cars backed up by two private entries, but the excursion was a disaster and only one finished, after spending a long time in a sand bank, and that was in 20th – and last – place. For Le Mans Lotus had two 750 cc cars both fitted with live rear axles to reduce friction loss, drum brakes and bolt-on alloy wheels. One had the FWC engine of the previous year (it was the car that finished) and one had a brand new Coventry Climax FWM s.o.h.c. engine,

enlarged from 650 cc to 742 cc, but it broke in practice and an FWA was substituted.

The Eleven perhaps won more races than any previous single model in the history of the sport and 156 were sold, 64 of them going to America. It was so firmly in control of the small-capacity classes there was no need to pursue development – until Eric Broadley's Lola appeared.

It is just as well that the Eleven could take care of itself, for other projects were taking Chapman's attention. During 1957 Lotus had introduced its Mk 12 front-engined F2 car, the Seven (a basic road/race car which continues in production to this day as the Caterham Super Seven), and the beautiful Elite with its fibreglass monocoque construction. Even then, Chapman was not finished, for nearing completion was the Lotus Fifteen.

In 1952 Coventry Climax began work on a 2½ litre V-8 engine for the Formula One which was to begin two years later. Connaught, Kieft, H.W.M. and Cooper all expressed interest in the unit and Kieft actually built a car for it, while Connaught was in the process of making a revolutionary rear-engined monocoque design, but Climax never released the engine. The company unfortunately believed the exaggerated power claims of the continental opposition and did not believe its FPE (Fire Pump Engine – a deliberate smokescreen) would be competitive. It was not until some time later that Climax learned its engine was at least as powerful as the best opposition and had a wider usable rev band. In test conditions it was reliable too.

Taking one bank of cylinders from the FPE, Climax made the FPF 1,475 cc (81.27 × 71.7 mm) 4-cylinder engine which produced 142 bhp and could be stretched to two litres. To accommodate this engine Chapman designed the Fifteen, which looked like an overweight Eleven. Frank Costin had become a freelance, severing his links with Lotus, and it was Charlie Williams of the body makers Williams and Pritchard who was responsible for the shape.

The space-frame followed established Lotus practice but was larger overall than the Eleven with a roomier cockpit, front suspension remained coil spring

143

and double wishbone but the independent rear springing was by 'Chapman struts' as used on the F2 car and the Elite. These were an adaptation of the Mc-Pherson strut and consisted of a long coil spring/damper unit and a lower wishbone, with the unsplined drive shafts giving lateral location.

Bolt-on alloy wheels were normally fitted, but knock-off wires were substituted for endurance races. On the works cars, and the first ones supplied to customers, a 5-speed gearbox designed for the F2 car by Colin Chapman and Harry Munday was fitted. This had ZF internals and a limited slip differential in unit and was located at the rear. Until he went off to found Cosworth with Mike Costin, Keith Duckworth's main occupation at Lotus was looking after these gearboxes.

In order to achieve a low bonnet line, the engine was canted over to the right, but their arrangement had to be revised early in the car's career. A Series Two version followed within months and this had an upright engine and conventionally mounted 4-speed BMC gearbox to make life easier for privateers, particularly those abroad.

The International racing career of the Fifteen was spasmodic and unsuccessful. A 2-litre version ran at Le Mans in 1958 and, though quick, lasted just three laps. They won a number of National and club events in Britain and elsewhere but cannot be regarded as a success. A revised version was made for 1959, with a stiffer frame and modified front suspension, but the rear-engined Cooper Monaco, based on Cooper's F1 car, came out in 1959 and was superior. Lotus followed suit the following year and made its own rear-engined sports car, the Mk 19.

While the Eleven had continued to carry all before it in 1958, the appearance of Eric Broadley's Lola Mk I gave warning that its days were numbered. In the few races in which the Lola competed it was so clearly superior to anything in the 1,100 cc class that an answer was required, especially since Broadley had a queue of drivers waving cheques at him.

Chapman's response, the Seventeen, was inadequate. While the Fifteen had not been a great success, the Seventeen was a disaster and it was the first hiccup in the Lotus success story so far as sports cars were concerned. The Seventeen was a Chapman concept drawn by Len Terry and was a smaller, lighter, version of the Eleven with a body which betrayed its ancestry. The problem was the front suspension, an adaptation of the 'Chapman strut'. When cornering hard it would flex, giving massive oversteer until enough speed was scrubbed off to release the front strut, whereupon the car went into understeer.

By the time the front suspension was modified Lola had control of the 1,100 cc class. Two Seventeens fitted with 742 cc Climax FWM engines ran at Le Mans in 1959, proving the fastest cars in their class ever to run there, but distributor trouble caused overheating and retirement in both cases. In the same race were two works Fifteens, a 2-litre car and one with a 2½-litre FPF engine developed for F1. Both retired.

Lotus's troubled F1 programme with the front-engined 16 was absorbing a great deal of energy as were the problems of putting the Elite into production (an Elite won the 1,500 cc class at Le Mans in 1959). It was beginning to look as though Chapman had lost his way through trying to fight on too many fronts but in the background was a new series of rear-engined sports and formula cars which were to revive Lotus's fortunes and change the face of International motor racing.

Strictly speaking, within the parameters of this book, Lotus deserves only a short entry because as a maker of classic sports-racing cars competing at an Inter-

national level its total achievement amounts to a few small-capacity, hence minor, class wins.

The achievement of Lotus and Chapman in our period was not to win races but to change the face of the motor racing industry and to lay down the bases of its future. D.B. Frazer Nash, OSCA, and any number of firms which were quantitatively more successful than Lotus in International racing in the Fifties are now only names and the subject for articles in the 'old car' press, but Lotus is still winning Grands Prix and, despite Chapman's death, winning them using the sort of innovative design techniques, such as computer-controlled 'active' suspension, of which he would have approved. Indeed, Chapman instigated the research programme which developed active suspension, so his influence is still with us.

Maserati

In the late 19th century there were born in Voghera, south of Milan, six brothers: Carlo, Bindo, Alfiero, Mario, Ettore and Ernesto Maserati. With the exception of Mario, who became a painter, all were to be associated with motor cars and motor racing.

The eldest brother, Carlo, designed and built a motor cycle as early as 1897 and this attracted patronage. These machines were sold and raced under the patron's name, 'Carcano', with Carlo himself winning several important events on them. He later worked for several car companies as a driver and engineer but tragically died in 1910.

Alfieri and Ettore spent some time in Argentina working in a subsidary of Isotta Fraschini and there they built a special based on Isotta components which they raced. During World War I the two brothers were home again and they and Bindo worked for Isotta on aero engines. In his spare time Alfieri designed a new type of sparking plug which he put into production in his Bologna workshop and this side-line became a prosperous business.

Once peace returned Alfieri was able to indulge his passion for motor racing and, building up an Isotta special, won several important races and hill-climbs. This led to Diatto, a company which built uninspired touring cars, approaching him to build a Diatto special in 1922. Once again, Alfieri's skill as an engineer and driver led to numerous successes, and a second Diatto special which performed as well as the first.

So impressed was Diatto with the transformation Alfieri was able to wring from its road cars that it commissioned him to start with a clean sheet of paper and design a new GP car. The result was a supercharged 2-litre straight-eight which was finished just in time for the 1925 Italian GP, where it retired.

Unfortunately Diatto was in financial difficulties and decided to withdraw from racing. Alfieri took over the GP project, converted the engine to 1,500 cc (supercharged) to comply with new GP regulations and in 1926 formed Officine Alfieri Maserati SpA Bologna. Maserati cars were not an instant success but began to make a significant mark from 1929. Both Alfieri and Ernesto regularly drove works cars in the early days, but from 1931 on were content to leave the driving to others. Then, in 1932, tragedy struck when Alfieri had to have an operation from which he did not recover.

Mille Miglia, 1954: Luigi Musso's Maserati A6GCS at the Ravenna control on his way to third overall.

In Ernesto, however, there was a worthy successor as chief designer and the firm went from strength to strength until, in 1938, the brothers were persuaded by Commendatore Adolfo Orsi, a wealthy industrialist, to sell the company. Orsi was particularly interested in buying the successful sparking plug business, but also realized that the racing car company could be a prestigious flagship to his industrial combine. As part of the deal the brothers were retained on a ten-year contract, though the company was run by Orsi's son, Omer.

Up to the outbreak of World War II, all Maseratis had been racing cars, though until 1932 these had two seats, for riding mechanics were carried, and some were also raced in sports form. In the period between the end of the war and the brothers' contract expiring, Ernesto created his first bespoke sports car, the Tipo A6. Its straight-six s.o.h.c. 1,488 cc (66 × 72.5 mm) engine was similar to the pre-war Tipo 6CM Voiturette motor. With a single twin-choke Weber carburettor it initially gave 65 bhp and was fitted in a ladder-frame with two large-diameter side members. Front suspension was by coil springs and unequal wishbones and the live rear axle was suspended on coil springs.

It first appeared at the 1947 Geneva Show with a simple, clean, coupé body by Pininfarina and a few months later made its competition debut, as the Tipo A6G (G = Ghersa or iron block), in the Mille Miglia. By this time it had an enlarged engine of 1,954 cc (72 × 80 mm) which gave 90 bhp, but Luigi Villoresi was forced to retire with a bearing failure. Some of these cars began to appear in Italian national events, scoring some wins, and at the end of September came the new A6GCS (C = Corsa, S = Sport).

Power had been increased to 125 bhp and lightweight cycle-wing bodies with a single central headlight were fitted to a shortened, stiffened, chassis. In place of the previous coil spring rear suspension, the live axle was spring on semi-elliptics with single trailing arms. Driven by Ascari and Villoresi they were holding first and second in the Circuit of Modena when the race was stopped because of an

Brian Naylor and his Tipo 150S at Silverstone, May 1956. The car proved no match for Coopers and Lotuses and the engine was transferred to a Lotus Eleven. (T.C. March)

accident. Both men drove the cars in the Turin GP a fortnight later but retired with broken gearboxes.

The following year the cars made a handful of appearances. Ascari, Amendola and Capelli drove them in the Mille Miglia, but all retired. Bracco and Villoresi scored a 1-2 in the Dolmite Gold Cup and Villoresi retired from the Coupe des Petites Cylindreés at Reims when fighting for the lead. Bracco also scored a number of wins in hill-climbs. At the end of 1948, although the design was promising, it was put on ice for several years, but private owners continued to race the existing cars.

Sixty A6 coupés were made up to the end of 1950, and a further 16 2-litre s.o.h.c. versions were made in 1951–53, but so far as competition was concerned, Maserati concentrated on single-seaters which were sold to privateers. With drivers of the calibre of Fangio, Ascari, Farina, Bira, Villoresi, Parnell and de Graffenried they took many wins especially in the period to the end of 1949. It was not until 1953 that the works again ran a team.

One of the reasons for the sudden gap in the history of the competition sports cars was that the three remaining Maserati brothers ended their contract in late 1947. Apparently they were not asked to renew and they made no efforts to continue the arrangement, but, instead, decamped to Bologna to found a new company, OSCA.

In 1951 the A6 engine was revived to be the basis of a new F2 car, the A6GCM, which was to be driven by, among others, Fangio and Gonzalez. There were extensive changes, for a start the old iron block was recast in light alloy and a new twin-plug d.o.h.c. cylinder head was made. 'Over-square' cylinder dimensions of 76.5 × 72 mm gave a total capacity of 1,985 cc. With three twin-choke Weber carburettors, the engine gave 177 bhp in F2 form (on an alcohol brew) and 165 bhp in sports trim.

The chassis was again a ladder-frame, with large-diameter main tubes, which pinched in at the rear and swept up over the live rear axle which was sprung on ¼-elliptics with hydraulic shock absorbers, radius rods, an A-bracket, and an anti-roll bar. Front suspension followed the earlier layout with unequal wishbones and coil springs, hydraulic shockers and an anti-roll bar. A tubular body frame was welded to the chassis and a graceful enveloping body shell built by Maserati's own Medardo Fantuzzi completed the car.

The first A6GCS was completed in 1952, but this was an interim car with a 'square' engine (75 × 75 mm) producing 140 bhp, semi-elliptical rear springs, and a cycle-wing body. It was sold to a Dutchman resident in the States who enjoyed some success with it. So far as the works was concerned, the first race was the 1953 Mille Miglia with three team cars driven by Musso, Mantovani and Giletti.

Musso led his class until crashing, but Giletti came in sixth overall and Sergio Mantovani tenth, the two cars finishing first and second in the 2,000 cc class. In the Targa Florio, Emilio Giletti finished second to Maglioli's Lancia with the Mantovani/Fangio car third. Some fine results in other Italian events followed and in August the team ventured abroad with the cars for the first time with a three-car entry in the Nürburgring 1,000 Km.

This time the cars had new Vignale bodies, but it was not a successful race. The Lang/Bertoni car expired with engine trouble, Herrmann/McAfee were disqualified for using a spare not carried on the car while Giletti/Marimon were leading their class with four miles to go when their engine broke. Back in Italy Mantovani finished second to Fangio's Alfa Romeo in the Supercortemaggiore GP.

Stirling Moss in a works Maserati 300S on his way to victory in the Sports Car race at Silverstone, July 1956. (LAT)

Meanwhile cars had been delivered to private owners and in Britain Roy Salvadori was successful in Sid Greene's Gilby Engineering car until Archie Scott-Brown's Lister-Bristol appeared in mid-1954. At the end of the year, Baron de Graffenried took his example to Brazil and won the Rio de Janeiro and São Paulo Grands Prix.

With the works concentrating most of its attention on F1, appearances of the sports car in 1954 tended to be infrequent. Giletti and Musso had a car for the Buenos Aires 1,000 Km, were outclassed by the opposition, and finished sixth. A single car was also entered at Sebring for Musso and Gatta, but it was never in the running and retired with brake failure.

Three cars were entered for the Mille Miglia for Musso, Venezian and Mantovani and while Venezian's was a standard A6GCS, Musso had an all-synchromesh (Porsche-type) gearbox on his and Mantovani's was fitted with an F1 2,493 cc engine and was designated 250S. The Mantovani car did not last long, but Musso had a race-long duel with Vittorio Marzotto's new 2-litre Ferrari Mondial, which he lost by just nine seconds. Still, he finished third overall, with Venezian fifth after a shunt, and a few weeks later in the Targa Florio, Musso came a good second to Taruffi's Lancia D24.

At Le Mans 'Fon' de Portago and Carlos Tomasi shared a car which was outpaced by the Bristol 450s let alone the 4.9 Ferraris and Jaguar D-types and it retired at about half-time with no oil pressure.

Three works cars entered the Tourist Trophy and were joined by Sid Greene's car for Cliff Davis and Horace Gould. Only one finished, that of Musso and Mantovani, and it came in a fine third on handicap (with the fifth highest race average). Works and private cars also appeared in lesser races during 1954 but the only victory was Musso's win in the Naples GP.

At the end of the year a road-going coupé version, the A6G2000 'Mille Miglia' was exhibited at the Paris Salon apparently with the intention of series production, but it did not get beyond the prototype stage. While A6GCSs had been popular with privateers and had turned in some respectable performances, they were always handicapped by lack of cubic capacity and so for 1955 Maserati created the Tipo 300S though they continued to run A6GCS models in selected races for some time afterwards.

It was virtually a sports-racing version of Giaocchino Colombo's 250F F1 car, but since Colombo had left at the end of 1953 to design Bugatti's abortive F1 car, the work was undertaken by Vittorio Bellentani. The engine had a capacity of 2,993 cc (84 × 90 mm) and a *claimed* output of 250 bhp and was fitted to a

chassis which closely followed the 250F. It had a ladder-frame with large-diameter main tubes, coil spring and unequal wishbone front suspension and, at the rear, a de Dion axle with a transverse leaf spring. Like its sister car, the 300S had a wonderful reputation for road-holding and its drivers remember it with the utmost affection. One thing it lacked throughout its life, however, was sheer horse power, for it could not be safely increased a great deal beyond 3 litres.

There was one other similarity to the 250F, its looks. Just as the F1 car has come to epitomize the style of F1 cars in the Fifties, so the 300S is the essence of sports-racing cars of the period. Its lines were beautifully balanced and were clearly aerodynamically efficient. Its looks did not flatter the car for it was one of the sweetest-handling of its time.

For Maserati, 1955 started well with the private A6GCS of Grandio and Faraoni finishing third in the Buenos Aires 1,000 Km behind two Ferraris with more than twice the engine size. On 13 March, the 300S debuted in two races, Jean Behra driving a works car in the Dakar GP (he led but retired with transmission troubles) while at Sebring Briggs Cunningham had what was really a works entry for Valenzano and Perdisa, and Bill Spear entered his car for himself and Sherwood Johnston. Both cars were impressively reliable, but outclassed for sheer speed, and Spear's finished third with the Cunningham car fourth.

Cesare Perdisa was entered in a single works car in the Mille Miglia and at one point held third before retiring with engine trouble. Grandio, however, brought one of the older cars home fourth, winning the 2-litre class, and his has been called one of the finest individual drives in the race. Two weeks later in the Bari GP Behra gave the 300S its first win, after Taruffi's Ferrari retired, and followed that with victory (with Musso) in the Supercortemaggiore GP at Monza after a fierce duel with the Hawthorn/Maglioli Ferrari 750S.

At Le Mans, however, both the works cars retired with transmission troubles, but even when they ran they were a long way off the pace. On the Mulsanne they were touching a shade under 154 mph, which compares to: Mercedes-Benz 168 mph, Jaguar 175 mph, 4.4 Ferrari 181 mph. They were, however, quicker than the 3-litre Aston Martin DB3S.

At the end of August, a new Maserati appeared at the Nürburgring 500 Km for 1,500 cc cars. This was the 150S and was in essence a shrunk 300S, though the de Dion tube was located by a central slide and vane-type shock absorbers replaced the 300S's hydraulic units. Its engine was virtually a 4-cylinder version of the 250F with a capacity of 1,484 cc (81 × 72 mm) and with its 'over-square' dimensions would rev up to 8,500 rpm, though maximum power (a claimed 135 bhp) was achieved at 8,000 rpm.

Maserati always had a policy of selling to privateers, and had identified the 1½-litre class as one in which it could make inroads. Behra performed sensationally with the little car, dominating practice and, after a slow start in the race, winning by over two minutes. The quality of every win is created by the opposition, and on this occasion Maserati had the strongest possible competition, which included not only works Porsches but the strong A.W.E. (E.M.W.) team from East Germany.

It was the only time in 1955 that the car raced and it flattered to deceive. In general it was not reliable enough to compete with Porsche in endurance events and in sprint races it proved too heavy to be competitive with the Coopers and Lotuses which were being sold in large numbers, particularly in America.

In the Tourist Trophy, the 300S was outclassed by the Mercedes-Benz and Jaguar teams and it proved an unhappy time. Behra crashed heavily, injured his arms badly and lost part of an ear. The second car finished a lacklustre fifth.

To complete its line-up, Maserati introduced the 200S at the last round of the WSCC, the Targa Florio. This was essentially a 150S with an enlarged engine of 1,992 cc (92 × 75 mm) which gave a claimed 175 bhp and drove through a 5-speed gearbox. It was a better car for its class than the 150S was in its and was generally thought superior to the Ferrari Tipo 500 Mondial, which caused Ferrari to introduce the Tipo 500 Testa Rossa. The works car crashed in both practice and the race while the private entry of Tony Parravano broke an oil pipe and ran its bearings. The 2-litre class was won by Giuseppe Musso (Luigi's younger brother), partnered by Rossi, in a A6GCS.

That November was held the first Venezuelan GP, which attracted works cars

from Ferrari and Maserati, and Fangio emerged a clear winner, by two laps, in his 300S.

The beginning of 1956 saw Maserati in good shape with Stirling Moss on the strength and a fair number of cars in private hands. Bellentani had moved to Ferrari and his place was taken by Giulio Alfieri, his former assistant. Alfieri was a designer of great imagination and depth who could turn his attention to any part of a car. With his later 'Birdcage' designs, he demonstrated a flair for those two most un-Italian design areas, chassis frames and aerodynamics, and it was Alfieri who laid down the design for the 3500GT which made Maserati a serious competitor to Ferrari in the production of road-going GT cars.

The cars that had gone to Venezuela stayed in South America and appeared in the Buenos Aires 1,000 Km in January 1956. There Moss and Carlos Menditeguy chased the 4.9 Ferraris until both retired with transmission troubles and stroked home to a clear win with the Gendebien/Hill 3.5 Ferrari two laps behind and Behra/Gonzalez third in a second 300S. It was Maserati's first WSCC victory.

At Sebring Menditeguy crashed one of the cars heavily, which kept him out of racing for the rest of the year, while Behra and Taruffi brought the other home a poor fifth. After so promising a start to the year it was a disappointing result, but Maserati was concentrating its best efforts on the Mille Miglia. In this it had its distractions, for the F1 team was taking a lot of attention and there were customer orders to fulfil, especially for the 150S. As if all that were not enough, there was a new engine under development.

As before this was a straight-six but had a capacity of 3,485 cc (86 × 100 mm) and was said to produce 270 bhp. It was not merely an extended 250F unit, for most of its components were new, and among other features it had step-down gears behind the clutch to lower the power line. While the lay-out followed the broad lines of the 300S, the frame itself marked a new departure for the team, being a multi-tubed space-frame, and there was a new rear suspension layout. It was still a de Dion system but located more precisely. Unfortunately it worked too well and showed up the inadequacies of the front suspension.

Worse, the front of the car tended to lift at speed and even the addition of a rudimentary front spoiler failed to cure it. Moss drove it in the Mille Miglia and he was holding sixth when, in heavy rain, the front wheels lost adhesion and he and Denis Jenkinson, his navigator, went over the side of a mountain but were fortunately saved by crashing into a tree. Neither of the works 300Ss finished.

In the later Reims 12 Hours race Umberto Maglioli drove a 350S, but when the rain came it proved so unstable it had to be withdrawn. Maglioli was a fine driver and Reims a relatively easy circuit so what it had been like for Moss in the Mille Miglia in the wet defies imagination. When Maserati conducted a back-to-back test with a 300S at Imola, the 350S proved slower by five seconds a lap. One was later fitted with 3- and 3½-litre versions of Maserati's F1 V-12 engine, but it was a brief flirtation.

A trio of 3-litre cars were entered in the Nürburgring 1,000 Km and against the strongest possible field, Moss built up a 25-second lead before handing over to Behra. The Frenchman was not long into his stint when the rear transverse leaf spring came away from its mounting. The Schell/Taruffi car, lying in third place, was called in by team manager Nello Ugolini and Behra moved it up to second before handing back to Moss, who rejoined the race 66 seconds behind Fangio's Ferrari.

Moss bit into the World Champion's lead at the rate of six seconds a lap and won by 26 seconds. It was one of many instances when Moss flattered the performance of a car; he did the same for Aston Martin and Porsche, and it is no coincidence that he shared the driving on the two occasions when a Maserati 300S won a WSCC event.

Taruffi brought a 300S home second to Maglioli's Porsche in the Targa Florio, but the fact that he was beaten by a car half the size did not reflect well on either car or driver and, worse, it would have been third except that Giulio Cabianca's 1,500 cc OSCA was disqualified on a technicality.

The Swiss privateer Benoit Musy, won the Grand Prix des Frontières and at les Sables d'Olonne in his private 300S and in the Bari GP Moss led throughout in a works example with Behra and Perdisa finishing second and third in their 200S models having already won the 2-litre race. These minor wins, welcome though they were, could not disguise the fact that Maserati desperately needed a bigger car, but work had long been in hand on the 4½-litre V-8 450S which first appeared in practice for the Swedish GP, the final round of the WSCC.

Maserati missed Le Mans, which had imposed a 2½-litre limit on prototypes, but were represented by two Maserati-powered Lago-Talbots, neither of which finished. In Sweden the team was a shambles, the pit stops were botched, and none of the cars finished.

The season ended on a mixture of tragedy and some good results. Musy crashed his new 200S at Monthléry and died. Behra and Schell scored a 1-2 in the Rome GP but the win was marred by an accident involving Villoresi which ended

153

his career. In the second Venezuelan GP Moss's 300S beat Fangio's Ferrari to win and repeated it in the Nassau Trophy against good opposition and, finally, in the Australian Tourist Trophy, Moss and Behra scored an easy 1-2.

At the beginning of 1955 Vittorio Bellentini and his engine designer, Guido Taddeucci, had laid down a 4½-litre d.o.h.c. V-8 engine, but work progressed slowly for it was initially only an alternative to the 3.5-litre straight-six. Then Tony Parravano approached the company for a 4.2-litre engine for Indianapolis. It was opportune so far as funding was concerned and also appealed to Maserati's sense of history, for a Maserati first ran at Indy in 1930 and won the race in 1939, 1940 and 1946.

When it emerged the engine had a capacity of 4,478 cc (93.8 × 81 mm) and with four twin-choked downdraught Webers and two plugs per cylinder, it produced so much power that the factory's 400 bhp dynamometer could not record it all. When it first ran in practice for the Swedish GP it was fitted into one of the 350S chassis and although the Tipo 54 450S series of cars retained that same basic layout, everything was beefed-up, the drum brakes massively increased, the suspension improved and transmission was via a 5-speed transaxle.

Parravano received the first new car, together with his two Indy engines, but he received a financial reverse and Ray Martinez took over his car. Fangio and Moss shared the driving on the model's debut in the 1957 Buenos Aires 1,000 Km and they led easily until the clutch went. The Behra/Menditeguy 300S was then brought in for Moss to take over and he set fastest lap on his way to second place behind a 3.5 Ferrari.

At Sebring Fangio teamed with Behra in the 450S and won easily from Moss/Schell in a 300S. After two rounds Maserati thus led the WSCC and had high hopes of winning its first Mille Miglia. On a practice run Behra's car was involved in a collision with a lorry, so both car and driver were out, but the team expected Moss to walk the race. His car was fitted with a 2-speed overdrive unit thus giving two sets of five ratios and it blasted away – for four miles. Then at 130 mph and approaching an 80 mph corner Moss had to put the car in a slide for the brake pedal had snapped off. Since 1957 was to be the last Mille Miglia following de Portago's fatal crash, Maserati was destined never to win the race it coveted above all others.

Two 450Ss were entered for the Nürburgring 1,000 Km and Fangio was sensational in practice. At the start Moss was slow away but soon took the lead, setting fastest lap in the process, but before he could hand over to Fangio a rear hub shaft broke. The other car, of Schell/Herrmann, ran third until its oil tank broke loose.

While driving for the Vanwall F1 team in 1957, Moss had become a great admirer of Frank Costin's aerodynamic work and persuaded Maserati to commission a coupé body from Costin for Le Mans. The shell was farmed out to Zagato, which made a complete mess of it. They reversed ducts so that instead of cool air coming into the car, the drivers got hot air from the engine bay; a hole for the radiator cap was cut in the nose, destroying the air flow; the wrong type of windscreen wiper was used and it blew off; the careful pressure area over the carburettors was altered and starved the engine of air, and, to cap it all, Zagato did not bother to fit the full-length undertray. Aerodynamics were not the Italians' strong suit. Costin took one look at the beast at Le Mans and disappeared into the nearest beer tent.

Moss ran second in the coupé until a universal joint seized on a half-shaft. André Simon in the open car led until the same thing happened and the third car, a 300S, had its clutch explode early in the race. Maserati had to win both remaining rounds, in Sweden and Venezuela, to win the Championship.

Moss and Behra obliged in Sweden while Schell's car retired with another UJ failure. Three 450Ss arrived in Caracas for the final round, two entered by the works, the third by Temple Buell, an American who was to run 250Fs in the 1958 F1 World Championship. The Championship was at stake and Ferrari arrived in force.

The race was to be the biggest disaster Maserati had ever had. On lap two Masten Gregory rolled the Temple Buell car. Moss led until a backmarker pulled across his bows and he was out in the resulting collision. Then Behra's car caught fire in the pits; it was quickly doused but Behra was burned. Moss and Schell took the singed car over and drove it back into contention. Schell was about to overtake Bonnier's 300S when it shed a wheel and slewed into the bigger car, which hit a wall and burst into flames, while Bonnier's car hit a lamp post. Ferraris finished in the first four places and took the Championship back to Maranello as a consolation prize for being completely outclassed in F1 by Maserati.

Maserati, however, was in a crisis. Although the sports cars had ultimately failed in 1957, Fangio had won the F1 World Championship at the wheel of a 250F, but it was clear the car had reached the end of its development and had already been made obsolete by Vanwall, which won three of the last four races. Its parent company had extensive trading interests with Argentina, but following the overthrow of Juan Perón had a lot of unpaid debts on its hands. Development costs of the V-12 F1 engine and the V-8 sports car engine had been heavy and at the end of 1957 sports car racing was restricted to 3-litre cars.

It was decided to close down the racing department but to continue work on customer cars. Simultaneously Maserati began to press harder in the production car market with its 3500 GT series derived from the 6-cylinder racing engine. Eventually, of course, it would make a production version of the big V-8.

1958 saw all the remaining 450Ss going to America, which was the only place for them, and while 300Ss still appeared in WSCC races, they did not distinguish themselves, being private entries and well past their prime. Maserati had a quiet year while its finances and those of the parent Orsi group were eased back from the edge of bankruptcy and sales of the 3500 GT started to generate some cash.

One result of the team going into suspended animation was that Valerio Colotti, who had been Maserati's engineer in charge of transmissions, left to set up his own business, Studio Tecnica Meccanica. From Colotti's studio came the 250F-based 'Tec-Mec' F1 car and, of course, the Colotti racing transmissions.

As things began to improve, Alfieri was allowed to begin work on a new design with the intention of building examples for customers. He chose as his starting point the components of the ill-starred 200S and, since money was tight, had to use a front-engined layout, though he would have preferred a rear location. He opted for the proven suspension of the 250F together with its 5-speed transaxle and, for the first time, disc brakes, which were by Maserati out of Girling. To produce a low bonnet line the engine was canted over at 45 degrees and in order to make the engine run more smoothly it was given a slightly larger bore and shorter stroke and, to allow it to be canted, the cylinder head was extensively redesigned. Eventually an output of 200 bhp would be claimed for this engine and since the car complete weighed just 1,100 lb it was a highly competitive package.

It was the chassis which caught the attention, however, it being a complex space-frame made up of over 200 small-gauge chrome-molybdenum tubes and this led it to be given several nicknames, but the one that stuck was 'Birdcage'.

Alfieri had taken note of the handling qualities of the Lotus Eleven and Maserati had even bought one for evaluation. At race meetings he had, too, discussed chassis design with Colin Chapman. His original intention had been to build a monocoque car, but he felt there was insufficient local expertise to build one. Most observers felt that Alfieri could have achieved the lightness and rigidity he desired with a less complicated design.

Stirling Moss drove the prototype in May 1959, enthused over it and suggested some detail modifications and later gave it a proper shake-down at the Nürburgring during practice for the 1,000 Km where he lapped under the 2-litre class record. Moss then gave the Tipo 60 its racing debut in the sports car race preceding the Rouen F2 race and, against strong works Lotus opposition, cantered home an easy winner.

Quite apart from the fact that the car had a power advantage, it also possessed outstanding road-holding and, unusually for a Maserati, excellent brakes. Its drivers were to describe it as the best handling car of its time.

The car impressed, but pressure came from America to build a 3-litre version and Alfieri set to work on enlarging the 250S unit, which was itself a development of the 200S. It was no easy matter, but eventually he came up with an engine of 2,890 cc (100 × 92 mm) which gave 250 bhp at 6,500 rpm. This was less than hoped, but since the car would still be lighter than the opposition, it would be competitive.

An initial batch of six Tipo 60s had been laid down, but these were now to be made up as 3-litre Tipo 61s and all had customers waiting for them, as did most of the second batch of six, and this before the 3-litre car had even turned a wheel.

In America, a fast talking wheeler-dealer, Lloyd 'Lucky' Casner, had been floating the idea of an American team which would take on the world in both sports cars and F1. His plans were grandiose particularly since he had no great financial resources himself, but he believed in his dream and plugged away. When he heard that the Goodyear tyre company was thinking of entering racing, which in the States was then dominated by Firestone, he sold it on the idea of sponsoring a WSCC team. Having got the backing he went to Maserati to buy three cars, was told they were all spoken for but that he might get one in the spring of 1960. This was a spanner in the works, but he was able to persuade

Maserati to convert a Tipo 60 to 3-litre specification for his Camoradi USA team. Another part of the deal was that Camoradi was to be, in effect, the Maserati works team.

With Aston Martin withdrawing, and Dan Gurney having quit Ferrari over a pay dispute, there were some fine drivers on the market and so with a superb car, sound backing and a first-rate driver line-up Camoradi started 1960 in a strong position. The single car was sent to the Buenos Aires 1,000 Km for Gurney and Gregory, and Gurney built up a good lead by the time he handed the car over to his co-driver.

Gregory continued to increase it until a rear shock absorber came adrift, which slowed him, and when later the crown wheel and pinion started to break up the car retired. A second Tipo 61 was soon delivered and Moss was entered in the non-Championship Cuban GP, where he scored a runaway win.

For Sebring Camoradi was up to three cars and Maserati's representation was strengthened by the appearance of some of the cars bought for US racing. One of the Camoradi cars blew up in practice and one blew up in the race after two laps. The third car, driven by Moss and Gurney, sailed into a commanding lead until, after eight hours, the crown wheel and pinion suddenly broke.

A single car was entered for the Targa Florio for Umberto Maglioli and Nino Vaccarella. At three-quarters distance they had a five-minute lead over the Bonnier/Herrmann Porsche, but a rock had pierced the fuel tank and Vaccarella suddenly found himself without power as he entered a corner and he finished in a ditch. 'Lucky' Casner was belying his nickname for his cars had led three WSCC races and on each occasion had failed to finish.

Piero Taruffi was engaged as team manager for the Nürburgring 1,000 Km and this gave everyone confidence. In practice both team cars suffered broken oil pipes, but this appeared to have been fixed for the race. By the time he handed over to Gurney, Moss had built up a two-minute lead, but three laps into his stint Gurney arrived at the pits covered in oil; another pipe had broken. Fortunately the engine was undamaged and he rejoined after a five-minute pit stop but half a lap behind the leader. Driving brilliantly in atrocious conditions, Gurney sliced away the deficit at a rate of 30 seconds a lap, but a slow pit stop meant Moss restarted in third place.

Moss was equal to the challenge, retook the lead, pulled away and set fastest lap to complete a personal hat-trick of wins in the race and give Camoradi its first major victory. Masten Gregory and Gino Munaron in the second car trailed in fifth.

Le Mans was the final round of the WSCC and three Camoradi cars were entered though the driver line-up was not as distinguished as previously – it appears that Casner and his drivers did not see eye to eye on fees. One of the cars, the one which crashed in the Targa Florio, had been re-built with an new aerodynamic body designed by Alfieri. While retaining the Birdcage's excellent handling, it was dramatically quick in a straight line and was timed on the Mulsanne Straight at 169 mph, faster than any previous 3-litre car at Le Mans.

Masten Gregory and Chuck Daigh had the 'streamliner' and Gregory set a cracking pace in the early stages, but on handing over, the starter motor refused to turn and an hour was lost replacing it. Daigh rejoined the race in last place. Then the car of Gino Munaron/Giorgio Scarlatti stopped, apparently on fire. When he investigated, Munaron discovered the starter motor had burned out, and since he could not restart the car it was abandoned.

The third car, driven by 'Lucky' Casner and Jim Jeffords, was called in and the starter changed as a precaution. On examining the replaced unit it was discovered that, like the others, the armature wire had been pulled too tightly in manufacture and had broken. Later Casner stuffed the car into a sand bank and sand got into the gear linkage causing the car's retirement.

Meanwhile Gregory and Daigh were going at a cracking pace and unlapping themselves at such a rate victory was still a possibility until, just before midnight, the rear wheels broke loose and the engine over-revved and popped.

Camoradi had begun the year in a strong position, but a combination of inexperience and Maserati's own errors had seen the effort finish with just the Cuban GP and Nürburgring 1,000 Km on the score board. It was not Casner's fault that he had been supplied with a batch of duff starter motors for Le Mans but some of the establishment were pleased to see the brash newcomer fall flat on his face.

Apart from its works-backed team's failure at the highest level, Maserati could be pleased with its car. By the end of 1960, 22 cars had been built of which five were 2-litre Tipo 60s and 16 Tipo 61s and there had also been the Tipo 60/61 supplied to Casner. Most of them went to America, where they scored many wins in SCCA racing and demonstrated that they were the outstanding 3-litre car of their day. Four Tipo 60s were sold in Italy and their drivers were repaid with equal success in races and hill-climbs.

Alfieri meanwhile received the green light to design the car he had wanted to all along, the Tipo 63. This was a rear-engined 'Birdcage' with independent rear suspension by coil springs and wishbones. Several versions of the 4-cylinder engine were used with different bore/stroke dimensions (70 × 64 mm, 75 × 56 mm, and 68 × 68 mm) and sometimes the cars were also run with a 2.9-litre development of the old F1 V-12 engine. Camoradi and Cunningham each bought Tipo 63s, as did Count Volpi's Scuderia Sernissima, but from the beginning these cars were dogged by ill-handling and were unreliable to boot.

The rear-engined Tipo 63 was the Tipo 61's successor and this developed example appeared in the 1962 Targa Florio as a Tipo 64 entered by the Scuderia Republica di Venezia for Colin Davis and Carlo Abate.

Sebring opened the 1961 WSCC and six Maseratis were entered, but only the 2-litre Tipo 60 of Briggs Cunningham and Bill Kimberley lasted to the end, in 11th place. They suffered broken engines, broken suspension and broken exhaust pipes. For Casner, Sebring spelt the end of a dream, for his sponsors were unimpressed by the cars' performance and withdrew support. The problem with the exhaust system was known and easily cured, but Casner had not got around to doing anything about it. Casner was in deep financial trouble and owed Maserati money, but the works did a deal whereby the Tipo 63 was returned and he kept the older car.

In the Targa Florio, three Maseratis were entered but were outpaced by the Ferraris and Porsches though the Scuderia Serenissima Tipo 63s of Vacarella/Trintignant and Maglioli/Scarlatti finished fourth and fifth.

Casner was really down on his luck and was in the process of cancelling his entry for the Nürburgring 1,000 Km, but on the strength of the previous year's win was able to put together a deal to finance his rather scruffy Tipo 61. Again the race was dogged by rain, but Masten Gregory had the car in third place when Casner took over. Then Moss's Porsche in second place had its engine seize and shortly afterwards the leading Ferrari crashed.

The Maserati was in the lead, but the little team had no spares and Gregory completed the race with his rear tyres dangerously worn, so much so that one exploded later in the paddock while the car was parked. With little more than a spare set of sparking plugs, Casner took the car to the Rouen Four Hours race and won.

Only one car, Briggs Cunningham's Tipo 60, turned out for Le Mans and it ran faultlessly to give the patron and Bill Kimberley eighth overall and third in class. In the final round of the WSCC, the Pescara Four Hours race, Casner nearly pulled of his second major win of the year. After bobbing up and down the leader board, he led easily until he slid on some gravel, hit a bank and flipped. Mennato Boffa brought his Tipo 60 home third behind a Ferrari and a Porsche.

Although Maserati's appearances in WSCC events had been spasmodic, and the front-engined cars had been overtaken by the competition, they remained successful in American racing during 1961, but thereafter slipped out of contention. Descendants of both the Tipo 61 and Tipo 63 were to appear in International racing in later years, but as serious contenders at the highest level Maserati was already a spent force. The corpse would not stay quiet, however, and in 1966 and 1967, Cooper F1 cars appeared with the V-12 engine and won a couple of Grands Prix.

In later years the company lurched from crisis to crisis, and had several different owners, but now seems to be fairly settled as a maker of quality sporting cars.

Mercedes-Benz

It is incredible that Mercedes-Benz's brilliant reputation in postwar sports car racing rests on just two, separated, seasons more than thirty years ago and the 300SLR, which has an unassailed position as one of the greatest of all sports-racing cars was entered in only four WSCC races.

In the Thirties, Mercedes and Auto Union had dominated Grand Prix racing to such an extent that they nearly killed it. The French huffily ran their Grand Prix for sports cars to give themselves a chance of winning.

Germany poured in vast resources, true, but as many teams have discovered, money can only help if the basic design is sound. One cannot point to Bugatti's designs and imagine that unlimited resources would ever have seen them competitive against the German cars.

In much the same way, when Mercedes returned to racing in the Fifties, it did so with the professionalism and resources of a major manufacturer, but that was not what made the return a success — it was superior design and technical flair. During both seasons, 1952 and 1955, Mercedes was able to dominate using engines of only 3 litres, which was a theoretical disadvantage of immense proportions.

It was not until 12 years after the start of World War II that the company was able to consider re-entering racing. It was not simply that the factories had to be rebuilt following Allied bombing and the business brought slowly and painfully back to health, but the political climate of the day would not, could not, allow the company to compete until a certain passage of time had elapsed. Since Mercedes had its 1939 V-12 1½-litre supercharged cars intact, it would have been theoretically possible for it to have entered Grand Prix racing almost immediately, but not until 1951 did the cars reappear, in Argentina, and their performance against Gonzalez's Ferrari (which won both races with Mercedes second and third) gave the racing department both valuable information and a perspective.

In mid-1951, the company decided to prepare for the 2½-litre F1, which was to be effective from 1954, and in the meantime gave the nod to put a toe into the water. Rudolf Uhlenhart and his team followed Jaguar's lead with the C-type and produced a car based on production components, in this case the Mercedes-Benz 300, and came up with the 300SL (Sport Leicht).

Uhlenhart, who oversaw all of Mercedes-Benz racing cars in the Fifties, was not only an engineer of the first order, certainly one of the greatest either motor racing or the motor industry has ever seen, he was also a superb driver. Stirling Moss, who should know, rated him as of Formula 1 standard. Being an employee of a large company, he did not stand out as an individual in the same way as, for example, Colin Chapman or Enzo Ferrari, but deserved to. All his cars were superb and set engineering standards by which others were judged and found wanting.

The 300SL followed the suspension layout of the production 300 saloon car range in having coil spring and wishbone front suspension and swing axle rear and a tuned (171 bhp) version of the 300's 6-cylinder s.o.h.v. engine which was

Maintenance work on Karl Kling's 300SL during the 1952 Carrera Panamericana Mexico. The broken windscreen was caused by a buzzard and for the rest of the race the 300SLs were fitted with protective bars.

canted over 50 degrees to the left and fitted with dry sump lubrication to achieve a low bonnet line. To the popular press of the day, however, the chief innovation was the use of 'gull-wing' doors which, 30 years later, became the main selling point of the disastrous De Lorean sports car.

De Lorean specified this arrangement as a marketing gimmick, but it was a necessity so far as Mercedes was concerned, for under the 300SL's sleek aluminium skin was a space-frame and it was to be more than 30 years before someone cracked the problem of building a rigid space-frame with conventional doors (Frank Costin and his TMC Costin component car).

As well as many pre-war technicians and, of course, Rennleiter Neubauer, Mercedes' all-German team of drivers included two of its leading pre-war drivers, Hermann Lang and the great Rudolf Caracciola. The Mille Miglia was chosen for the car's debut and, typical of Mercedes-Benz's thoroughness the team spent two months in Italy learning the course.

Mercedes' main opposition came from the Ferraris of Giovanni Bracco and Piero Taruffi. In a wet race, Karl Kling's 300SL led at Rome, but Bracco was driving like a man inspired, and overcoming early tyre troubles he won by five minutes. Kling was second and fourth was Caracciola, at that time the only non-Italian ever to have won a real Mille Miglia (in 1931 with a Mercedes-Benz SSKL). In 1940 a 927-mile race called the Mille Miglia was run over nine laps of a 103-mile course and it was won by a German driver in a German car bearing the infamous insignia of the SS, but entries were naturally restricted.

From Italy the team headed to Switzerland and the Preis von Bern at Bremgarten, where Kling, Lang and Riess scored an easy 1-2-3 against opposition not of the first rank. During the race Caracciola crashed heavily and, aged 51, retired from the sport. It was a sad end to the career of a man who is high on anyone's list of the ten greatest drivers.

Then came Le Mans and in practice one of the 300SLs sported an air brake on its roof, but it was not used in the race, though it was revived three years later when the team returned. It was not the only example of radical thinking going on

in the team; one 300SL was made with a glass-fibre body which *may* have been the first time the material was used for a car body, but the finish did not please and so it was never made public. Later in the season, supercharged cars were entered for the German GP 'curtain-raiser' but were withdrawn after practice.

The appearance and performance of the new cars from Mercedes panicked Jaguar into making a low-line front for the works C-types which was the team's undoing, for the cars all retired early on with cooling problems. Apart from Jaguar, Mercedes saw the chief threat coming from Cunningham, but when that team had to revert to 3-speed transmissions for the race (a 5-speed gearbox prov-

A 300SLR stripped bare.

ing unreliable in practice) its cars were hobbled.

After most of the Ferraris retired, it turned out to be Pierre Levegh's Talbot which so nearly carried off the honours until, close to the end, he missed a gear and over-revved his engine. The Mercedes cars were running to strict team order, aiming for a finish, but when Levegh went out, the Lang/Riess car went on to win, with a record distance of 2,320 miles, followed by the sister car of Helfrich and Niedermayer.

The only other important race in which the cars appeared was the incredible Carrera Panamericana, a 1,934-mile thrash across Mexico run in eight stages, an event which bears more than a passing resemblance to a modern rally. Mercedes' reliability and superb technical support won the race, for the faster Ferraris fell by the wayside, mainly with transmission failures, and victory finally went to the 300SL of Karl Kling and Hans Klenk with Lang and Riess second while the third entry, driven by John Fitch, was disqualified from fourth place for receiving outside assistance.

At the end of the year, Mercedes-Benz retired from racing in order to concentrate on the forthcoming 2½-litre Formula 1. In 1954, a production version of the car was made available and 3,250, mainly open models, had been sold when production ended in 1962. The glamour of the 'gull wing' continues, for though the roadster (introduced in 1957 after the coupé had ceased production) had improved rear suspension, and disc brakes were fitted in 1961, it does not attract the (inflated) prices of the car with the distinctive doors.

After Mercedes-Benz established its superiority in F1 in 1954, it turned to the 300SLR sports car using an enlarged (2,982 cc) version of the same straight-eight desmodronic-valved engine. This was made in two banks of four cylinders with the timing gear in the middle feeding from a ten-bearing crankshaft, had two plugs per cylinder and Bosch fuel injection. Compared to the F1 engine, it had a slightly wider bore and much longer stroke (78 × 78 mm as opposed to 76 × 68.8 mm), and would give up to 300 bhp.

This engine was slanted at 33 degrees from the horizontal in a chassis based on the W196 F1 car, being a space-frame with front suspension by double wishbones and longitudinal torsion bars with low-pivot swing axles and longitudinal torsion bars at the rear. Its drum brakes were mounted inboard front and rear.

Interestingly enough, the chassis had provision for four-wheel drive and had Mercedes continued beyond 1955 it would have implemented a programme to evaluate disc brakes.

For Mercedes-Benz, the World Sports Car Championship must have appeared like taking sweets from baby. In terms of pure engineering its only rival was Porsche, which did not count for it was making only 1,500 cc cars. Jaguar could be a threat, and its cars were on the whole more advanced, but Jaguar was interested only in Le Mans. Ferrari was in a trough, demoralized by poor performances in F1 and internal strife, Maserati had no serious car ready and Aston Martin was making so many fundamental errors (e.g. the Lagonda V-12 engine) that it could safely be discounted.

Mercedes-Benz made its debut on 1 May in the Mille Miglia, having missed the opening two rounds of the WSCC, Buenos Aires and Sebring. Though late into the fray, the team could call on some of the best drivers in the world, notably Stirling Moss, who had no peer in sports cars.

His first victory, in the Mille Miglia, is too celebrated to need any reiteration, for the account published by his passenger, Denis Jenkinson, who guided him with the first known example of pace notes, is one of the classics of sports writing. It is as though Bjorn Borg's racquet could speak.

Although facing stiff opposition from the Ferraris of Taruffi and Castellotti, Moss and Jenkinson won with thirty minutes in hand over Fangio, whose 300SLR had a fuel injection fault. Their winning average of 97.99 mph was 10 mph faster than the previous best and Moss became only the second non-Italian to win a real Mille Miglia.

In the non-Championship Eifelrennen meeting at the Nürburgring, Fangio managed to beat Moss by one-tenth of a second (team orders?) with Kling's 300SLR fourth behind Masten Gregory's Ferrari.

At Le Mans Moss and Fangio were paired and all three team cars were fitted with a pop-up flap to act as an air brake at the end of the Mulsanne Straight. Though often spoken of approvingly, this device was a crude compensation for the fact that Mercedes-Benz could not match the braking power of the Dunlop discs. Like gull-wing doors, this expediency has caught the imagination.

Pairings in the other cars were Kling/Simon and Levegh/Fitch. Although really only an amateur driver of limited racing experience, Levegh was included in recognition of his great 1952 drive at Le Mans, a rare instance of sentimentality entering the thoroughly professional approach of the team, but it was one which was to cost dearly.

For the first 2½ hours, Fangio diced with Hawthorn's D-type, a fierce duel which was more in the spirit of a sprint race rather than the beginning of a 24-hour endurance event. The Jaguar was slightly faster down the Mulsanne Straight (175 mph to the 300SLR's 168 mph) but the Mercedes had better handling. Hawthorn held a slight lead when he appeared to be ready to make his first pit stop, changed his mind, and moved across the bow of Lance Macklin's Austin-Healey 100S. Macklin jinked to the left, which brought him in front of Levegh's much faster 300SLR. Levegh's car glanced off the Healey, hit a bank, took off into the crowd, and exploded. Over eighty people, including the unfortunate driver, were killed.

Though Moss and Fangio led by two clear laps after eight hours, with Kling/Simon third, the team was withdrawn on orders from Stuttgart.

Another non-Championship race, the Swedish GP on the Bebelov circuit at Kristianstad, followed and again the air brakes were used, for the second and last time. Fangio won by a tenth of a second from Moss (team orders again?), who had had a stone shatter his goggles and finished the race in some pain.

Moss and Fitch took the Tourist Trophy at Dundrod after winning a fierce duel with the Hawthorn/Titterington Jaguar, which suffered a seized engine close to the end when in second place and led home a Mercedes 1-2-3 from Fangio/Kling and von Trips/Simon.

Two cars were entered for the final round of the WSCC, the Targa Florio. This time Moss was paired with Peter Collins, a bright young prospect who had been part of the Aston Martin team (which did not run in Sicily) and who would drive for Ferrari in 1956 and win two Grands Prix. In the race, Moss came close to disaster when avoiding a spinning Ferrari, his car going through a wall and nearly toppling down a cliff. He managed to rejoin the race, losing nine minutes, and, with severely damaged bodywork, he and Collins won by five minutes from Fangio/Kling.

At the start of the Targa Florio, Ferrari had led the Championship, but at the end of the race, Mercedes took the title, the points denied Ferrari by the second car being critical. Mercedes-Benz also won the series' GT title with the 300SL and, of course, Fangio and Moss finished 1-2 in the F1 Drivers' Championship.

Had there been a Sports Car Drivers' Championship Moss would have won it.

During 1955 two coupé 300SLRs were built, one used by Rudolf Uhlenhart as his own transport, and both were prepared in readiness for the Carrera Panamericana, which was cancelled. The race's future had been in doubt after a number of fatal accidents in 1954 and the Le Mans tragedy settled the matter.

Having proved its point, Mercedes withdrew from racing. The decision was taken at board level and surprised the racing team, which had a programme of engine and suspension developments prepared for the winter.

Mercedes-Benz's great reputation in postwar sports car racing rests on two seasons, only seven classic races and five major victories. It was not quantity of success which established the reputation, but their quality. No team has ever gone sports car racing with an approach so clearly in a higher league to the opposition.

The company has never returned to racing, though every magazine has the headline 'Mercedes Return!' set up ready to use, and the headline has been used quite often over the years as wishful thinking translates the vaguest rumour into 'fact'. As the most profitable company in Germany, Daimler-Benz has no need for the kudos of race wins and now prefers to make its technical advances, which are considerable, via an R&D department which has 7,000 employees.

Some indication of how M-B went racing in 1955 may be gauged by the fact that no fewer than ten cars were built for a seven-race programme in which a maximum of four were entered in any one event. All ten are retained at Stuttgart and are occasionally to be seen demonstrated at circuits, though the car often presented as the 1955 Mille Miglia winner is, in fact, a team spare with the number '722' painted on.

Nardi

Nardi was one of the more interesting of the small Italian specialist manufacturers which flourished in the Fifties, firms such as Giaur, Ermini, Stanguellini, Moretti, Siata and Bandini. Frequently they based their cars on Fiat components and almost always demonstrated Italy's two great motoring traditions: engine tuning and body styling.

While their British equivalents tended to concentrate on sports-racers, these companies often marketed exquisite GT cars whose styling has withstood the test of time and which were aerodynamically advanced for their day. Their chassis design, however, tended to be rugged rather than imaginative. This was partly due to the popularity of pure street racing in Italy, and partly due to a different emphasis in the Italian tradition.

An exception to this rough rule was Enrico Nardi, who first came to national attention in 1932 with an attractive lightweight special, the Nardi-Monaco. Later Nardi was employed by Enzo Ferrari on the development of his first car, the Auto Avio 815 and was entrusted with much of the test driving.

Postwar he formed a partnership with Renato Danese and in 1947 marketed his first car and a range of tuning equipment. Unlike most Italian makers, Nardi was catholic in his choice of engines and his cars featured Panhard, Universal, Crosley, and B.M.W. (ex-motor cycle) units, as well as Fiat. Almost from the beginning, his chassis were unusual in that they were multi-tubular frames at a time when most designers began with two large-diameter steel tubes. These were not true space-frames but, rather, stressed rectangular constructions of low height.

They were also of low weight and Nardi's cars soon gained a reputation in Italian National races and hill-climbs. In 1950 he displayed a variety of chassis to take anything from a 500 cc engine up to one of 4½ litres, all of which featured transverse leaf and torsion bar front suspension, with quarter elliptics at the rear.

That year he also tried his hand at a 500 cc F3 car, which in common with other Italian attempts was unsuccessful; provided the chassis for Count Rossi's Alfa Romeo special; and split with Danese.

Re-formed as Officine Enrico Nardi, the company continued to make small numbers of more or less bespoke cars, the majority having small-capacity engines. In 1952 a Nardi F2 car was made using Lancia Aurelia components and this had a genuine space-frame, a rarity anywhere at the time, let alone Italy. It was not, however, a success.

A Crosley-engined Nardi appeared at Le Mans in 1954, without notable success, but it was the following year that the marque caught the racing world's attention.

Taking advantage of a rule which allowed prototypes, Nardi stretched his imagination, and the regulations, to the limit by making a 'twin-boom' car along the lines of Taruffi's Italcorsa record car, Tarf II. Although outlandish, it was a logical development of the man's preoccupations and, at the time, was received with respectful interest. After all, Pegaso had already shown the way with its Bi-Torpedo.

Nardi had always ploughed his own furrow when designing chassis, but though his cars were successful on his home patch, they were not outstandingly so. He was, however, moving in the right direction and his ideas on chassis design were ahead of other small Italian makers, but he did not realize the potential of his schemes.

The twin-boom Nardi entered at Le Mans in 1955 and driven by Damonte/Crovetto. It was built to Damonte's requirement and differed vastly from the lightweight, well-handling, cars usually built by Nardi. (Motor)

The Nardi 'twin-boom' was created for a Doctor Damonte, a Turin chemist who regularly raced at Le Mans and who had previously used other expressions of the Italian specialist car industry such as Stanguellini and OSCA. It appears that Damonte was the inspiration of the design, but it was an extension, albeit an unorthodox one, of Enrico Nardi's thinking. He had always been conscious of weight (and its distribution), and aerodynamic drag. With the 'twin-boom' car he took these preoccupations too far, at the expense of other, more fundamental, considerations such as handling and drive-line friction losses.

Whereas the Taruffi car had been a genuine 'twin-boom', developed in a wind tunnel, with the two pods joined by spars, the Nardi merely took the outline of the 'twin boom' notion and the space between the two pods was filled in. While Taruffi's car was designed to lap a banked circuit, Nardi's was supposed to go round corners as well and the weight distribution which had worked well on record attempts was not perhaps ideal for road racing.

The Nardi had a multi-tubular frame with the driver sitting in the right-hand pod with his centre-line directly over the centre-line of the right-hand wheels. In the left-hand pod was a d.o.h.c. Giannini engine of 735 cc which produced 64 bhp at 7,000 rpm. Giannini had designed the Moto Guzzi water-cooled 4-cylinder motor cycle engine and the engine Nardi used had been designed originally for another small Italian car maker, Taraschi.

This engine was located along the centre-line of the left-hand wheels so that the drive shaft had to be articulated to allow it to pass under the live rear axle to a cluster of step gears starting beneath and behind the axle, which then transferred the power to a reversed differential hard against the left-hand rear wheel.

This complicated arrangement not only lost power but caused axle hop. It is difficult to see how any suspension layout could have coped with so offset a final drive, but Nardi is not the only designer to have tripped over a complicated power line. Colin Chapman and Brian Lister both came unstuck with the power lines on later F2 cars.

Front suspension was by sliding pillars, modified from the Lancia Ardea, with, at the rear, ¼-elliptics, upper radius arms, and hydraulic vane-type dampers. The central section of the car contained the radiator and battery.

With the driver seated so far to the right, the steering column had to be cranked first to the right, through about 60 degrees, then to the left, by about 70 degrees. It was not an arrangement made for precise steering.

Aerodynamically the Nardi was suspect, its 63 in. width (front track was only 43½ in.) gave it a relatively large frontal area. The mechanical compromises and losses of the layout were not, then, compensated by improved air flow. As one contemporary commentator noted, 'The designer appears to have gained nothing but a curious shape...'

The scrutineers at Le Mans examined the car, and then the rule books, and decided they would pass it only if a main frame tube was cut and hinged to allow access from the driver's seat to a notional passenger seat in the central section. If this did not damage the overall rigidity of the car, then there was none to speak of in the first place.

At Le Mans it was driven by Damonte and Crovetto, and proved to be pathetically slow. After the first hour it was established in last position until approaching midnight when it retired after a minor shunt which was caused by it being blown off course when overtaken by a faster car. By that time nobody cared, for the race was already in the shadow of the sport's most terrible accident.

Considering that the Nardi was a make-weight at Le Mans '55, a race etched into the consciousness of the sport for different reasons, it aroused a great deal of interest. Some muttered that it was not in the spirit of the regulations. Others took the line that it was an innovation which, with development, could be made to work. They were wrong, it never could have worked.

Nardi continued to make cars in small numbers and followed the 'twin-boom' with a rear-engined design using a modified Renault 4CV unit. In 1958 he produced a Vignale-bodied GT car based on a modified Fiat 600 floorpan which was intended for series production, but few were made. From then until 1964 he made just a few one-offs including a startling GT car with a 350 bhp Plymouth engine and Michelotti body, but the company name is still alive with a range of accessories.

The 'twin-boom' car was nothing if not interesting, but it's a shame that it is the most memorable Nardi for its creator had a history of sound design.

Nash-Healey

By world standards, Nash-Kelvinator was a very large and successful combine in 1945, but compared to other American corporations, it was a middleweight. It had prospered on government contracts during World War II when inter-company rivalries were, on the surface at least, submerged. Come the peace it was vulnerable after the immediate postwar sellers' market.

On the other side of the ocean, the motto in Britain was 'Export or Die' and

British businessmen crossed the Atlantic to explore opportunities in the only healthy export market in the world. Among them was Donald Healey, a noted pre-war competitor and designer, who had set up his own motor company in 1946. His was a small-scale operation and, at the time of his crossing on the *Queen Elizabeth* in 1949, was looking for the means to expand.

Also on the boat was George Mason, head of Nash-Kelvinator, who was looking for ways in which his company could find an edge over the giants. British sports cars had been making an impact in America and Mason was well aware of the drawing power of a sports model in the showrooms. Mason and Healey met and were soon engaged in conversation about the possibility of a Nash-engined Healey.

From both sides the idea made sense and Healey proposed a Nash version of his own Riley-engined Silverstone sports car which had just arrived on the market and was already making a good reputation for itself. So it was that the tiny English manufacturer slipped into partnership with the American giant and the car they made joined the long list of Anglo-American hybrids.

Healey set to work installing a 6-cylinder 3.8-litre Nash Ambassador engine and 3-speed Nash gearbox (with overdrive top) into a Silverstone chassis which was a light (160 lb) box section affair with trailing link front suspension. It was similar in design to the Healey A-type which, with an Elliott body, was the fastest 4-door saloon made in Britain and which had had a fine competition career which included class wins in the 1949 Mille Miglia (the first class win by a British car in the race) and the Targa Florio.

The styling of the first car was odd, being an adaptation of the cycle-winged Silverstone but with an enveloping body. With a decent 138 bhp on tap (the standard Silverstone had 104 bhp) it had competition potential and since Healey himself had been a Mille Miglia competitor before the war it was natural that he entered the new car in the 1950 event.

It was not a wonderful debut. Healey was forced off the road by a truck which

The Nash-Healey team at Le Mans, 1952. No 11, driven by Veyron/Giraud-Cabantous, retired with transmission trouble, while No 10, driven by Johnson/Wisdom, finished third. (Geoffrey Goddard)

This Nash-Healey, driven by Leslie Johnson and Bill Hadley, finished 11th at Le Mans in 1953. (Geoffrey Goddard)

had strayed on the course and he and his son, Geoffrey, had to drive on with a damaged transmission with no overdrive. Restricted to what was effectively third gear out of four, they finished in 177th place.

Next up was Le Mans, where the car was entered for Tony Rolt and Duncan Hamilton. It finished a respectable fourth behind two Talbots and an Allard and covered 2,103 miles, which was a fair performance given that the car was the prototype of a series production model and not a dedicated racer.

Meanwhile work went ahead on productionizing the car and orders were taken in 1951. Nash components were shipped to England, where they were fitted into a modified Silverstone chassis and clothed with an aluminium body made by Panelcraft. Performance was brisk with 0–60 mph achieved in 11.5 seconds, which was marginally better than the Jaguar XK120, but its 106 mph top speed was lower than the Jaguar's 126 mph. Since the two cars cost about the same in America it is not surprising that the Jaguar had the edge in the market, for its looks were sassy and there was no arguing with the 120+ mph.

In 1951, Donald and Geoffrey Healey again ran a car in the Mille Miglia and finished 30th overall, 4th in class, an improvement on the first year but not a sensational result. An aerodynamic coupé, which had something of the later Bristol 450 about it, was prepared for Rolt and Hamilton to drive at Le Mans and they brought it home sixth. During the race the Nash-Healey covered 2,142.58 miles, which, though it was just over 100 miles short of the winning Jaguar C-type, compares well with the 2,153.12 miles covered by the winning Talbot the previous year.

A few Nash-Healeys began to appear in SCCA events, but the marque's next important race was the 1952 Mille Miglia, where Leslie Johnson and Bill McKenzie finished a fine seventh overall, and the first British car home. Quite apart from the fact that the Brits were short on the sort of intimate knowledge of the route which was the natural advantage of any Italian driver, practice was made more difficult by severe currency restrictions.

For Le Mans the 1951 coupé was converted into a roadster and a larger (4.2-litre) engine was installed, and the 1950 prototype car was given a modified engine which produced a *claimed* 200 bhp.

This special engine, with a new cylinder head designed by Donald Healey's partner, A. C. Sampietro, failed in the race, but Leslie Johnson and Tommy Wisdom brought the other car home a splendid third behind the leading brace of Mercedes-Benz 300SLs. For a lightly modified production car it was an excellent performance, with a class win and second in the Index of Performance thrown in for good measure.

Despite the success, sales remained slow and Nash lost money on every car sold. With hindsight it seems clear that Nash should have taken over Healey's design and mass produced it to a keen price, just as Austin did with another Healey design. The 104 sold in the first year of production might have been excellent by Healey's standards but was not the sort of impact Nash was looking for. Production of the road car was suspended until a revised version, with Farina styling, came on stream in 1952.

In terms of sales this did little better. Its styling was admired but the $5,000 it cost told against it. Donald Healey had become involved with the Austin-Healey and Nash was undergoing a merger with Hudson. The car was not high on anyone's list of priorities.

Nash-Healeys appeared in two more classic races, both in 1953. John Fitch drove a roadster in the Mille Miglia, but retired early on with a broken brake pipe. Two appeared at Le Mans, one retired early in the race with falling oil pressure and the other finished 11th.

Production of the car ended the following year with a total of just 506 made.

OSCA

The early story of the remarkable Maserati brothers is told briefly under 'Maserati'. In 1947 the three surviving brothers, Ernesto, Ettore and Bindo, were serving out the last few months of their ten-year contract with Officine Alfieri Maserati SpA Modena and there was no sign of their term being extended. As soon as they were free agents they returned to Bologna to start their own company, which they registered on 1 December, 1947, as Officine Specializzate per la Costruzione di Automobile – Fratelli Maserati SpA which abbreviated to OSCA.

The talents of the three brothers admirably complemented each other. Ernesto was the designer, Bindo the businessman and Ettore supervised the workshop. Work began in 1948 on the first car, the MT (Maserati Tipo) 4 – like some other

The 1500cc OSCA entered for Jackie Reece in the 1500cc Sports Car race at Silverstone, July 1954. (T.C. March)

companies the brothers did not want to start with Mk I for that suggests that the customers are guinea pigs for a first effort. Ernesto picked the popular 1,100 cc sports car class and designed a Fiat-based engine of 1,092 cc (70 × 71 mm) with a s.o.h.c. head which produced 55 bhp.

The chassis followed typical Maserati practice and was a simple ladder-frame with cruciform front bracing and the main tubes reduced in size behind the driving compartment and then kicked up over the live rear axle, which was suspended by ¼-elliptics and radius arms. Front suspension was by coil springs and this broad outline was to form the basis for most OSCA cars with coil spring rear suspension first appearing in 1956. Frua made the body, a simple aluminium shell over a tubular steel framework which had cycle wings and a near-circular radiator grille which became an OSCA trademark.

The first car, designated MT4, appeared in August 1948 and the following month Luigi Villoresi ran it in the F2 Naples GP against Ferrari works opposition, and won. Later that year Dorino Serafini won the Circuit of Garda. It was a promising debut by any standards.

Ernesto was meanwhile working on a new engine. The Fiat block was discarded and a new alloy one substituted, with twin overhead camshafts (with typical Maserati 'finger' followers) and a hemispherical cylinder head replaced the earlier s.o.h.c. layout. Crankshafts were milled from solid billets and, like the rest of the car, were beautifully made and finished. All of OSCA's subsequent 4-cylinder engines derive from this unit though most were made with iron blocks.

In 1951 OSCA built a V-12 4,472 cc (78 × 78 mm) engine for F1 and the first one was fitted to a Maserati 4CLT/48 chassis for B. Bira. This engine derived from the 4-cylinder 1,490 cc Maserati 4CLT engine but with simplified cylinder heads which were s.o.h.c. with two valves per cylinder in place of the original d.o.h.c. four-valve heads. A second engine went into a new OSCA chassis which had a large-diameter tube ladder-frame, coil spring and wishbone front suspension and a de Dion rear axle suspended on torsion bars. Designated Tipo 4500-G it was finished in time for Franco Rol to drive to ninth in the Italian GP which, though nobody at the time knew it, was the penultimate race to be run to the old 4½-litre/1½-litre supercharged F1.

Apparently Amédée Gordini was due to take delivery of a couple of engines (OSCA built four but projected a run of eight), but the old formula collapsed before he was ready to take delivery of them. A single bank of the V-12 engine

bore a certain resemblance to Gordini's own 'six'.

Neither car was a success for they were already dated by comparison to the 4½-litre Ferraris and with only about 300 bhp on tap they were decidedly under-powered. Bira won a minor race in the 1951 Easter Monday Goodwood Meeting against thin opposition but appeared in only one World Championship event, the Spanish GP. There it practised half a minute slower than Ascari's Ferrari and it retired on lap one with engine troubles. It later had a varied life in Australia and Britain and is now to be seen in the Donington Park Museum. Rol's OSCA was later converted into a central-seater sports car.

A third Tipo 4500-G was sold to Cordero di Montezemole Paole, who had it made into an r.h.d. sports car with an extensively revised rear end. This car is now in a French museum.

From the V-12 engine OSCA derived a straight-six 160 bhp 1,987 cc (76 × 73 mm) twin-plug dry-sumped F2 engine which was mated to a ladder-frame chassis with coil spring and double wishbone front suspension and a de Dion rear axle suspended on ¼-elliptics. Driven by Louis Chiron, who was then well into his fifties, and Élie Bayol, they appeared during 1952–3 almost exclusively in non-Championship races where starting money could more than cover expenses. Even at that level they were not particularly successful and on the couple of occasions that they appeared in World Championship Grands Prix their performance was embarrassing. Chiron's car now has coupé bodywork and is in France.

Later, in 1954, three 2-litre sports cars (Tipo 2000S) were built along the lines of the F2 car but were bought by amateurs and neither cars nor drivers made any impression in International racing. This was an unusual occurrence in OSCA's history, at least so far as sports cars were concerned, for the reputation of the Maserati brothers tended to attract a very nice class of customer.

While its foray into single-seaters was ill-starred, from its start OSCA was very successful in Italian sports car racing. Luigi Fagioli used one to win the 1,100 cc class in the 1950 and 1951 Mille Miglias. In 1950, Fagioli also finished an excellent seventh overall. Giulio Cabianca carried on the Mille Miglia tradition in 1952 and also led the Targa Florio until three-quarters distance when the back axle broke. OSCAs continued to win the 1,100 cc class in the Mille Miglia every year up to, and including, the last race in 1957.

Also in 1952, an OSCA appeared for the first time at Le Mans. It was a Frua-bodied 1,350 cc coupé in the hands of Damonte/Martial and it was leading the 1,500 cc class when its clutch went. The following year Damonte, who later became known for the 'twin-boom' Nardi, won the 1,500 cc class with the car in partnership with one 'Helde'. 1,350 cc OSCAs also won the 1,500 cc class in the 1952 and 1953 Sebring 12 Hours races.

173

Briggs Cunningham and Bob Said were just two drivers who imported 1,453 cc (78 × 76 mm) OSCAs to the States and in 1953–4 they had a lot of success with them, until the Porsche 550s began to appear. In March 1954, Cunningham managed to persuade Stirling Moss to drive his OSCA in the Sebring 12 Hours race and, partnered by Bill Lloyd, Moss kept going when all about him were dropping out. Moss and Lloyd went on to score a sensational victory, but it was not without its troubles for they drove most of the distance with no brakes to speak of. It was probably OSCA's finest hour and was certainly the first time so small a car won a WSCC race, though Porsche was to ensure that it would not be the last.

The following year the same car, driven by Lloyd and Huntoon, finished seventh overall at Sebring and first in the 1,500 cc class.

At Le Mans in 1954 the Porsche team hit trouble with a plethora of holed pistons and late in the race OSCAs held first and second in the 1,100 cc class. Unfortunately their drivers were so intent on individual glory that both crashed. That year Cabianca led the Tour of Sicily in a 1500 ahead of 2- and 3-litre Maseratis and Ferraris but retired with engine troubles. Later in the year Cabianca won the Coppa della Dolomite ahead of Gendebien's Ferrari.

OSCAs found homes mainly in two countries, Italy and America, and in both countries set the standard in the 1,100 cc and 1,500 cc classes. From time to time they faced opposition at home and Ermini and Stanguellini both had periods when they were more successful in Italian national 1,100 cc events, but neither company was able to approach OSCA in the classic races.

For 1955 OSCA offered a twin-plug head on the 1500 which was then renamed the 1500TN (tipo nuove), but that same year saw the beginning of a decline in OSCA's fortunes as customers increasingly turned to Porsche for 1,500

Winner of the Index of Performance at Sebring in 1958 was this superbly aerodynamic 750cc Osca driven by de Tomaso and his wife.

cc racing and Cooper and Lotus in the 1,100 cc class. The British cars, however, were no match for OSCA in the rugged road-racing events on the Continent. There OSCA's comparatively old-fashioned, but sturdy, chassis was ideally suited to coping with potholes, manhole covers and cobblestones.

Indeed, although the cars increasingly came under pressure in airfield club events, 1956 was to be one of OSCA's best years. In the Mille Miglia not only was the 1,100 cc class taken (of course) but OSCAs also won the 1500 and 750 cc classes. Luigi Musso, on loan from Ferrari, won an hour-long 1,500 cc race at the Rome GP meeting, beating Behra's Maserati 150S and Brabham's 1,500 cc Cooper-Climax, while in the Targa Florio, Cabianca had his finest hour. Maglioli won the race in a 1.5 Porsche, but the OSCA finished a close second ahead of the surviving Ferraris and Maseratis. Then he was disqualified on a footling technicality involving the nomination of a co-driver. It was a cruel end to a magnificent performance.

The OSCA engine caught the attention of the former Ferrari designer Aurelio Lampredi, who was then at Fiat, and he arranged for Fiat to make a production version in much the same way that Ford was later to take on the Cosworth FVA engine and make from it the Ford BDA. As made by Fiat, however, its power was deliberately kept in check and with a single Weber carburettor gave just 80 bhp, a long way short of its potential. Fitted in a very pretty Farina-style cabriolet, it was available from late 1959 on as the Fiat 1500S and stayed in production for six years. From 1957 onwards, this project took a great deal of Ernesto's time, which is one reason why his new desmodromic engine took a back seat and some of the energy went out from OSCA's overall programme just at the time when it faced serious competition in the 1,100 cc and 1,500 cc sports car classes.

OSCA was too small a company (it never had more than 50 employees) to take on the might of Porsche in the 1,500 cc class, though cars continued to give a good account of themselves. The brothers realized, too, that in the 1,100 cc category they had no answer to the energetic and innovative British constructors using the Coventry Climax FWA engine. Their strength had always been their engines rather than their chassis. They turned instead to the 750 cc class, where their opposition at home came from such as Stanguellini and, abroad, from the increasingly dated Panhard-engined French cars.

Thus came the 747 cc (62 × 62 mm) d.o.h.c. Tipo 187 engine which had such a successful debut in the 1956 Mille Miglia. The following year such a car won its class again in the Mille Miglia and appeared at Le Mans, where it was beaten into third in class by the little Lotus Eleven and a D.B. This led to a completely new engine, the 187N, which departed from Ernesto Maserati's usual practice in that it had 'over-square' (65 × 58 mm) dimensions.

It was a little jewel of a motor with its block cast in light alloy and it developed a claimed 76 bhp at 7,700 rpm (the earlier 750 had given 70 bhp at 7,400 rpm). The chassis followed established OSCA practice but with coil spring rear suspension and the all-up weight was claimed to be only 757 lb. Alejandro de Tomaso partnered by his wife, Isobel, and Bob Ferguson, entered one in the 1958 Sebring 12 Hours race and won the 750 cc class and Index of Performance despite Ferguson having to drive for several hours without a clutch.

Two such cars appeared at Le Mans, where they faced no fewer than fourteen other cars in the 750 cc class. These not only included two Lotuses but several Panhard-based cars fitted with new d.o.h.c. cylinder heads. One of the pair of OSCAs, driven by de Tomaso and works driver Colin Davis, son of the great journalist and former Le Mans winner 'Sammy' Davis, won through against this formidable array to finish a magnificent tenth overall, first in class and winner of the Index of Performance. During the 24 Hours it covered over 2,100 miles, more than the winning Ferrari in 1949.

These little cars became popular in SCCA racing, where they won the Class H Modified Championship in 1959 and 1960, while an OSCA-engined Lola won in 1961. A 750 was made for 1959 and this broke new ground for the Maseratis in that it was a rear-engined space-frame car with a Porsche gearbox and all-independent suspension by transverse leaf springs and lower wishbones. Apparently it was built at the instigation of de Tomaso and the brothers did not really have their heart in it for they were 'engine men' who felt themselves out of their depth with so radical a departure from their established practice. It was sold to the Rodriguez brothers and ran at Le Mans where, like the front-engined 750 which also ran, it retired.

The great days of OSCA were coming to an end though work continued on desmodromic cylinder heads. A 750 finished third in the Index of Performance in the 1960 Sebring race and the same year Lodovico Scarfiotti won an Italian hill-climb with a 2-litre 'desmo' sports car. A 1,600 GT 'production' car using a tuned version of the Fiat/OSCA engine was offered for sale and this not only offered disc brakes on all four wheels but a 6-speed gearbox was listed as an option.

OSCA was not quite finished for Bini and Rigamonti came a splendid fifth overall, and first in the 1-litre class, in the 1961 Targa Florio with a 950 cc car. In the same race a works 1,500 ran with independent rear suspension by transverse leaf spring and lower wishbones but failed to finish. Fitted with the 2-litre 'desmo' engine Scarfiotti ran this car in the Pescara Four Hours Sports Car race but was outclassed.

Experiments continued with i.r.s. and desmodromic heads in both 1,500 cc and 2-litre forms and cars fitted with these engines made occasional appearances in sports and F2 events from as early as 1957, when the 1,500 cc unit was claimed to give 160 bhp and rev to over 8,000 rpm, but these units did not distinguish themselves and the project was never satisfactorily developed. A 1½-litre 'desmo' OSCA-engined de Tomaso F2 car, bearing more than a slight resemblance to a Cooper, appeared in 1960 but was not a success.

In fact the energy had gone out of the firm. All of the brothers were in their late sixties or early seventies and maintaining the company at all had often been a struggle. In 1963 the *fratelli* sold out to M.V. Agusta, which continued to make the GT cars in small numbers until 1967, though the last ones were offered with Ford V-4 engines, which was a sad end to an illustrious line.

Between them, the Maserati brothers had graced over sixty years of motor sport history with distinction. Although they competed in the small-capacity classes, often against special builders, the cars they made were thoroughbreds of impeccable pedigree.

Pegaso

Though Spain was neutral in World War II, its Civil War of 1936–8 had devastated its economy and industry, and both had been weak by European standards in the first place. In 1954, for example, Spain's total production of cars and commercial vehicles amounted to only 6,500 units and many of those were motor cycle-engined mini-cars. It may appear odd, then, that it was from Spain whence came one of the most expensive cars of the Fifties, Pegaso.

While the country's industry was in poor shape, ENASA (Empresa Nacional de Automamioes SA), the company which had inherited the remains of Hispano–Suiza in Barcelona, was making a reputation with its Pegaso trucks and had attracted former Alfa Romeo designer Wilfredo Ricart back to his homeland.

Ricart had the apparently bizarre idea that Spain, one of the poorest countries in Europe, should build 'jewels for the rich'. Perhaps he had in mind a car which would demonstrate that Spain was capable of the standards of engineering achieved in the rest of Europe. Perhaps he had in mind low labour costs, which would make the building of a hand-crafted car a more immediate reality than a mass-produced model for the home market.

Ricart drew a d.o.h.c. V-8 light-alloy engine with a five-bearing crankshaft and dry sump lubrication. The 5-speed gearbox was mounted at the rear, in unit with a limited slip differential. Front suspension was by double wishbones and torsion bars, with a de Dion rear axle. Huge (12¾ in.) Al-fin drum brakes were used and these were mounted inboard at the rear.

When the Pegaso Z102 was first announced in 1951, the buyer could choose between a 2.8-litre normally aspirated engine giving a claimed 170 bhp or a supercharged 2.5-litre engine which gave 255 bhp.

On specification alone, it should have attracted buyers, for it followed existing racing practice and, by all accounts, the car was a delight to drive. Unfortunately

Joaquin Palacios competing with a 2.8-litre Pegaso in the 1954 Rabassada hill-climb.   177

Pegasos were very noisy and not well finished. They also lacked any form of pedigree, yet the asking price was £3,000, well over twice the cost of a Jaguar XK120 and though Jaguar had no great pedigree at the time, it had won Le Mans that year.

Only about 125 cars were made and it is hard to find two alike for many coachbuilders made bodies for the cars. A bewildering variety of engines were also used, the d.o.h.c. unit reaching 3.2-litres and available in normally aspirated form or with one- or two-stage supercharging. A 3.2-litre supercharged spyder was entered in the sports car race at the 1954 Spanish GP meeting and was timed at 183 mph on the Pedralbes straight before it retired with a broken fuel pipe.

Pegaso's competition debut came in 1953 at the Rabassada hill-climb and works test driver Joaquin Palacios drove an open 2-seater to FTD while fellow tester Celso Fernandez took the first prototype to fourth. Since every Pegaso was tested for 3,000 miles before being handed over to a customer, the works testers did get a little practice in driving the cars.

A prototype sports-racer was built for the 1953 season and, like the later Nardi, was inspired by the 'twin-boom' Tarf record breaker. In the 'Bi-Torpedo',

The Pegaso Bi-Torpedo twin-boom car was built for Le Mans but was damaged before the race. Later it was successfully used for some record attempts. (Autosport)

the driver was to sit in line with the right-hand wheels under a perspex bubble canopy, the notional passenger in line with the right wheels, while the 300 bhp supercharged 2.5-litre engine occupied the centre section.

Entered for Le Mans in 1953, the Bi-Torpedo was badly damaged in a fire not long before the race. It was probably a mercy. Two Barchettas with 260 bhp engines were entered instead and proved very quick down the Mulsanne Straight in practice, but one inexplicably slewed and crashed, badly injuring the driver and leaving the car a non-starter. The second Pegaso was withdrawn.

The Bi-Torpedo was restored to health for some record attempts and achieved 148.6 mph on public roads in Spain. Encouraged, Pegaso took it and a Barchetta to the Jabbeke (Belgium) dual carriageway in September 1953. The Bi-Torpedo blew its engine but the Barchetta recorded 149.75 mph for the flying mile and 151 mph for the flying kilometre, beating the times set by a Jaguar C-type the previous year.

In the 1954 Carrera Pan-Americana, a 3.2-litre supercharged Barchetta appeared driven by Palacios and Fernandez and entered by a son of Trujillo, the dictator of the Dominican Republic. Despite encountering some initial problems with the local fuel, they put up a good performance, finishing fourth on the second stage and third on the third stage. The Pegaso was in seventh place overall when it crashed on the Mexico City to León section.

That was Pegaso's only appearance in a WSCC round, but they continued to be raced in Spain and in the 1955 Montjuich Cup in Barcelona, for example, Fernandez and Bay brought two 3.1 Pegasos home second and third to Daetwyler's Ferrari, but the Swiss visitor had a very easy race.

Push-rod V-8 engines of 3.9-, 4.5- or 4.7-litres were offered for the Z-103 model introduced in 1955 but there were few takers and production officially ceased in 1957. Thereafter Pegaso concentrated on commercial vehicles which today enjoy a high reputation. The cars cannot be counted a success but they did draw attention to Spanish engineering and the name 'Pegaso', and created a favourable image for both.

Porsche

1948 saw Dr Ferdinand Porsche, one of the greatest engineers of the twentieth century, working from a collection of sheds in Gmünd, in the British occupied zone of Austria. On the site of an old saw mill members of his great design studio, Dr Ing. h.c. Ferdinand Porsche GmbH., Konstruktionsburo für Motoren und Fahrzeugbau, devoted themselves to designing and making barrows and farm implements and repairing ex-Wehrmacht Volkswagens. It was inexacting work for the man who had created the Mercedes-Benz SSKL, the Volkswagen, the Auto Union Grand Prix car, the Leopard, Tiger and Maus tanks, and who had once turned down an offer from Stalin to be Czar of Industrial Russia with an unlimited design budget, but Porsche was in poor health.

At the end of 1945, the French had invited him to Paris to advise on the Renault 4CV, a VW crib, which was being prepared for production. Having picked his brains the French authorities arrested him as a war criminal (an entirely trumped-up charge) and threw him in gaol together with his son, Ferry, and his son-in-law, Dr Piëch. Intervention by Raymond Sommer and Charles Faroux, the journalist who had dreamed up the idea of Le Mans, obtained the release of the younger men, but the French held on to Ferdinand Porsche, then aged 70, and demanded a ransom of one million francs.

Porsche's design studio was physically in Stuttgart, an occupied city, to which access was denied to Porsche's son, Ferry, and the rest of his staff. In order to raise the ransom, they undertook a commission from Piero Dusio, an Italian industrialist and sometime racing driver, to design a new Grand Prix car, the Cisitalia.

It was not a Porsche design in the sense that Ferdinand oversaw it, but was drawn by members of his studio under Karl Rabe and what emerged was typically 'Porsche'. It was also one of the most radical F1 designs ever built with a space-frame chassis (one of the first examples of the structure used for a car), a 1½-litre supercharged flat-12 engine (with over-square cylinder dimensions) mounted amidships, and four-wheel drive.

It also had, and this was significant for Porsche's long-term prosperity, a new form of synchromesh designed by Leopold Schmid. Dusio's business collapsed before the Cisitalia could race, but it at least raised the money to spring Porsche from gaol. One of the engineers who went from Austria to Italy to supervise the project was Carl Abarth, who stayed on to create his own cars and reputation.

Ferry Porsche, who was 39 in 1948, had been driving an ex-army Volkswagen but found it less than satisfactory and so decided to build a VW-based sports car for his own use. Since it was Porsche Design No. 356 it would be called the Porsche 356 but it was not the first Porsche-designed special VW. Pre-war Ferdinand had overseen production of three coupés (Type 64) which had been built for a proposed Berlin-Rome race in 1940.

Materials were scarce, hence the choice of a second-hand VW base, and some items had to be literally smuggled into Austria. Careful work to the 1,131 cc engine raised its power output from 25 to 40 bhp. A simple box-section frame was built using VW suspension components, brakes and wheels, and the engine was mounted behind the driver with the gearbox behind the rear axle line.

Porsche's debut at Le Mans came in 1951 when Auguste Veuillet and Edmond Mouche drove this 356 to victory in the 1100cc class. (Louis Klementaski)

An all-enveloping open body, looking remarkably like later production Porsches, was designed by Erwin Kommenda, who had been taken on as one of the key men when Porsche had started his own design studio in 1930. Its panels were made from aluminium and there was a bench seat to enable three people to squeeze in. With a weight of about 1,300 lb, the little car would do an honest 84 mph.

There was apparently no idea of building more than the one car, but it attracted so much attention and favourable comment that the team decided to build a limited number of cars. To raise money for the venture, the original special was sold to Switzerland and the proud owner, a Herr von Senger, allowed the Swiss magazine *Automobil Revue* to test it. The resulting article brought orders flooding in and work started on a run of coupés which were tested aerodynamically by running prototypes with tufts of wool attached.

These 'Gmünd' cars had shorter wheelbases than the original and the engine hung behind the rear axle line with the gearbox in front. The box-section frame was welded to the body frame to give greater rigidity and the body shell itself was of aluminium. It was first shown at the 1949 Geneva Show and most of the fifty cars made in Gmünd were sold in Switzerland though four were retained by the works.

In the meantime two important things had happened, Porsche had reached an agreement with VW which brought him a royalty on every car, a guaranteed supply of components for his own cars, and an agreement that Porsches would be serviced by VW agents. The other was the promise by the US Army to hand back his factory in Stuttgart, though this was delayed for years with the onset of the Korean War.

Having chosen the nearby coachbuilder Reutter to supply steel bodies, Porsche was allowed about 5,000 sq ft of Reutter's factory to begin production which got under way in 1950. At first only the 1,131 cc engine was available, but this was soon reduced to 1,086 cc in order to qualify for the 1,100 cc competition class and with two Solex carburettors maintained the larger engine's 40 bhp. By the end of 1950 a 1,300 cc 44 bhp engine was offered and the brakes (previous standard VW cable-operated devices) were improved.

Also in 1950, some of the first customers began to enter their cars in competition and began scoring class wins in some important rallies. The first works Porsche appeared at Le Mans in 1951 at the specific invitation of Charles Faroux and it was an invitation accepted with some hesitation for it was the first post-war appearance by a German car in France.

Two cars were entered, these being of the four Gmünd cars retained by the firm, but accidents to the designated entries left only the reserve car as a starter. These cars were designated 356SLs (Porsche Type 514) and featured aluminium spats over all four wheels while a slatted aluminium panel (à la pre-war VW) replaced the normal glass rear window. With the single car two French drivers, Auguste Veuillet and Edmond Mouche, had a trouble-free run to win the 1,100 cc class ahead of the winner of the 1,500 cc class.

Later that year a 1,500 cc engine was fitted to a car which was run in the Liège-Rome-Liège Rally and it finished third overall and first in class. A 1,500 was also used, along with two other cars, to take a series of records at Monthléry and before the year was out it had become a production engine.

The other two cars at Monthléry were an 1,100 cc coupé and a Porsche-based sports-racer built for Walter Glöcker, the Frankfurt VW agent. German motor racing at the time largely consisted of small-capacity specials and for the 1950

This Porsche 550 Spyder driven by Polensky/von Frankenberg finished fourth overall at Le Mans in 1955 and won the 1500cc class. It is seen leading the Frazer Nash Sebring of Dickie Stoop and Marcel Bequart which finished tenth. (T.C. March)

season, Glöcker, who had the assistance of an ex-Adler engineer called Ramelow, built a short-wheelbase tubular frame covered with a neat and professionally finished slipper body. The engine was mounted 'about face' ahead of the rear axle line, with the gearbox behind it, and by using an alcohol brew, Glöcker obtained 48 bhp.

The following year he made an improved model with a much higher compression ratio which gave 58 bhp and Hermann Kathrein used the car to easily win his class in the national championship. Meanwhile a further Glöcker-Porsche was in hand, this time with a 1,500 cc engine which was tuned to give 85 bhp, and with it Glöcker won the German 1,500 cc Championship. It was this car which joined the works record breakers at Monthléry, which it set three International records including 500 km at over 121 mph.

In 1952 Glöcker easily won the German Championship, while the earlier car, driven by Heinz Brendel who had had a brief pre-war career as a Mercedes-Benz 'cadet' driver, easily won the 1,100 cc class. While the works continued to enter its remaining Gmünd cars in races and rallies, the Glöcker cars gave the works a great deal of food for thought. They showed what could be achieved with production parts and a relatively simple car.

The Gmünd cars continued to be competitive during 1952, and Count Lurani and Count Berckheim won the 1,500 cc class in the Mille Miglia with one, despite having to drive the last 200 miles in third gear only. The early Porsches had non-synchromesh transmissions and the gearbox, as well as having an awkward change, was fragile. After all, it was a VW unit designed to take 25 bhp, not the 60+ bhp which production cars were giving. At Le Mans, Veuillet/Mouche repeated their 1951 class win with an 1,100 cc version.

Ferdinand Porsche himself was not to witness the burgeoning success of the cars which bore his name or, to be more accurate, his son's name. He had been 70 years old when imprisoned by the perfidious French (a trial in his absence cleared him of all charges but the ransom was never returned) and his internment had broken his health. He suffered a stroke in 1951 and died on 30 January, 1952.

Wolfgang von Trips and Umberto Maglioli finished fourth overall and first in class in the 1956 Nürburgring 1000 Km driving this Porsche 550 Spyder. (Leica-Studio Wörner)

While customers continued to be successful in rallies and races, and improvements to the basic 356 design were constantly being incorporated, the works both appreciated the value of competition success and realized that a new car was required if Porsche was to maintain its initiative. Meanwhile the production cars had improved brakes, a synchromesh gearbox of such excellence that the system was built under licence by many major manufacturers, and a 70 bhp 1,500 cc engine option.

Porsche Design No. 550 was a simple ladder-frame chassis with all-independent torsion bar suspension. A neat two-seater aluminium body was built by Weidenhausen, the company which had built Glöcker's bodies, and a 1,500 cc push-rod engine mounted 'about face' as on the Glöcker specials. At the same time, Dr Ernst Fuhrmann, who had been responsible for much of the increased power from what were becoming increasingly distant cousins from the original VW units, was set to work on a new engine, Porsche Design No. 547.

When it was finally ready, in 1953, No. 547 was a 1,498 cc (85 × 66 mm) air-cooled flat-four with twin overhead camshafts, driven by a complicated system of shafts and bevel gears, and two plugs per cylinder. When it first ran it gave 110 bhp (which would increase over its life to 180 bhp) and since the overall weight of the car was just over 1,200 lb, its power/weight ratio was three times better than the first Porsche special. This engine would be mated to a 4-speed all-synchromesh transmission which incorporated a ZF limited slip differential.

Until No. 547 was ready to race, the works built up two 550s with tuned 1,500 cc push-rod engines. In the very wet 1953 Eifelrennen run in late May, Helm Glöcker, a cousin of Walter, scored a narrow win from two works Borgwards with 550-1. Then this car and a second example were prepared for Le Mans.

The relatively poor quality of the fuel at Le Mans caused Porsche to lower the engines' compression ratios which limited power to about 77 bhp (on alcohol they gave up to 98 bhp), but coupé tops were fitted and the cars were timed at just under 124 mph on the Mulsanne Straight. The two cars staged an impressive high-speed demonstration run to cross the finishing line together, easy winners of the 1,500 cc class. The organizers decided that the car driven by Paul Frère and Richard von Frankenberg had covered the greater distance in the time (we are talking about a few feet) and awarded them the class ahead of Helm Glöcker and Hans Herrmann.

After appearing in several German races and hill-climbs, with satisfying re-sults, the cars were sold to Jaroslav Juhan in Guatemala, who entered them in the 1953 Carrera Panamericana. Juhan himself crashed but José Herrate won the 1,500 cc class and so the name 'Carrera' entered the Porsche vocabulary.

A 550 fitted with the No. 547 engine first appeared during practice for the sports car race at the 1954 German GP meeting, where it intrigued observers by its unusual exhaust note (the bonnet remained tightly shut) but was actually slower than the 'push-rod' cars. A week later it was loaned to Hans Stuck for the Freiburg-Schauinsland hill-climb but Stuck found it hard to cope with the peaky power curve, there was little below 5,000 rpm though the engine revved to 7,500 rpm, and could do no better than third behind Herrmann, in a push-rod 550, and Günter Bechem's Borgward.

By the time the 550 was ready for its first 'real' competition appearance, the 1954 Mille Miglia, a number of subtle changes had been made. The rear torsion bars were moved forward to the front of the engine and Kommanda had refined the body to arrive at the definitive 550 shape. In the Mille Miglia, Hans Herr-mann and Herbert Linge, a Porsche engineer and works driver, were delayed for 20 minutes with a damp ignition system and once had to duck as they came across a railway level crossing to find the barrier being lowered, but they motored on to finish sixth overall and first in class.

A single car, for Herrmann, was run in the Eifelrennen but he retired after a single lap with a misfiring engine and suspension trouble and the Borgwards of Bechem and Hartmann no longer had anything standing between them and a fine 1–2. Ignition troubles also beset the four cars entered at Le Mans, one with an 1,100 cc 547 engine. Two of the 1,500s retired with holed pistons and the third (Claes/Stasse) car ran the last four laps on three cylinders well out of contention until the two leading 1,500 cc OSCAS decided to fight between themselves and both were eliminated by crashes, leaving the Porsche to limp around in 12th and the only 1,500 cc finisher. The 1,100 cc car (Duntov/Olivier) had a trouble-free run to finish 14th and the only survivor in its class.

A fortnight later in the Reims 12 Hours race, von Frankenberg/Polensky redressed the poor (by Porsche standards) showing at Le Mans with an easy class win to which, later, were added Porsche class wins in the Nürburgring 1,000 Km and the Carrera Panamericana in which Herrmann finished third overall.

Seen before the 1956 Le Mans race, the RS1500 hard top driven by Umberto Maglioli and Hans Herrmann. It retired in the race. (LAT)

At the end of 1954 the first of about 100 customer cars began to be delivered with the majority going to the States, where the 500/1500RS (Rennsport) was immediately dubbed 'Spyder'. In SCCA racing these cars swept the board especially in the hands of English 'ex-pat' Ken Miles.

It is at this point that trying to keep track of Porsche successes becomes difficult for not only did the works have win after win but private owners did their fair share. 1,500 cc class wins were taken in five of the six 1955 WSCC rounds: Buenos Aires, Sebring, Mille Miglia, Le Mans and the Tourist Trophy. At Le Mans, von Frankenberg/Polensky won the 1,500 cc class and Biennial Cup, finished fourth overall and won the Index of Performance, the first 1½-litre to do so since World War II. Following the von Frankenberg/Polensky car, two more 1½-litre cars finished fifth and sixth overall while two 1,100 cc versions finished 1–2 in their class.

A look at the Porsche's 1955 results suggests a steam-roller, but some strong opposition was flexing its muscles. The East German A.W.E./E.M.W.s gave Porsche a hard time at home (for political reasons they did not race outside of Germany) as did Jean Behra's Maserati 150S which sprung a surprise victory in the Nürburgring 500 Km. Though often dogged by reliability in long-distance events, the light and nimble Cooper and Lotus cars gave food for thought for on tight circuits they demonstrated superior road-holding and, indeed, in 1954, Herrmann had taken a 550 to Silverstone for the British GP meeting and had been soundly trounced by Colin Chapman's Lotus Mk 8-M.G.

In the meantime, the production road cars had been undergoing steady development in the wake of the competition models and been performing well in all manner of races and rallies. Despite its high profile in International racing, however, total Porsche production was still less than 8,000 cars by the end of 1955. This situation was to change dramatically over the next four years during which time 22,500 road cars were made.

For 1956 the works prepared a new model designated 550A (or 1500RS) which featured a space-frame which was lighter and considerably stiffer than the old ladder-frame, a 5-speed gearbox, improvements to the engine which allowed it to produce 130 bhp, and a new low-pivot i.r.s. system. Later that year the 'Carrera' appeared which was basically an amalgam of the competition chassis with a slightly tamer engine, and the standard coupé body and trim. About 700 were

made over its four-year production life and in 1,500 cc and 1,600 cc forms they dominated small-capacity GT racing.

The 550A made its debut in the Mille Miglia, where it retired, but in the meantime the existing cars had continued to win and Porsche added another 1–2 in the 1,500 cc class at Sebring. In the Nürburgring 1,000 Km Wolfgang von Trips and Umberto Maglioli not only won their class but finished fourth overall on the same lap as the winning Maserati of Moss/Behra, and ahead of the Collins/Brooks Aston Martin DB3S. Herrmann and von Frankenberg brought their car home in sixth and second in class.

At the Nürburgring a Swiss amateur called Michael May (who was to become the first International Formula Junior Champion in 1959 and who also designed the 'fireball' cylinder head for the Jaguar V-12 engine) appeared with a strange device on his 550. Oddly enough it did not attract a great deal of attention in the press at the time, but it was a high-mounted wing controlled from the cockpit which could be feathered on the straights and give downforce in the corners. In practice May lapped faster than the works Porsches but the team and the organizers (it was in Germany, after all) joined forces to ban it. It was to be more than ten years before the idea was rediscovered.

Porsche had the 1,500 cc class by the throat and its cars had started to make a habit of humbling much larger and more powerful machinery, but nobody could have been prepared for what was to happen in Sicily on 10 June. Due to an error in filling out the entry forms Maglioli had to drive the Targa Florio without a co-driver. It was a non-Championship race but the teams which mattered were represented, though not with their very best drivers, and Maglioli outdrove and outlasted them all to score an astounding victory. 'Targa' was added to Porsche's vocabulary and it was the first of what was to be eleven wins in the race until the last Targa Florio was run in 1973.

A problem with writing about these 4-cylinder Porsches is that as soon as a new model made its debut and got into its stride it became dull for it simply steam-rollered the opposition. The design team was not brilliantly innovative (it *could* be as the Cisitalia proved) but, rather, erred on the conservative side. There was no need for Porsche to try trick aerodynamics or pare its cars' weight to the limit. What it made worked, and worked better than the opposition. Moreover the cars were incredibly reliable: they did not throw wheels or break chassis, they were not temperamental, and they did not need star drivers to wring the best from them. In an age of special builders, Porsche made masterpieces of engineering.

It would have been a brave man who, in the Fifties, had predicted that Porsche would today hold its eminent position in production sports cars, but all the ingredients of future success as a considerable manufacturer and development consultancy were apparent from Ferry Porsche's first VW special.

So 1956 continued with the inevitable class win at Le Mans (and fifth overall) and the only hiccup was when the factory tried a shorter, narrower, prototype which was nicknamed 'Micky Mouse'. With a smaller frontal area, it was quick in a straight line but after a couple of unsatisfactory appearances it was driven by von Frankenberg in the Avusrennen and, while leading, disappeared over the top of the North Loop, apparently due to a breakage, and eventually destroyed itself when it hit the ground which was a long way below. The driver escaped with minor injuries but 'Micky Mouse' was seen no more.

As with the 550, its successor was put into limited production and about 30 reached private hands. 1957 continued as before with a succession of class wins in important races, and fourth overall in both the Mille Miglia and Nürburgring 1,000 Km, to say nothing of numerous successes in lesser events. During that year a new prototype appeared in hill-climb events and though externally it was marked by a lower, by four inches, shell and small fins at the rear, it was the arrangement of an experimental front suspension system which caught the attention. The top tubes which contained the upper torsion bars were angled down to the centre of the bottom tubes which appeared from some angles to represent the letter 'K'. Although this was a short-lived arrangement, the Porsche No. 718 was known thereafter as the RSK.

While front suspension remained by torsion bars at the rear, the low-pivot swing axles were now sprung by coil springs and Koni dampers. In the comparative privacy of hill-climbs in 1957, Porsche also experimented with 1,586 cc and 1,679 cc versions of the No. 547 engine. One other idea was also in the pipeline, the conversion of the basic car to the new Formula 2. This indeed was done after first running Edgar Barth in an 'F2' 550A in the F2 category in the 1957 German GP. Barth managed to qualify as the quickest F2 car, ahead of a couple of private Maserati 250Fs, and he won the F2 section in a sports car with a cover over the passenger seat.

This encouraged Porsche to make single-seat open-wheeled F2 versions of the RSK, but while initially the cars had a power advantage to offset the lower frontal area and greater lightness of the Climax-powered cars, development of the Coventry Climax FPF engine narrowed the gap and in the main these cars were relegated behind first the Coopers and then, decisively, behind the Lotus 18s.

Some of these cars continued into the 1½-litre F1 and picked up occasional wins in both categories, but in the main, the special builders demonstrated that formula racing was completely different to sports cars. A bespoke Porsche F1 car with an air-cooled flat eight engine was largely a failure though Dan Gurney managed to win the 1962 French GP after the main opposition retired.

The 1958 sports car season began with a wonderful result in the Buenos Aires 1,000 Km when Moss and Behra found themselves without a car after their Maserati was damaged in practice. They were invited to take over a 1.6-litre 550A and Moss went quicker in it than anyone at Porsche dared imagine. The Anglo-

French partnership brought it home third overall behind two works 3-litre Ferraris, but on the same lap, and was considered Porsche's finest performance to date.

The second round of the WSCC at Sebring brought another third place, this time with Harry Schell and Wolfgang Seidel driving a 1.6-litre car, but it was a demonstration of reliable speed rather than brilliance. Earlier in the race, though, Behra and Barth in an RSK had run with the leaders until forced out with a leaking oil seal. Back to the Targa Florio, which had replaced the defunct Mille Miglia as Italy's WSCC round, and the Behra/Scarlatti 1.6 finished an excellent second, though some way behind the Musso/Gendebien 3.0 Ferrari.

The Nürburgring 1,000 Km brought fourth place (and first in class, naturally) for Maglioli and Herrmann, and Behra and Herrmann finished third at Le Mans not far behind the Aston Martin DB3S of the Whitehead brothers and with the RSKs of Barth/Frère and de Beaufort/Linge fourth and fifth. The WSCC season finished with a class win in the Tourist Trophy so ending a year in which Porsche won its class in every round. Remarkably, Porsche also tied with Aston Martin for second place in the final Championship placings which were decided on overall finishes and not class wins. It was a fine performance for a team of 1,600 cc cars running in a 3-litre formula.

Porsche went into the final round of the following year's Championship, the Tourist Trophy at Goodwood, with an outside chance of winning the title though still running cars with half the engine capacity of its opponents. The works 1959 cars had a further rear suspension modification, the swing axles were abandoned and a coil spring and wishbone system substituted.

Von Trips and Bonnier had opened the score at Sebring with another third overall (and, need one add, a class win) and in the second round, the Targa Florio, works and private Porsches saw off a strong team of Ferraris to score a wonderful 1–2–3 with the 1,500 cc RSK of Barth/Seidel heading the 550A of Strahle/Mahle/Linge and the private 1,500 cc Carrera of Baron Pucci/von Hanstein.

An Aston Martin and two Ferraris filled the first three places at the Nürburgring 1,000 Km, but Maglioli and Herrmann came in fourth. For once Le Mans was a disaster for though by half-time Porsches held the places between fourth and seventh, none were to last the distance. It was a rare failure caused by running a different camshaft which delivered more power but over-stressed the engine. It was a mistake which was to cost Porsche the WSCC.

Goodwood hosted the final round and when the leading Aston Martin caught fire during a pit stop, the RSK of von Trips and Bonnier led the race and, hence, the Championship. When the flag fell, however, Porsche had to be content with a fine second ahead of a works Ferrari. They had no answer to the brilliance of Moss and the Aston Martin DBR1/300 on the circuit where both marque and driver had enjoyed some of their finest hours. The final points tally was: Aston Martin 24, Ferrari 22, Porsche 21.

1960 saw a change in the WSCC's regulations and Porsche remodelled the RSK as the RS60 with a longer wheelbase, wider space-frame and smaller wheels. These cars were immediately available to private owners for the earlier models were no longer eligible for International competition. In 1,500 cc form they had 160 bhp on tap and this rose to 180 bhp for the 1.7-litre engine which also had better torque characteristics. During 1960 Porsches appeared for the first time with disc brakes and it was typical that the company produced its own system rather than rely on proprietary suppliers.

The story of the season closely followed 1959 with Porsche again in contention for the WSCC but again let down by a disastrous showing at Le Mans. The five-round championship kicked off at Buenos Aires where Jo Bonnier and Graham Hill brought a 1.6 home third behind two Ferraris. At Sebring it looked as though Moss and his 'Birdcage' Maserati had the race in the bag until the back axle let go after eight hours so handing the race to the 1.5 RS60 of Oliver Gendebien and Hans Herrmann with the private car of Holbert/Schechter/Fowler a fine second. The Targa Florio had become a happy hunting ground for Porsche and the 1.6 cars of Bonnier/Herrmann and Gendebien/Herrmann (no misprint, Hans drove both cars) finished first and third.

Using a 1.7-litre engine, Bonnier and Gendebien came second in the Nürburgring 1000 km to the Moss/Gurney 'Birdcage' and other Porsches finished fourth and sixth, so with one round remaining, Porsche led the WSCC. At Le Mans, however, only two of the four cars finished and then down in 11th and 12th places. The fact that they scored a 1–2 in class was beside the point, Ferrari came first and second in the race and clinched the Championship by four points.

In the last year of the sports-racing WSCC, 1961 (it was replaced by a new, restructured, GT championship the following year) Porsche had a thinnish time. During the year Ferrari introduced its new rear-engined 2.4-litre Dino model which had a distinct power advantage and the revised RS61 may have had refinements to its body and, on occasion, a 1,987 cc engine but it was still the same basic car which had first appeared in 1953.

At Sebring the private Penske/Holbert RS60 came home fifth (and first in class) and that was followed by the Targa Florio, but Ferrari had its new car and it won. Bonnier/Gurney in a 2-litre Porsche came second and the 1.7 car of Herrmann/Barth third. No fewer than four drivers (Linge, Gregory, Moss and Hill) shared the Porsche which finished eighth (and first in class) in the Nürburgring 1,000 Km and the other good result that year was fifth at Le Mans and first in the 2-litre class (Gregory/Holbert).

1961 was a poor year by Porsche standards but it was still a season which would have been regarded as brilliant by most of the manufacturers listed in this book. The company had been active in sports car racing throughout the period of the WSCC (1953–61) and not only had it distinguished itself throughout, it had seen its road car operation expand beyond anything which could have been imagined when the first VW special was built in Gmünd in 1948.

Although the first works Porsches were a long way removed from the RS61s, they were both of a continuing series. Like the axe which beheaded Queen Anne

Boleyn it had had a few new heads, and a few new shafts, but the line was continuous. It was the greatest line ever seen in sports car racing.

Had Porsche retired from racing in 1961, it would have done so honourably, having achieved much, much more than could ever have been expected from a maker of small-engined cars. Its place in motor racing history would have been assured for its cars were the most consistently competitive during the period and a tribute to consistent development. As we now know, far from having thoughts of resting on its laurels, Porsche's competition career was only just beginning.

Salmson

Before World War II, France had a tradition of sporting and quality cars the equal of any other country in the world. Makers such as Bugatti, Delahaye, Delage, Hotchkiss, Salmson, Amilcar, Hispano-Suiza, Chenard Walcker, Talbot, Lorraine and Delaunay-Belleville went hand in glove with a parallel, distinguished, coachbuilding tradition.

Some of these makers folded in the financial depression of the Thirties but most survived the war, at least nominally. In 1945, however, the industry was almost in ruins along with the French economy. Still, the surviving companies struggled to get back on their feet and French cars were fairly successful in both racing and rallying in the immediate postwar years.

Then, in 1951, the French government introduced a series of fiscal measures designed to encourage the mass production of small, cheap, cars in order to get France back on four wheels. These measures had their desired effect for, by the

The 2.3 litre Salmson driven by Colas/Dewez at Le Mans in 1955. It was little more than a re-bodied Salmson 2300S which, at the time, was highly successful in rallying. In the background is the 1500cc Kieft-Turner of Baxter/Deeley. (Motor)

Another view of the Salmson at Le Mans. (T.C. March)

end of the Fifties, France was again a major motor car producer and exporter.

These same measures, however, killed the specialist car industry. Not only did larger cars attract hefty road taxes, but a swingeing levy was imposed on companies for every worker they employed. This naturally encouraged capital-intensive mass production at the expense of the labour-intensive methods employed by the specialist car makers. With these taxes went levies on personal wealth for it was reasoned, not without some justification, that personal wealth may have been acquired during the war through collaboration or the black market.

Specialist companies found themselves unable to finance new models while their pre-war-based designs were terribly expensive compared with new cars from abroad. Salmson's modest S641, a 4-seater drophead with a top speed of 75 mph, was a pre-war design which soldiered on into the Fifties but after the employment levy was introduced, production tumbled for the car cost 20 per cent more than a Jaguar XK120.

These fiscal measures cut into Salmson's car production. In 1950, it sold 3,000 cars but by 1955 its output was down to double figures. Still, the company overall remained healthy for most of its business was aero engines.

Salmson had made d.o.h.c. engines since the late Twenties and, in 1951, introduced a lightweight 4-cylinder 2.2-litre unit for a new model, the Randonnée. Two years later this was slightly enlarged to 2.3-litres (84 x 105 mm) and put into the 2300S, a pretty, Italianate, GT car. With a large Solex twin-choke carburettor, the unit gave 110 bhp at 5,000 rpm, though its bottom end power was not good. The result was a top speed of 105 mph and reasonable acceleration with a 0-60 mph time of 12.5 seconds.

A Cotal 4-speed gearbox was used, with electromagnetic gear selection activated by a lever under the steering wheel. There was a sturdy box-section chassis with front suspension by wishbones and torsion bars with a torque tube and cantilever springs at the rear, hardly advanced engineering.

Still, the car handled well and examples performed creditably, one finishing second in the 1955 Lyons-Charbonnières Rally and another second in the Liège-Rome-Liège (to Gendebien's Mercedes-Benz 300SL), as well as scoring successes in French national events.

For Le Mans, 1955, the factory made its one excursion into postwar motor racing producing a lightly modified 2300S with a two-seat sports body officially entered by one of the drivers, J. P. Colas. It is not hard to imagine Salmson's motivation for, on the one hand, sales were negligible while, on the other, its main model was performing well in rallies. In the background was a take-over by Renault.

A good result at Le Mans might boost sales and persuade the new owners to maintain the car division. It was a gamble taken with the heart, not the head, for the car had to compete in the 3,000 cc class against the likes of the works Mercedes–Benz and Aston Martin teams.

At that level it proved painfully slow with a recorded top speed of just 117.44 mph. To put that figure into perspective, a 750 cc Panhard achieved 118.69 mph. In fairness, though, the Salmson should really be compared to the modified Austin-Healeys which raced at Le Mans two years previously and achieved 111.9 mph. In that light, the Salmson turned in a creditable performance.

Driven by Colas and Dewez, the car circulated at the tail end of the field in the company of the tiddlers until retiring in the ninth hour with engine problems. It was an unfitting last racing appearance by a company which had been making twin-cam production engines longer than any other and whose 1,094 cc cars had won the Index of Performance at Le Mans in 1927 and 1928.

Renault acquired Salmson and the marque was defunct by 1957. Right up to the end, though, it produced new ideas. A 1.5-litre version of the Randonnée engine was exhibited at the 1955 Paris Show and, shortly before production ceased, a 4-seater saloon version of the 2300S was made.

Scarab

Although Scarab sports cars raced as a team for only a single season and then only in their native America, and though they were not even eligible for WSCC events, let alone competed in any, the spirit of these cars is such that they belong in this book. Historically, they are interesting too for they were the first sign that the American and European racing traditions might merge.

It is true that Briggs Cunningham had pioneered the 'hands across the sea' but Cunningham had been a one-off and when he finally stopped making his own cars there was nobody else in America who was prepared to follow.

Pre-war there were three distinct motor racing traditions in the Western Hemisphere – Britain, Europe and America – and there was little overlap between them. Britain was dominated by Brooklands and tended to breed specials built for that one venue. Europe had a rich tradition of genuine road racing while the sport in America was largely confined to oval circuits where the emphasis was not on 'improving the breed' but providing close competition for the drivers and the maximum excitement for spectators.

Postwar in Britain, Brooklands had gone and in its place were ex-military airfields, which provided a form of road racing and so Britain moved towards the European tradition. Much the same situation existed in America except that the airfields were operational, but the powers in Strategic Air Command were open to the idea of using parts of their airfields for racing. With that refreshing attitude, the ready availability of a large variety of European sports cars, and with the dollars to buy them, it was natural that a road racing tradition would grow. Starting at Watkins Glen in 1948, one did indeed begin.

By the late Fifties, America had begun to send over a number of gifted drivers such as John Fitch, Phil Hill, Dan Gurney and Carroll Shelby, all of whom had purely a sports car background. Races were staged at Monza, where Indy roadsters met the Europeans. Stock car, dragster, and kart racing crossed the Atlantic, too, and there was a general cross-fertilization which was to enrich racing on both sides of the Big Pond.

Lance Reventlow's Scarab team was an early and important manifestation of that process. Lance was rich by anyone's standards, being a Woolworth heir who inherited the equivalent in today's terms of about £60 million on his 21st birthday. He enjoyed his money in a flash way, gravitating to fast cars and Hollywood starlets, but was very serious about motor racing.

While still only 19, two years under the 'legal' age for SCCA racing, he began to enter races and achieved some success with an 1,100 cc Cooper 'Bobtail' and a Maserati 200S. He was discovered, however, and banned for a year.

During a trip to Europe in 1957, during which he managed to write off the Maserati at Snetterton, Lance and his close friend Bruce Kessler visited Maserati, and were not impressed by the Italian approach. It was a long way from Yankee efficiency. They visited Brian Lister, too, with the idea of buying a Lister chassis and installing a Chevy engine, but were not impressed by Lister's admittedly rudimentary chassis.

Having possibly been overawed by European makers before his visit, Reventlow now thought they were not as special as he'd supposed and, if he could gather the right people around him, he could make an all-American car which could be as good as anything from Europe. He was wrong. America did not lack expertise, it lacked a tradition.

Back in California he formed Reventlow Automobiles Inc. and set about recruiting the best available talent. The original intention appears to have been to contest the WSCC, but when the FIA imposed a 3-litre limit for 1958, and a deal with Maserati to supply V-12 engines evaporated, Reventlow decided to proceed with the Chevrolet 283 cu in. (4½-litre) V-8 and concentrate on American racing while keeping the idea of a 3-litre car on the back boiler.

The chassis he had designed by Dick Troutman, Dick Barnes, and Chuck Daigh, the chief mechanic and designated No. 1 driver, was a cranked ladder-frame with coil spring and unequal wishbone front suspension and an adjustable de Dion rear end. Mercury 11 in. drum brakes, inboard at the rear, were used initially but these were later enlarged and Al-fin drums cast. A Halibrand limited slip differential and Halibrand alloy wheels were fitted and, with Hillborn fuel injection the engine gave an easy 350 bhp. About the only non-American component on the car was the Morris Minor rack and pinion steering box, but by 1958 that had become required wear for every special.

While the design of the car was fairly conservative, it was superbly engineered, everything worked in harmony, and visually this harmony was underscored by a stunning body designed by an art student, Charles Pelly. It was not, however, aerodynamically sound and the front tended to lift at high speeds.

Although Reventlow's personality apparently underwent a change for the worse when, on his inheritance, he went from being merely a very rich kid to a fabulously wealthy man in his own right, he did retain a sense of humour and the name 'Scarab' (a dung beetle) was a private joke, a reaction against the macho and exotic names other cars were called.

The Scarab in its 1959 form with Lance Reventlow at the wheel and American motor racing journalist Hans Tanner in the passenger seat.

The first Scarab was built with left-hand drive but cars No. 2 and No. 3 had r.h.d. (to gain a smoother gear change) and engines of 339 cu in. (5½-litres). The two new cars then raced with Daigh and Reventlow as drivers. In SCCA racing in 1958 the two cars, running in the B/Modified class, simply steam-rollered the opposition and its European cars. It has to be said, though, that RAI competed through a loophole in the regulations. It was a professional team competing against amateurs and keeping its amateur status by not directly paying its drivers.

Daigh was a gifted, but not top-rate, driver and a useful man to have on the strength for he was skilled with fuel injection systems. In 1958, Daigh swept everything before him in his class of SCCA racing and took twelve successive wins. Reventlow apparently gave him orders not to sandbag in favour of the patron, he'd been given so much he felt he had to *earn* his wins and, indeed, he took wins at five US circuits and in the Governor's Cup in the Nassau Speed Week.

Nothing in America could touch the Scarabs in 1958 though it has to be said that the team as a whole was in a different class to its opposition. The acid test came with the sports car *Riverside Times* Grand Prix which attracted a strong field.

Daigh's Scarab battled for the lead with Phil Hill's 4.1-litre Ferrari until Hill fell by the wayside and Daigh went on to win. At the time Hill had already established himself as a Ferrari sports car and F1 driver so was no push-over, but a 200-mile race at Riverside is not the same as Le Mans or the Targa Florio. At Riverside Daigh's Scarab was timed at 174 mph on the one-mile straight, which compares to 169 mph for a 4.9 Ferrari and 165 mph achieved by a Maserati 450S.

It is interesting to speculate how Scarabs might have performed in the WSCC had there not been a 3-litre limit in 1958. The hard truth is the team would probably have been out of its depth. Though the chassis was sweet and forgiving, and the engine was not lacking in power, the classic sports car races were a world apart from airfield sprints and the team completely lacked experience of long-distance racing.

Reventlow did seriously consider building 3-litre cars for 1959 and ran car No. 3 with a 3-litre Offenhauser at Santa Barbara. It was naturally slower than the larger-engined car but not by very much. This promising project got no further than the one race before Reventlow, buoyed by success, decided to tackle the Europeans at the highest level.

After one glorious season the three Scarabs were sold and continued to perform well in private hands. Reventlow then turned his attention to Formula 1, an adventure which was to prove a disaster. One of Offenhauser's designers, Leo Goossen, drew an engine, with desmodromic valve gear and markedly 'over-square' dimensions (95.25 × 85.73 mm). This was intended to be both an F1 engine and a unit for a later serious assault on the WCM.

While the sports cars had been relatively simple, the F1 project was too complex for the team's resources and instead of appearing in 1959, it did not show until a year later, by which time the rear-engined revolution had made the front-engined Scarab obsolete. The planned 3-litre sports-racer was quietly dropped in the wake of the team's brief, traumatic, F1 career during which Reventlow was to learn that, although certain factories could appear a shambles and the cars so simple, when it came to racing he was a long way from being ready to take on the Europeans at their own game.

Reventlow was later to maintain that his F1 cars would have been competitive if ready on schedule, and it has become popular to maintain that it was the 'rear engine revolution' which caught Scarab out. A look at Scarab's practice lap times, however, belies the notion. In terms of times, Scarabs were at least four years behind the opposition and the team packed up and went home after three races. Reventlow and Daigh failed to qualify for the first two and Daigh's Scarab lasted just two laps in the Belgian GP having qualified last.

In practice at Monaco, Stirling Moss drove one of the cars and managed 1 min 45 secs. This was seven seconds a lap better than Daigh or Reventlow but it still would not have seen him on the grid. In fact it was nearly nine seconds off his own pole time. Stirling reported, 'The handling is too delicate and the suspension is too hard.' His time said, 'The car's a dog.' It was a dog which went home with its tail between its legs.

A car with a rear-mounted Buick engine was later built for the Inter-Continental Formula which died before it could race. Reventlow then decided to quit racing and he wound up his team. Jim Hall then commissioned Troutman and Barnes to design the first Chapparal which, not surprisingly, followed the lines of the Scarab.

Scarab's later history does not, however, detract from its marvellous 1958 SCCA season and two of the three cars are now to be seen in American Historic racing in the hands of Don Orosco and Augie Pabst.

Skoda

Of all the manufacturers in the Eastern Bloc, the most interesting is Skoda. Its ancestral company, Laurin & Klement, was founded in 1894 as a bicycle maker and within twenty years had grown to be a considerable engineering concern and one of the most important in the Austro-Hungarian Empire. Czechoslovakia has been something of a football in European politics over the past 100 years but the national character has remained resilient and even though current Skodas are not good cars by Western standards they are at least individual.

Czechoslovakia has both a distinctive engineering tradition (*vide* the Bren gun, Jawa and Tatra) and a motor sport tradition which has long maintained international racing at Brno. Two Aero Minor cycle-winged sports cars (derived from a Jawa design) which were based on the firm's little f.w.d. saloons with 615 cc 2-stroke 2-cylinder engines ran at Le Mans in 1949. Both finished (15th and 19th) and the quicker car won the 750 cc class. They returned to Le Mans in 1950,

The Czechoslovakian Aero Minor was a successful contender in the 750cc class in 1949/ 50. This photograph was taken at the works.

together with a Skoda special, and a single entry ran in 1951.

Skodas still appear in International rallies and their frequent successes, albeit in a minor class, indicates that Czech motor engineers are a good deal better than their road cars suggest, but then production Skodas are made under the constraints of a bureaucracy.

At the end of 1958 Skoda unveiled an 1,100 cc sports-racing car designed by Frantisek Sajdl, which, if claims made for it are true, would have been the fastest car of its engine size in the world. Its engine, based on that used in the Skoda 440 saloon, was a d.o.h.c. all-aluminium unit of 1,089 cc (68 × 75 mm) with hemispherical combustion chambers and valves inclined at 90 degrees. There were two plugs per cylinder, supplied by twin Scintilla Vertex magneti, and two twin-choke Jirav carburettors which were copies of Webers.

Another Czechoslovakian project was this 1100cc. Skoda, probably that which ran at Le Mans in 1951. (Haymarket Motoring Photo Library)

The Sports-racing Tatra, with, to the left, the Skoda. (Haymarket Motoring Photo Library)

Claimed maximum output was 92 bhp at 7,300 rpm (and that on poor-quality fuel) which fed through a 5-speed gearbox mounted in unit with the final drive. There was a beautifully made, if substantial, space-frame which was extensively drilled for lightness, but still the car's weight, 1,280 lb, was nearly 50 per cent more than a Lotus Eleven.

Suspension was independent all round, by double wishbones and torsion bars at the front, and torsion bars and swing axles at the rear. Iron drum brakes with alloy fins were mounted outboard at the front, inboard at the rear.

Top speed was *claimed* in press releases to be 160 mph, but this must be taken with a pinch of salt. Frantisek Sajdl, the designer, put its maximum at a more modest 130+ mph but even that seems optimistic. If the claimed power output was accurate and, given the engine's advanced specification it does not seem unreasonable, Skoda had perhaps 5 bhp over the best Coventry Climax FWA engines. That advantage would have been more than absorbed by the car's weight and though the fibreglass body looked slippery enough, there was no way it was on a par with the Lotus Eleven and yet the Eleven's maximum speed on the Mulsanne Straight was 128 mph.

We have no information about the engine's overall power characteristics or reliability and unfortunately it was never seen in competition outside of Czechoslovakia, Hungary and Poland. No information is available as to how the cars performed but the opposition must have been amateurish at best.

Two sports-racers were built (and two GT cars along the same lines) and both were retained by the works until, in the Sixties, a young student named Martin Svetnicka was able to acquire one of the cars, thanks to family connections. He raced it in Czechoslovakia but after the Russian invasion of 1968 decided to defect to the West. In the middle of winter, Svetnicka drove the car across Europe and eventually landed in England, where he enrolled at London University to continue his studies, using the Skoda as his everyday transport.

Later the car went to the Midlands Motor Museum, but it is now in the hands of Duncan Rabagliati, a collector who specializes in the unusual. Its sister car is in Skoda's own museum.

In the late Fifties there were many rumours of Eastern Bloc manufacturers poised to enter international motor racing, the Russians released details of their 'Kharkov' and various production car-based 'record' cars, for example, and the Czech Tatra company made several racing cars including a rear-engined space-

197

frame single-seater with a 2½-litre V-8 which produced 200 bhp and a rear-engined sports-racer with an air-cooled 636 cc V-twin.

It was only Skoda, though, which appears to have made a car ready for international racing, but in the late Fifties the political climate was not such that it could emerge from behind the Iron Curtain and show its mettle.

Stanguellini

Until the arrival of Formula Junior in 1958, most of the efforts of the small Italian constructors were directed to 750 cc and 1,100 cc sports car racing and Italy's own version of F3. When the 500 cc single-seater class became International F3 in 1951, a number of Italian firms built cars for the class, but instead of following the lead of the British constructors with their lightweight rear-engined cars, most made miniature F1 cars which were lovely to look at but no match for the Cooper, Kieft and J.B.S. cars which continued to dominate the category.

Although Italy made some exquisite multi-cylinder motor cycle engines, they were either not available to F3 car builders or else, when they were fitted to F3 cars, proved not to have the power, or perhaps the right power characteristics to compete with the all-conquering single-pot Norton. The Italians thought that importing Cooper-Nortons to race was no fun at all and so devised a 750 cc 'Formula 3'.

Most of the cars in this class were closely related to the sports cars built by the same maker, indeed the Bandini was a dual-purpose car, you simply removed the mudguards and covered the passenger seat to convert your sports car into an F3 car. The Bandini, in common with other Italian cars, had a lightweight ladder-frame chassis with coil spring and unequal double wishbone front suspension and a live rear axle suspended on semi-elliptical springs. It was usually fitted with a modified Fiat engine with a special twin overhead cam head, though sometimes the 750 cc s.o.h.c. American Crosley engine was used.

The Giaur was built on similar lines to the Bandini and came about as collaboration between Domenico Giannini, a Fiat tuner since 1925, and Bernardo Taraschi, a driver/constructor. This again had a d.o.h.c. Fiat-based engine. Giaurs were very successful in Italian 750 cc sports and formula racing between 1950 and 1955. In 1954 Taraschi supercharged a Giaur 750, which made it an

F1 car, and entered it in the Rome GP. It proved both slow and fragile but was one of only two types to use the 750 cc s/c option in the 1954–60 F1, the other being D.B. Later Taraschi was to build his own Formula Junior cars which were similar in concept to those of Stanguellini and, for a time, were Stanguellini's most forceful competitor.

Pasquale Ermini concentrated mainly on the 1,100 cc sports car class and initially was very successful. Piero Scotti, who later drove a Connaught Type B in a brief F1 career, took an Ermini to three important class wins in 1950 in the Pescara 4 Hours race, the Tour of Sicily and the Targa Florio. Two years later Aldo Terigi came fourth overall behind three works Lancias in the Targa Florio. Ermini's fortunes then went into decline but continued to make cars in small numbers for some years.

Siata was another company which transformed other makers' cars, particularly those of Fiat, but it tended to concentrate on road-going cars. Nardi is dealt with elsewhere in this book. Moretti, which currently makes Jeep-like vehicles based on Fiat parts (and distributed through Fiat dealers in Italy) built a small number of Fiat-based sports and GT cars in the Fifties and made the occasional foray into International motor racing.

Of all the small Italian companies, the name which became best known outside its native land was Stanguellini. The cars were attractive and, if fragile, were often quick. Stanguellini was anyway a good name for a racing car, the sort of name which a script writer might choose. In much the same way the name 'Tojeiro' was quicker than any of the cars.

It was Stanguellini which, in 1959, the first truly International season of Formula Junior, set the standard the others had to beat. So it was that the company briefly stood out above its fellows and in the minds of those outside Italy became the epitome of the small Italian constructor.

Vittorio Stanguellini was born in Modena in 1901, a contemporary of Enzo Ferrari. His father was the first car owner in Modena (in 1910) and later Vittorio became a Fiat dealer and, pre-war, modified Fiat Balillas which he raced.

In 1946 he founded Officine Stanguellini Transformazioni Auto Sport Corsa which made and sold bolt-on 'go faster' parts for cars as well as various truck and van conversions, though his main business remained the selling of Fiats.

Stanguellini was an 'engine man' and he extensively developed Fiat 750 cc and 1,100 cc units, giving them d.o.h.c. heads and strengthened bottom ends. His chassis, by contrast, were conventional twin-tube ladder constructions, and his earliest car, in 1947, used Fiat Topolino suspension. It was not long before Stanguellinis were making a name for themselves in national racing, particularly when driven by Sesto Leonardi.

In 1951 Stanguellini announced the 'Bialbero', a road-going 2-seat sports car with an enveloping body and 80 bhp from its modified Fiat 1100 engine. On this occasion, coils spring and wishbone front suspension was specified, with a live rear axle suspended on semi-elliptical springs. Despite sometimes being bodied by top-class stylists such as Bertone, road-going Stanguellinis sold in very small numbers.

Briggs Cunningham imported a 750 cc Stanguellini into the States but sold it at once when he found it could not compete with home-grown specials using the Crosley engine. We must therefore assume that claims of up to 70 bhp for the 750 cc engine were wishful thinking. Similarly claims of 92 bhp from the 1,100 cc engine were not borne out when one was imported into Britain and fitted to a Lotus Eleven.

The 1953 Stanguellini 750 cc twin-cam sports-racing car. (Duncan Rabagliati)

Another view of a 1953 Stanguellini, this time with a single headlamp mounted behind the air intake. (Duncan Rabagliati)

Stanguellinis appeared quite often in classic races outside Italy but were not particularly successful, tending to come second or third in class rather than winning. For Le Mans 1956, a team of three 750 cc cars was entered with space-frames and rubber-band springing. Writing in *Autosport* John Bolster commented drily that the cars did not look as though they had the 72 bhp claimed for them and, for Le Mans, reliability was more important than innovative suspension. One crashed, one broke its crankshaft in the third hour and the third car struggled around on three cylinders for the final part of the race to finish in penultimate position.

Stanguellini had long supported the Italian 750 Monosport Championship which had sprung from the 500 cc F3 when the Italians found they could neither

This 750 cc Stanguellini engine is fitted with twin Weber 32 DCO single-choke carburettors, but others were equipped with Del'Orto carburettors.

build chassis to match the Cooper, nor obtain home-grown engines to match the Norton. It was natural that the firm should take to Formula Junior when it started in 1958 and its first car, with a ladder-frame, Fiat engine, and looking like a miniature GP car, was enormously successful, at first. Cammarota won the first Italian FJ Championship with a Stanguellini in 1958 and when, the following year, the category expanded abroad, Michael May used a Stanguellini to become the first International FJ Champion. Sports cars were then largely forgotten though Stanguellinis continued to appear at Le Mans, without success, until 1960.

At the end of 1957 Stanguellini announced this 750cc car with bodywork by Scaglietti. It was not particularly successful and soon afterwards Stanguellini began to concentrate on Formula Junior in which it was successful until British makers joined in.

1960 saw the Brits take to FJ and in common with all the other European FJ constructors (there were over 100), Stanguellini was shown up in the biggest possible way. Lotus and Cooper cars in particular demonstrated how terribly outdated was Stanguellini's chassis design while both BMC and Ford engines were more powerful than Stanguellini's Fiat-based units.

By the end of 1960 British FJ cars had dealt such a blow to the small European constructors that they never recovered and many went out of business. Stanguellini staggered on a little longer and made a rear-engined FJ car in 1961, and an F2 car in 1964, but neither was successful.

Talbot

It's a curious thing, but three of the greatest names in French motor racing have been Italian: Bugatti, Gordini and Lago. To Antonio Lago, a Venetian by birth but French by adoption, it fell to keep alive the last vestiges of the great pre-war French tradition of quality sporting cars and *Grands Routiers*. In the Twenties he had been based in London, where he became well known for his L.A.P. o.h.v. conversions. After a spell with the Wilson Self-Changing Gear Co, Lago joined

Driven by Louis Rosier and his son, this 4.5 litre Talbot won Le Mans in 1950. (Motor)

the old Sunbeam-Talbot-Darracq concern in 1933. When the company failed two years later, Lago had been able to raise the capital to salvage part of it and launch SA Automobiles Talbot.

An engineer by training, and a motor racing enthusiast by inclination, Lago used his firm's successful participation in sports car racing to enhance its image. By the time the war broke out Talbot was an established constructor of *Grands Routiers*, which were bodied by leading French *cassories*.

In the immediate postwar climate, however, displays of ostentatious wealth were regarded with suspicion in France since they often carried the imputation of collaboration or black market profiteering. In purely practical terms, France did not need labour-intensive cars for the wealthy few, it needed a broadly-based motor industry making cheap mass-produced cars both to replace the vast number of cars lost in the war and to generate industrial expansion and exports. It is estimated there were only 300,000 working vehicles of any description in France in 1945.

When, in 1950, a swingeing tax was imposed on every employee in a company, it had the effect of making hand-built French cars prohibitively expensive to buy. A Frenchman had to be a chauvinist indeed to pay more for a Delahaye (still basically a pre-war design, complete with cable brakes) than for a Bentley Mk 6. As for exports, there were few takers for not only were the cars expensive, they stuck to r.h.d., a feature of most pre-war quality cars in Europe, for when Sir wanted to drive over Alpine passes, it was desirable that he sat on the near side of the road. It cut no ice in California.

Sales declined rapidly from 1950 onwards and with them the profits which might have financed re-tooling and new designs to meet the changing circumstances. One by one the old marques like Delahaye, Hotchkiss, and Delage folded while Lago, in an increasingly decrepit factory at Suresnes, soldiered on.

Talbot re-entered motor racing in 1947 with an update of its 1939 single-seater which had been good enough to finish third in the Pau GP behind two Mercedes-Benz and third and fourth in the French GP behind two Auto Unions and on both occasions beat Raymond Sommer's works Alfa Romeo. Driving this car, Louis Chiron scored a fine win in the 1947 French GP.

In 1948 the marque began to be called 'Talbot-Lago' and that year Lago and his engineer, Marchetti, created a new version of Talbot's pre-war straight-six 4,483 cc engine which had a single camshaft mounted high in the crankcase. The overall dimensions and layout remained the same but a second camshaft was added, the overall effect being similar to that of the classic Riley layout, with short push-rods activating inclined valves. In this form it gave 240 bhp at 4,700 rpm but, by 1950, this figure had risen to 280 bhp at 5,000 rpm.

These engines powered Talbot's road cars and a new Grand Prix design, a development of the firm's 1939 car. The revised chassis retained the old independent front suspension using a transverse leaf spring, with a live rear axle suspended on semi-elliptical springs (there was no other form of rear axle location). Lockheed hydraulic drum brakes replaced the Bendix cable layout of the earlier car but transmission remained via a 4-speed Wilson preselector gearbox.

Though less powerful and considerably heavier than the leading opposition, the Talbots were reliable and easy on fuel. Consequently they frequently figured in the results and, in 1949, with Alfa Romeo in retirement for a season, Talbots won the Belgian and French Grands Prix driven by Louis Rosier and Louis Chiron respectively. Early in 1951 Lago was forced to withdraw his F1 works team, but privateers continued until the end of the season.

By converting this car, the T-26C, into a narrow 2-seater and adding mudguards and lights, it became a sports car and three Talbots were entered in the 1950 Le Mans race. After the main opposition, from Ferrari, fell by the wayside, Louis Rosier, assisted by his son who drove just a couple of laps to give his father a break, won from the older (1939) Talbot of Meyrat/Mairesse with the third car, a production Grand Sport model driven by Chambas and Morel, third.

It was not an inherited victory – Rosier led from the third hour apart from a brief period when the Meyrat/Mairesse car moved ahead. He also set new records for average speed, distance covered and fastest lap which, at 102.83 mph, was the first time the record had risen above 100 mph.

Next year there were six Talbots in the race and the driving talent was strengthened by Fangio and Gonzalez, but the opposition was stiffer too, and Jaguar arrived with its team of C-types. Three of the six cars dropped out but Meyrat and Mairesse finished second once more, though nine laps behind the winning Jaguar. Levegh and Marchand finished fourth and Chambas and Morel brought their Grand Sport to the finish again, but this time in 13th.

Pierre Levegh's real surname was Bouillon, but he had adopted the pseudonym. His entire racing career covered only a few races, and he was certainly not a driver of the first rank, but he had a burning ambition to win Le Mans at the wheel of a French car. He was entered in the car Gonzalez had driven in 1951 but

Louis Rosier and Yves Giraud-Cabantous finished second in the 1953 Reims 12 Hours with this streamlined Talbot. (LAT)

which now had a graceful, fully-enveloping, body. His nominated co-driver was Marchand but that is a matter of academic interest only for Levegh was determined to drive the whole distance.

Panicked by the arrival of the Mercedes-Benz 300SL coupes, Jaguar rebodied the C-types with a low nose which caused overheating and all the cars were out within four hours. The Ferraris dropped by the wayside and Levegh found himself in the lead just after half-time with two Mercedes following him. Levegh led, single-handedly, until the last hour when he apparently missed a gear change, over-revved the engine, and was out. Given the pace of progress, it was Talbot's last chance.

Three works cars were entered in 1953 but only that of Levegh/Charles Pozzi

One of the two over-weight Maserati-powered Talbots entered at Le Mans in 1956. Driven by Jean Behra and Louis Rosier, this car survived until late in the race before succumbing to transmission problems. (LAT)

finished, in eighth. The following year there were three private cars, but none finished. No Talbots appeared at Le Mans in 1955.

1956 saw two Talbots back at Sarthe, this time based on the smaller 'Sport' chassis, which retained the traditional layout, but using sports versions of the Maserati 250F engine for, as prototypes, the cars were restricted by the 2½-litre upper limit imposed at Le Mans that year. Both cars had a new 4-speed ZF gearbox and bodywork by Pichon et Parat which was very much in the idiom of contemporary Maserati and Ferrari sports racers.

At the time Lago and Maserati were in negotiation with a view to Talbot building a Maserati-engined production car and Talbot's new competitions manager, the veteran Italian driver Goffredo Zehender, had put together the deal. Two cars were entered for Louis Rosier and Jean Behra and Zehender/Jean Lucas. Lucas crashed early in the race and the other car survived just over eight hours before retiring with rear axle failure but while it had been going it recorded eighth fastest speed on the Mulsanne Straight.

In the meantime, Tony Lago was trying to save his company with a pretty coupé which first had a 4-cylinder version of the Talbot straight six then, when the Maserati deal did not come to fruition, with a BMW 2.5-litre V-8. This latter car was the only French *grand routier* made with left-hand drive. This concession to marketing sense was too late, only twelve BMW-powered 'Americas' were made. They were not prohibitively expensive but suffered from an 'economy' interior and the fact that the styling was compromised by the necessary use of proprietary parts such as a Simca Vedette windscreen and a Jensen 541 rear window.

A little confusingly, the badges of these cars bore the name 'Lago-Talbot' rather than 'Talbot-Lago' and sometimes the cars were simply called 'Lago' though the company's registered name remained Automobiles Talbot.

In 1957 came Talbot's last appearance at Le Mans. It was a private entry, financed by André Dubonnet, and was based on the Talbot-Maseratis of the previous year, with a very pretty body by Reggiani which resembled contemporary Stanguellinis. It was fitted, however, with an impossibly high rear axle ratio to obtain maximum speed on the Mulsanne Straight and when Bruce Halford sprinted across the tarmac at Le Mans he found he could not get it off the line for the high gearing burned out the clutch.

It was an ignominious end in competition for a marque which had won the race so convincingly in 1950 and had come so close, with Levegh, two years later. Talbot remains the only company to have won Le Mans and a major Grand Prix with what was basically the same car.

By 1959, the company had passed into the hands of Simca, which tried selling the 'America' with a version of the Ford Pilot s.v. V-8 engine which was used in its Vedette saloons. Just as Talbot did not deserve the ignominy of the last car to appear at Le Mans bearing its name, so it did not deserve so mundane a motor. Apparently the buying public concurred for there were few takers and the marque died in 1960, a few months before Tony Lago.

Tojeiro

Like so many British constructors, John Tojeiro began by building a special for his own use and then was asked to make replicas by others who wanted to go racing. In fact, he never did race the first car which might properly be called a 'Tojeiro' for Chris Sears saw it under construction and bought it.

Early Tojeiros were rolling chassis which an enthusiast could buy and fit with his own engine, transmission and body. Later such a builder would be classified as a 'component supplier'. These cars had a simple ladder-frame with fabricated castles at each end which carried transverse leaf springs, in the style of contemporary Cooper sports cars. Tojeiro had had access to Brian Lister's Cooper-M.G. and there was some cross-fertilization of ideas.

Of early Tojeiros, two stand out. The first was one built for his near neighbour and ex-school friend Brian Lister. This was fitted with a rudimentary body and a Robin Blackburn-tuned 1,100 cc V-twin J.A.P. engine and nicknamed 'Asteroid'. The second outstanding car (LOY 500) was Bristol-engined and raced by Cliff Davis, it scored numerous wins and led to A.C. taking over Tojeiro's design and making of it the A.C. Ace.

Though LOY 500 and 'Asteroid' were both no more than successful club racing specials, each in its own way played an important role as a catalyst (see A.C. Ace and Lister) and they represent John Tojeiro's major contribution to the sport.

Tojeiro made about a dozen ladder-framed chassis but at the back of his mind was an idea to build a Jaguar-engined car which, he reasoned, would need to be more sophisticated than his previous efforts. Besides, A.C. had acquired the rights to the ladder chassis.

In 1955, Tojeiro produced a new car with a multi-tube frame, de Dion back axle and front suspension by coil springs and unequal wishbones and began trading as Tojeiro Automotive Developments Ltd. Two cars were built that year, one with a Bristol engine, the other with a 2½-litre Lea Francis unit, though later a Jaguar engine was substituted.

An improved, lighter, frame followed for 1956 and four were made. Two were fitted with Bristol engines, one with a Coventry Climax FWA engine (it was not a success, being much heavier than the new Lotus Eleven which quickly took charge of the 1,100 cc class) while a fourth was sold to a club racer, R. R. C. Palmer, who gave it a Microplas 'Mistral' glass-fibre body and a flat-four, air-cooled, A.J.B. engine.

After the initial success of the ladder-framed cars, the competition careers of Tojeiro's designs were on the wane. It was due in part to the fact that as an *intuitive* designer, he picked up his expertise as a fitter in the Fleet Air Arm during the war; it was partly due to his only occasionally attracting a good driver; and it was partly the cumulative effect of making so few cars in a 'factory' which was really a glorified shed with a workforce of one.

Meanwhile Tojeiro was approached by a wealthy amateur, John Ogier, who was prepared to commission a lightweight Jaguar-engined car. This was built along the lines of the other 1956 chassis with coil spring and double wishbone front suspension, and a coil-spring de Dion tube at the rear located by parallel trailing arms and central bronze slide block. Transmission was via a 4-speed Moss gearbox and a chassis-mounted ZF limited slip differential.

Registered 7 GNO, the car appeared in May 1956, and was driven that year by Ogier and Dick Protheroe, a competent club racer. It did not, however, take racing by storm and its sole win was in a seven-lap race at Crystal Palace against negligible opposition. On the same day, Cliff Allison's 1,100 cc Lotus Eleven lapped 1.6 seconds quicker. There were two main reasons for its lack of performance. Its wheelbase was only 7 ft 3 in., and its track just 4 ft 2 in., which made it difficult to tame and, though pretty, the body was aerodynamically deficient.

Ogier was not discouraged, however, and in 1957 he became a shareholder in T.A.D. while creating, with Tojeiro, the Tojeiro Car Company which looked after the racing side. If nothing else the cars were extremely handsome, being styled by an architect, Cavendish Morton, a man with a sure eye for a car's lines, though whether they were aerodynamically sound is another, unresolved, matter. When A.C. wanted a special car for Le Mans in 1958, the company turned to Tojeiro, who built a Bristol-engined car along the lines of his 'production' models and Morton styled it.

Tojeiro's second Jaguar-engined car had a 3 in. longer wheelbase and 1¼ in. wider track than 7 GNO, wire wheels replaced alloy Dunlops, and its de Dion tube was located by a Watts linkage instead of a sliding block.

Driven by Dick Protheroe, its first race saw it ranged against a moderate field at Snetterton which included Archie Scott-Brown's new Lister-Jaguar. When the Lister retired, Protheroe went on to win. Any win is good, but it soon became clear that the Snetterton success was a hollow victory. The car simply was not up to the opposition and since both Jack Brabham and Graham Hill were hired to race it there are no excuses.

John Ogier used it for a hill-climb at Stapleford in October 1957, crashed, and totalled it, but fortunately he was thrown clear and suffered 'only' a broken leg. In the meantime, 7 GNO had been sold to Frank Cantwell in New Zealand, but though he was successful at first in it, it was not long before the marginal handling got the better of him and he crashed heavily. It was rebuilt, passed through several hands, and is now back in Britain.

1958 arrived with no Tojeiro-Jaguar in Britain but Ecurie Ecosse wanted a replacement for its D-types and hedged its bets by ordering both a new Lister and a new Tojeiro which did not appear until mid-year. With Ivor Bueb at the wheel, the Ecurie Ecosse 'Toj' took fourth in the sports car race at the British Grand Prix but was beaten by Moss in the works Lister and, significantly, the 1,500 cc Lotuses of Roy Salvadori and Cliff Allison. The day of the 'big banger' special was coming to an end.

Car No. 3 raced rarely and its results were indifferent. With a 3-litre Jaguar engine (a bored-out 2.4) Jock Lawrence managed fifth at the 1959 Easter Monday meeting, and Ron Flockhart, with a 3.8-litre engine, inherited a couple of fourth places at Aintree and Silverstone. On Whit Monday, however, Flock-

Ivor Bueb with the third Tojeiro-Jaguar to be built which was loaned to Ecurie Ecosse. It is seen on its way to fourth place in the Sports Car race at the 1958 British Grand Prix meeting at Silverstone.

Chris Threlfall with his 1100cc Tojeiro-Climax at Brands Hatch in May, 1959. (NMM)

hart scored a lucky win at Goodwood when Jim Clark's 3.4 Lister-Jaguar ran out of fuel before half distance.

Tojeiro's continental debut came at the Nürburgring 1,000 Km, but early in the race Flockhart crashed heavily while avoiding a back marker.

That year, four lightweight 1,100 cc Climax-powered cars were made and those driven by Chris Threlfall and Richard Utley gave a reasonably good account of themselves in a class dominated by the Series II Lotus Eleven. One ran at Le Mans but retired with rear axle trouble.

In 1959 there was a 1,500 cc Climax-powered sports car which had a number of interesting ideas, not least the central one of making a lightweight car which would blast between corners and to Hell with handling. John Whitmore tried it, without success. A scientific designer might have toyed with such a notion but would never have allowed it out of the cage.

A new 'Toj' was commissioned by Ecurie Ecosse specially for Le Mans and though it was on the heavy side, it ran in the top half-dozen until its 3-litre Jaguar engine cooked itself. The car reappeared at Goodwood for the Tourist Trophy in the hands of Masten Gregory and Jim Clark.

It was lying in seventh place when Gregory arrived at Woodcote Corner with defective steering. Realizing he wasn't going to make the bend, he had started to climb on to the back of the car. It hit the banking at Woodcote and broke its back but Gregory was thrown clear, lucky to escape with a broken collar bone. The car was a write-off.

The one Tojeiro-Jaguar left in Britain, No. 3, enjoyed a chequered career. Peter Blond crashed it during a downpour at the British Grand Prix Meeting at Aintree. Repaired, Tony Maggs took it home to South Africa to race it successfully against negligible opposition in the embryo Springbok series.

Back it came to Britain where it raced briefly and unsuccessfully before appearing in the film *The Green Helmet*, in which it was crashed. Repaired again, it was bought by the Lewis brothers, mainly for use in hill-climbs and sprints, but in 1963, David Lewis's wife, Vivienne, crashed at the end of a run in the Brighton Speed Trials. She lost her life and the car was burned out, but the bits and pieces have since been reassembled.

Tojeiro did not make many more cars under his own name, though he did design the Britannia GT, a pretty car with a tuned Ford Zephyr engine commissioned by one Acland Geddes, who proved unequal to the task of putting it into production. To put the company's name before the public, Tojeiro designed a rear-engined Formula Junior which never amounted to much. When Britannia folded he bought a number of frames and assembled them as 'Tojeiros', but they faired no better.

Then there was the Ford Anglia-engined Berkeley Bandit, intended as an extension of the caravan firm's embryo sports car range, but though a decent little car, the company folded before it could be put into production.

For the 1962 Le Mans race, Ecurie Ecosse commissioned Tojeiro to build two mid-engined coupés. These had 2½-litre Coventry Climax engines, Cooper/Jack Knight gearboxes, independent suspension all round by coil springs and unequal wishbones, and a Cavendish Morton-styled body. They were built in a rush, not properly tested, and only one made Le Mans (retired, gearbox, eight hours).

The following year the two cars were given Ford and Buick V-8 engines and, thanks to a bright young driver called Jackie Stewart, managed decent showings in British club races. While they advanced Stewart's brilliant career, the races in which they succeeded were a long way from the classic events for which they were designed.

They were the last competition cars John Tojeiro made. Later he advanced some way towards making a Corvette-engined road car, the 'Corveiro', with styling by Dennis Adams, who styled the acceptable Marcos. Recently, after a gap of nearly a quarter of a century, Tojeiro again became involved with car building, as Technical Director of a kit car company, Dax, which has incorporated 'Tojeiro' in its name.

There is a rough justice in this since Dax makes Doppelganger* Cobras, a car which descended from the A.C. Ace which, in turn, came from Cliff Davis's Tojeiro-Bristol, a car which was a combination of a Cooper-style chassis and a copy of the Ferrari 166 Barchetta body.

A further irony is that the car Cliff Davis owned before LOY 500 was a Cooper-M.G. (JOY 500) built by Lionel Leonard which also had a Barchetta body and in 1954 Leonard was one of the very first people to offer a glass-fibre body to special builders. It was a Barchetta copy.

---

* Doppelganger – from Teutonic mythology, a spirit which resembles a living being but without its substance.